David Tennant and the Gargoyle Years

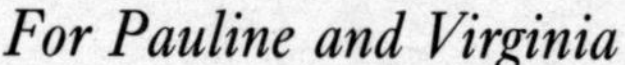

For Pauline and Virginia

David Tennant and the GARGOYLE Years

MICHAEL LUKE

Weidenfeld and Nicolson
London

First published in Great Britain in 1991 by
George Weidenfeld and Nicolson,
91 Clapham High Street, London SW4 7TA

British Library Cataloguing in Publication Data
Luke, Michael
David Tennant and the Gargoyle years.
1. London. Westminster (London Borough). Clubs.
Gargoyle Club, history
I. Title
367.942132

ISBN 0-297-81124-X

Printed and bound in Great Britain by
The Bath Press, Avon

Contents

Illustrations

Acknowledgements

To all the people mentioned and quoted from in the text I owe much indeed, and I am glad to recognize this debt here. I would also like to thank the following for their generosity and helpfulness: Simon Blow, Angela Culme-Seymour, Caroline Dakers, Ginette Darwin, Margaret de Wend-Fenton, Anne Dixon, Glur Dyson-Taylor, Rosalind Fox, Derek Horne, Christopher Moorsom, Jennifer Ross, Christopher Todd for permission to quote from his father Ruthven's papers, and Margot Walmsley.

Particularly, I would like to thank Michael Law, a gallant survivor of the Gargoyle campaign, for help and support beyond the call of any duty; to thank, also, Clarissa Luke for her vital seminal role; Robert Kee for some very salutary, and at the time most unwelcome, advice given at the outset; and my brother Peter for his constant encouragement and apt criticism.

Sadly, I have to record the names of the following friends who, to a greater or lesser extent, contributed to the book and who died in the period between conception and execution: Hermione and Ciggie Baddeley, Barley Allison, Freddie Ayer, Bobby Buhler, Adrian Daintry, Mark Culme-Seymour, Paul Potts, Reed de Rouen, Feliks Topolski. This book, in its modest way, is offered in memoriam of them.

Introduction

The Gargoyle was a club but it was much more than a club while also managing to be something of an anti-club. It was certainly unique and its span of influence long outlasted its existence. There are still distinguished veterans of the Gargoyle years active today in letters and the arts for whom the Gargoyle has been a watchword and a lodestone.

The Gargoyle Club came into being in the mid-twenties, reached its zenith during the Second World War, and died slowly in its aftermath. The Club's elegant and somewhat eccentric setting overlooked the rooftops of Soho. The Moorish interior of its ballroom, where an infinity of mirrored mosaic around the walls fragmented reflections from the dance-floor, had been inspired by a Club member, Henri Matisse.

The Gargoyle's principal singularity, however, lay in an eclectic membership combining robustness with an Attic quality which gave it a very addictive appeal. Recruited from the most diverse sources irrespective of sex – another unique aspect at the time – this membership nevertheless endowed the Club with an exclusiveness that made it appear infinitely desirable to outsiders.

Contradiction – perhaps echoing the elusive and unpredictable character of its owner – also contributed much to the Club's appeal. By day the Gargoyle was a sober luncheon club patronized by politicians and their wives, by distinguished servants of the State, by literati and nobility – and by the occasional spy. But at night the place became a cosmopolitan arena; an antic theatre of social, sexual and intellectual challenge – of thrust and counter thrust, of bravura display and emotional piracy.

After the decline of the Café Royal as the favourite rendezvous of London's Bohemia, the Gargoyle remained the only common ground where all branches of the arts and the media might meet; and through its tolerance of age, class, and of sex in all its variants, the Club established an emphatic social breakthrough.

The Club's landscape is a densely populated one. However, the single, the lone figure of David Tennant stands in an eminent and central position, and remains so throughout the Gargoyle years. David Tennant 'was' the Gargoyle, and as such has been identified with his club rather more than any other founder-owner of his day.

1

As this century moved into its second quarter, there was a general, if muted, sense of optimism that the 'war to end wars' might indeed have done just that.

1925 was the year when the dance craze really established itself in London. The places to go were Ciro's, where you could dine and dance after the theatre and which also offered a cabaret with 'speciality dancers', the Café de Paris, the Criterion restaurant, Oddenino's and the Piccadilly Hotel with Jack Hylton's band playing in the ballroom. At the Savoy, Carol Gibbons, with the Savoy Orpheans and the Savoy Havana Band, played simultaneously on different floors, while the Vincent Lopez Orchestra from the USA played the new Kit-Cat Club in the Haymarket. George Gershwin, the 'song-writer who composes dignified jazz', arrived in London for the broadcast of 'Rhapsody in Blue' by the Savoy Orpheans.

This explosion of night and late-night life did not escape the disapproval of the leader writer of *The Times*. 'Not for the first time in the history of London the minds of some of its inhabitants are at the present moment much exercised on the subject of night clubs. Among the more youthful and, therefore, more numerous of the frequenters there seems to be an idea that, like shingled hair or wireless telephony, they are a product of the age. It is this delusion, common to the young of each generation in its turn, which partly accounts for the strength of the lure that keeps them up to all hours, as their aunts would say, dancing and supping, when older and perhaps saner people are in bed and asleep. They think they are doing something that is new, and, therefore, dashing and Bohemian. Just now, because of the craze for dancing and the one-partner habit evolved by the war and its reactions, they are enjoying a renewed vogue, and the night clubs (and their proprietors) are making hay while the fever lasts.'

In defiance of the Thunderer's growl a 'happening' was celebrated as the year began by a surprisingly distinguished gathering given the, then, unsalubrious venue in which it was held. This was the opening, by a young student recently down from Cambridge, of a club in Soho on premises where once Nell Gwynne had owned a house. David Tennant, who chose to call this new club The Gargoyle, had no intention of 'making hay'. But the timing was propitious. 1925, as Hemingway observed, was also 'the year the rich showed up'.

The intentions of the youthful founder of this new club were made clear. 'The Gargoyle will be', David Tennant announced to the Press, 'a chic night-club for dancing but also an "avant-garde" place open during the day where still struggling writers, painters, poets and musicians will be offered the best food and wine at prices they can afford. Above all, it will be a place without the usual rules where people can express themselves freely.' There were to be rules, of course – David's – but not the usual ones.

This patrician concept was, on the face of it, a singular and, even for the twenties, almost bizarre ambition to be found in one so young, so apparently *un*sophisticated, and from a background so particular. Moreover, the ambition was not only broadly fulfilled but, in spite of many vicissitudes, it was sustained for the better part of a lifetime. The Club survived the war and even flourished, suffering only a few bomb-shattered windows. As with the Windmill Theatre around the corner, the only licensed rendezvous in wartime London where naked lovelies might be admired in the flesh just so long as they were never seen to move, the Gargoyle Club, too, 'never closed', or only very briefly. It survived, also, a period of great social and economic change. A change to which, it might be said, David acquiesced with reluctant grace.

David Tennant was exceedingly handsome, rich, clever and had, at a time when they still counted for much, enviable family connections. His father, Edward Tennant, a man of noble looks, had been raised from his inherited baronetcy to the peerage as the first Lord Glenconner. Pamela, his mother, a greatly admired beauty, was the third daughter of the Honourable Percy and Madeline Wyndham. On the death of David's father she married Viscount Grey of Fallodon, the Liberal statesman. David's aunt, Margot Tennant, had married Herbert Henry Asquith, later to become Prime Minister of the Liberal government and Earl of Oxford. While the Tennants were rich, the Wyndhams were aristocratic. Both belonged to that élite group of families – movers of politicians, shakers of intellectuals – whose blood was spilt in such profusion in the First World War. A group to become so bound with the weed of self-love and admiration that many of its younger shoots struggled to escape its stifling embrace. This might in part explain the calm resignation, in some cases not far short of joyous acceptance expressed in the stream of letters sent home from the Front, with which these golden boys, as members of the largest volunteer army ever fielded in the history of warfare, welcomed death in battle. Suspicion lurks, too, that this romantic death-wish, cloaked in the mystic cult of chivalry, might have been an unconscious act of grace born of a sense that there would be no place for them in a future world. War had opened the door to an heroic and early exit thus allowing another, and a better world, to emerge which, had they remained, they would have impeded. Such a one was David's eldest brother Edward (nicknamed Bimbo – Bim for short), killed on the Somme at the age of nineteen. Then there were his cousins, Percy Wyndham, Charles and Thomas Lister, Ivo and Hugo Charteris, and, by marriage, Raymond Asquith, none of whom survived the Great War.

The wit, the aesthetic sensibilities and intellectual attainments of the social group known as the Souls, described by that formidable American lady of letters, Edith Wharton, as 'the very flower and pinnacle of the London world', must have provided a welcome relief in late nineteenth-century Britain from the Prince of Wales' philistine court, the Marlborough House Set. The Souls provided, in their several large country houses, stimulating *caravanserais* where innovators and practitioners of the arts might gather, attracting, among others, Oscar Wilde, Henry James, Max Beerbohm and his marginally more famous actor/manager half-brother, Sir Herbert Beerbohm Tree, Mrs Patrick Campbell, James McNeill Whistler, Sir Edward Burne-Jones and John Singer Sargent. These houses provided an opportunity not to be found elsewhere for political opponents to meet and intermingle on purely social ground. The High Priest of this exclusive world – or 'gang' as they so described themselves until Lord Charles Beresford decided that, as their public intercourse was an unceasing examination of each others' souls, he would henceforth refer to them as 'The Souls', was the urbane, metaphysical pessimist Arthur Balfour, whose deceptively languid manner concealed keen political skills and a certain visionary statesmanship. These were exercised in the interests of the Conservative Party, and of the country as a whole, when he became Prime Minister in 1902 in succession to his uncle, Lord Salisbury. That 'most superior person' George Nathaniel Curzon, who in 1899 became Viceroy of India, a lofty perch from which he was eventually toppled by Kitchener, might be described as their master of ceremonies, if ceremony itself was not something the Souls felt themselves to be above.

Of the principal players in this arcane masque two men made a similar mark by virtue of exceptional promise which had been largely unfulfilled. Additionally, they both died in middle age, although it was unlikely that longevity would have redeemed the situation. They each enjoyed exceptional good looks carried with the haughty, careless elegance of the born dandy. Both had been described as 'the handsomest man in England'. Predictably, each was a compulsive and, except by one another, unrivalled '*coureur des femmes*'. Both had political careers, Harry Cust's less successful than George Wyndham; the latter, however, attracted considerable odium as Chief Secretary to Ireland, a post given him by his political protector, Arthur Balfour. Each was high born. Wyndham was descended on his mother's side from the quixotic and doomed Irish patriot, Lord Edward Fitzgerald, and 'La Belle Pamela', a legendary beauty, the illegitimate daughter of Philippe Egalité and Madame de Genlis; and, on his father's side, from Lord Leconfield, owner of Petworth House, one of the great houses of England. Harry Cust was the heir to Belton, the beautiful seventeenth-century property in Lincolnshire belonging to his cousin, Lord Brownlow. Further, there was the great Gothic pile of Ashridge, which would have been Harry's had he survived, where life was lived very much in the grand manner.

The relationship of these men to David Tennant was two-fold: in George Wyndham's case it was simple, he was his mother's brother; where Harry Cust was concerned it was less so, since he was Pamela Tennant's lover. At least, Harry made no secret of the fact that he loved Pamela and wept copiously over the matter when the occasion arose.

The brilliance of the Souls flowered only briefly and did not survive the outbreak of the First World War. But what made the Souls so distinct in the English society of their time was the degree to which the source of its energy came from its women, many of whom were David's own relations. As Daisy, Countess of Warwick – one of the better of the Prince of Wales' 'good friends' – observed later: 'Our unenlightened aristocracy was actually perturbed by the discovery that there were clever women in its ranks.' At a Souls gathering outstanding beauty could be allied with intelligence in high degree; high spirits sparked with wit and fantasy; learning leavened with artistry. Most notable, in this latter aspect, was the disturbingly elusive beauty, Violet, Duchess of Rutland, mother of Diana Manners, who exhibited her work professionally from an early age and whose drawings and sculpture were admired by Rodin. There was Ettie, Lady Desborough, of whom Diana wrote in *The Times* obituary: '. . . in the years before 1914 Lady Desborough held a position in the worlds of wit and fashion that nobody has occupied since.' And the ravishing and erudite Wyndham sisters were immortalized by John Singer Sargent in a painting dubbed by the Prince of Wales 'The Three Graces'. David's mother, Pamela, being the most 'Soulish' of the trio. The most forceful, original, outrageous, vivacious and intrepid of these emancipated ladies, however, was David's diminutive aunt Margot, the youngest of the four famous daughters of that redoubtable patriarch Sir Charles Tennant. By the time E. F. Benson's best seller *Dodo* was published in 1893, of which she was the instantly recognizable if somewhat satirized heroine, Margot's strength of character had so imposed itself upon society that she had become an accepted hostess in her own right – a unique situation for a young unmarried woman. Her candour, her social anarchy, her dazzling and scandalous wit and very un-English indulgence in high fashion were a godsend to a Press only too ready to exploit such refreshing attributes.

The Tennant ancestry was one of proud, God-fearing, independent men – typical nonconformist lowland Scots farmers. The founder of the family's fortune was David's great-great-grandfather Charles, born in 1768. He was a gifted chemist and the first to solve a domestic problem that had defied even the ingenuity of the Romans. With this discovery the Senators' togas would always have been immaculate, the shifts of the Vestal Virgins whiter than white – in short, bleaching powder. The financial energy generated by the marketing of the bleaching process was channelled, with the instinct of an inspired entrepreneur, into various richly rewarding industrial and monetary fields by the Liberal MP and Baronet, Sir Charles Tennant – known within the family as 'The Bart'. As with his forebears, The Bart's procreative energy was handsomely rewarded by the fathering of sixteen children through the agency of two wives, the second being taken when he was at the ripe age of seventy-five. So a dynasty, too, was founded.

The Bart was generous in the extreme and endowed his daughters in a manner which could bear comparison with the millionaire fathers of the young American beauties then welcomed into English society. One of the few to recognize this generosity openly was his son-in-law Lord Ribblesdale married to Charlotte, known throughout her lifetime as 'Charty'. He, for his part, was always referred to as 'The Ancestor' in recognition of the elegance of his Olympian form which provided the subject for another of Sargent's most celebrated paintings. The Bart's generosity allowed The Ancestor to accept one of the more romantic appointments in the Queen's Household, that of Master of the Queen's Buckhounds.

The most artistically talented of the daughters was Lucy, whose gifts were almost completely extinguished under the bushel of a long, unwelcomed by The Bart, and not particularly happy marriage to Thomas Graham Smith. He took her with him to the country and kept her there. Laura and Margot, the two youngest, were brought up as twins. They must have seemed amazing, sharing an unbounded zest for life and the same reckless vitality which made them, wrote Lady Elcho, '... quite unlike anyone London had seen before ....' The two girls had innumerable suitors, the most persuasive of them being Alfred Lyttelton, the seventh of Lord Cobham's sons. Alfred won the heart of the mercurial, wide-eyed and deeply susceptible Laura. Within a year they were married. A perfect partnership it was declared by all. Within another year she was dead following the birth of a son, who was himself to die shortly after. Alfred, having fulfilled one of his father's ambitions through his excellence as a cricketer, fell on that field rather than the one of battle when he was hit on the head by a cricket ball a year before war broke out. Charty, too, died while still only in middle age from the then incurable tuberculosis, a disease which had killed her two half-sisters.

Meantime, Margot was very much alive. And she hung on to her independence – if not to her virginity. When this last became an aggravation she arranged for its disposal at the hands of a Soul 'fellow traveller', the poet and explorer Wilfrid Scawen Blunt, a close friend and cousin of the Wyndhams. Thus released, she determined upon marriage. The object of her attentions was the lawyer and politician Herbert Henry Asquith, whose formal exterior concealed a man of strong passions. 'Squiffy', as Asquith widely and indulgently came to be known, had fallen in love with Margot after the death of his first wife by whom he had five children, the eldest, Raymond, destined to be killed like Edward Tennant on the Somme in 1916. Margot and Squiffy were married in 1894 when she was already twenty-eight. The marriage drew her outside the central circle of the Souls but, since Squiffy was then Home Secretary and would soon be Prime Minister in the Liberal administration, it broadened the scope of her influence. She admitted that she felt an acute nostalgia for the world of the Souls, a loss which may have been assuaged when two of her step-sons married into the coterie. The Tennant girls, high-minded, high-spirited, high-handed, were the very stuff of which the Souls were made. It was only later a rather jaundiced view came to be taken of them, succinctly expressed by one of their descendants: 'Inter-married, inter-bred, inter-financed, interfering.'

Unquestionably, David Tennant was himself a child of the Souls, with the dominant influence in the female house, a house firmly ruled by Pamela. His father, Edward, whom Pamela had been encouraged to marry on her return from India where she had been sent to 'get over' Harry Cust, seems to have been rather an austere man, conscientious and public spirited. No doubt he deserved his peerage, although without the machinations of his determined little sister, Margot, it might well have slipped him by. What paternal affection David was to acknowledge came from the man to whom Pamela gave the love that had failed to materialize for her husband. He was Edward Grey, later to become Lord Grey of Fallodon. Indeed, Grey might well have been David's true father. David himself felt that he had detected certain clues to support this possibility, one which did not displease the dark romantic in his nature. However that might be, the two Edwards and Pamela formed an amicable 'ménage à trois', embracing Pamela's five children during the last years of Glenconner's life – a situation the Souls tended to condone within their own orbit.

The four boys – Edward (Bim), Christopher, David, Stephen – and the eldest child, Clarissa (Clare) were brought up with a similar lack of restraint, formality and convention to that Pamela herself had enjoyed in her idyllic childhood at Clouds, the great house her parents had built in Wiltshire. They were consciously exposed to all that was held to be most elevating to the spirit and poetic sensibility was encouraged at all times. After a visit to Glen, the Tennants' Scottish baronial mansion in Peeblesshire, Arthur Balfour described the children as being like 'hot-house orchids'. It was Pamela's conceit to receive visitors with all the children arranged tastefully around her, while she sat like Penelope at her loom. If arrival was delayed no respite was allowed. They had to be caught in this 'natural' pose. Kathleen (Kakoo), Duchess of Rutland, née Tennant, was welcomed on one occasion in this manner. Bim rose with a sigh from his cramped kneeling posture: 'Oh, thank God you've arrived, cousin Kakoo. We've been preperating [sic] so long.'

But it was Bim, the eldest son, a gifted boy of exceptional sensitivity, who proved most responsive to this hot-house atmosphere that Pamela had created. Pamela and Bim held each other in an affection which was intense. When Bim was killed at nineteen her greatest dread was realized. But, as with other Soul mothers, a deep concern for themselves found a certain sense of atonement in the spreading of their sons' blood over the battlefields.

For consolation, Pamela turned to spiritualism. She was encouraged in this by Sir Oliver Lodge, an eminent scientist turned spiritualist, whom she had first encountered at Clouds. The mantle of maternal devotion now fell upon David, Christopher having not been found sufficiently malleable, Stephen being too young, and Clare, being a girl, whom Pamela had never found it in her to like. Wriggle as he might David could not escape the intensity of this attention. Perhaps he did not altogether want to. Pamela must have been an entrancing as well as a deeply attentive parent. She was beautiful, intelligent, adventurous and romantic with a strong leaning towards the Bohemian in her artistic devotions, taking the children on long, horse-drawn caravan trips through the West Country, playing the guitar and singing to them by the light of an oil lamp while their dinner simmered on the primus stove. This, again, might have been an echo of early days at Clouds when her father's cousin, Wilfrid Blunt, would arrive in a caravan and pitch his tent in the grounds.

At this time, when David came sharply into Pamela's focus, he had pressing problems of his own which he felt she alone could solve and for which he felt she was responsible. Until he was thirteen David had never been exposed to any formal education. Then it was decided that he should be sent as a boarder to Sherborne, a public school whose principal merit in Pamela's eye was its proximity to Wilsford Manor, the Wiltshire home she had commissioned from the architect Detmar Blow to be built as a lesser Clouds. The experience was a short sharp shock. By his second term David was writing to his mother in anguish: 'They hate me here! This is the most terrible experience of my life! Why do you have to torment me so?' His fellow pupils could well have been exasperated by what might strike them as David's precocity. There was something about him, at any rate, with which they were quite unfamiliar, something that irked. Accordingly, they threw the astonished boy into a gorse bush.

The timely intervention of an attack of diphtheria released David from his Sherborne dilemma and gave Pamela the excuse to repossess her now favourite son. Thenceforth he was to remain at home where, with Clare breeding and bolting – she was to be thrice married – Bim dead, Christopher at sea, Stephen absorbed in his experiments with the pots and paints and powders on Pamela's dressing table, David was free to concentrate on such healthy pursuits as carpentry and his developing fascination with the internal combustion engine. In between, there were bouts of private education to prepare him for university.

By the time David, at eighteen, was ready to go up to Cambridge, the humiliating prick of the Sherborne gorse bush had been buried beneath a confident veneer. As his younger brother claimed for all of Pamela's children – but presumably with himself principally in mind: 'We Tennants have the fatal gift of beauty.' At least David had escaped the fate which befell Stephen of being dressed by Pamela as a girl – a fate not necessarily unwelcome given the predilections, and subsequent development, of the young Narcissus. But unlike the epicene Stephen, on whom Cecil Beaton was to model his persona, David's looks were virile and masculine with a touch of the matinée idol. Slimly built and tall, over six foot, David's impression of height was enhanced by an explosion of luxuriant dark hair waving from the top of his head. This wave would later be repressed by the application of a special product from Messrs Trumpers, hairdressers to gentlemen from the upper crust, bringing him more into line with the Pierrot-like silhouette of the twenties dandy.

Meanwhile Pamela looked at what she regarded as her creation with satisfaction. 'It wouldn't displease me at all to have a child by you. Yes, I can quite imagine it,' she told him. A wistful, throw-away line that might have slipped from the painted lips of one of the Queens of ancient Egypt, or been written by Noël Coward for Gertrude Lawrence to exhale throatily on a cloud of cigarette smoke. Not, anyway, quite the voice heard in her own book, *The Sayings of the Children*, with the following pious quote: 'Every child comes with the message that God is not yet discouraged of Man.'

In 1920, a little over a year after the Armistice, David arrived up at Trinity. The university was still licking the fearful wounds the Great War had inflicted, wherein more than half of its young graduates had been either killed or wounded. Now a fair number of the first- and second-year undergraduates, J. B. Priestley among them, had been 'blooded' in the trenches or served in the war as commissioned officers and thus become 'men'. This must have had a sobering and restraining influence on potential young bloods such as David. There was a feeling of discomfiture and disillusion abroad. David shared rooms in Bridge Street with his brother Christopher. Hoping to pursue a policy of political, emotional and social non-involvement, he chose to read the Mechanical Sciences Tripos. It was a subject in which he was interested and for which he had some natural aptitude, but it was still a rare choice to be found in a college dominated by Old Etonians and members of the Apostles, that clandestine and self-perpetuating élitist Cambridge society, comprised of radicals and many of the best minds in literature, philosophy and economics.

Two distinguished living contemporaries, Sir Steven Runciman and

George 'Dadie' Rylands, remember David from Cambridge days. Both formed part of the aesthetic élite there and were, respectively, Byzantine scholar-historian and a man of the theatre, who became the active inspiration of the dramatic group founded by Rupert Brooke, the Marlowe Society. As Rylands points out, the university was 'a totally different affair from what it is to-day'. 'Colleges were essentially individual each one *sui generis*. You were "a Jesus man", "a Kings man", "a Trinity man". The life-styles, as it is now called, of Tennant and myself ("a Kings man") were very unlike. He was well-off, fashionable, belonging to a higher social status, etc. As undergraduates we had very little in common.' That was to change later when living in London on little more than £300 a year Rylands would go at night with friends to the Gargoyle the most popular club in those carefree days and discovered that he shared with David a strong addiction to the theatre.

Runciman's view of David, although a fellow 'Trinity man', was not confined to Cambridge. The two families knew each other well and Steven's father, the first Viscount Runciman, was a close friend of Edward Grey. Steven found David rather a dull dog compared to the more mercurial Stephen who was 'eccentric and fantastic and in those days full of charm'. That David was then – if not for all of his life – a deeply shy man, beneath a charming manner much of the time masking a Soul-ish sense of superiority, is rather borne out by what Runciman says, in echo of Rylands: 'David was always friendly, and I certainly didn't dislike him. But we had little in common.'

David came down from Cambridge in 1922 with an acceptable second-class degree in his chosen subject and without acquiring affectations of manner from the prevailing climate of aesthetic sensibility – he had been exposed to enough of that at home. However, he did acquire a reputation for sartorial daring by adopting corduroy trousers, for daily wear: unusual enough at the time to draw comment from the popular press. Meanwhile Lord Glenconner had died suddenly after an operation and Christopher had inherited the title and with it the responsibility of directing a considerable industrial empire. It was something for which he was admirably suited by temperament. He threaded his often wayward relations through the frequent bogs and quick-sands of their financial affairs with familial devotion. He was not really interested in what motivated people, only in the outcome of their actions. The financial portfolio was the security blanket in which all those for whom he felt responsible should be securely wrapped. Even if only limited to the family this was already a considerable undertaking.

Glenconner's death while he was still up at Trinity relieved David of any obligation for conventional acts of filial defiance. It was the latter-day Jocasta, in the form of Pamela, who was a much greater threat to his sense of identity. Time and power, in the sense of the control she exercised over his finances, were running out for Pamela. In little over a year David would attain his majority and then enjoy the independence of a very large income from one of the trusts set up by The Bart – £15,000 a year, today's equivalent of rather more than £225,000. Perhaps to strengthen her hand, Pamela decided to regularize the union with the surviving base of her domestic triangle. Shortly after David came down, she and Lord Grey married.

David found himself cast upon a delighted metropolis. In all respects he was regarded as a highly desirable catch. He had every reason to believe that the world was about to become his oyster, but his social cavortings were very strictly monitored by Pamela. To take care of the dangerous nights – he was living in her London house – she would buy tickets for the theatre – the theatre was considered safe so long as you remained on the right side of the footlights – to which he would supposedly escort some carefully selected companion. Ursula Grosvenor, a cousin by marriage, was very well-considered in this regard. David would frequently play hookey by selling the tickets back to the box-office and go off in pursuit of something less demanding. Dancing, like as not, and dry at that. He had pledged himself to his mother to remain teetotal until he was twenty-one. David's twenty-first birthday celebrations came and went calmly without any physical or emotional entanglements to ruffle the surface of maternal omnipotence. Pamela shied away from the thought of any binding alliance, but the possibility of a *mésalliance* was for her a real dread. 'Thank God he hasn't married an actress,' she congratulated herself to a friend. She was not to know what (or who) was waiting in the wings.

2

The next dramatic and decisive influence in David's life, and one that was to lead him inevitably up to the Gargoyle heights, owed more to the inspiration of *commedia del arte* than to the Olympian calm of the lofty Souls. Late in 1923, a box in the St Martin's theatre enclosed David and his formidable aunt Margot. They were there to see *The Likes of 'Er*, one of the hits of the season. Of the play's sensational new star, the critic, James Agate, had written: 'A young actress flew across our stage last night with more latent capacity than any other young actress living.' Florrie Small, the furious little ball of cockney-gamine fire, was played by the diminutive Hermione Baddeley, aged just seventeen. George Bernard Shaw had seen her act when she was twelve and was so impressed that he instantly shot her off a postcard saying she acted twice as well as people twice her age and suggested, rather tweely, that from now on she should change her name from Baddeley to Goodeley. She failed to impress Mrs Asquith, however. 'What an odious child', was her comment after the performance. 'Really? I found her rather endearing', David had replied.

Hermione was the fourth daughter of a gifted but feckless composer, William Clinton-Baddeley, and his stage-struck wife Louise, of French Catholic descent. Louise Baddeley was a resourceful and determined woman who, when patience with the failure of her husband's artistic ambitions was exhausted, abandoned him in the country and brought her children to London. To her daughters' delight, she opened a boarding house for gentlefolk near Hyde Park and there they lived and grew up throughout the First World War. Divining the artistic potential of her daughters very early, Louise sent them to the newly opened Margaret Morris School of Dancing, more of an arts centre than just a theatre school. So precocious was the strain of theatrical genius handed down from Robert Baddeley, who had appeared with David Garrick at Drury Lane in the eighteenth century, that the two youngest girls, Hermione and Angela, were to make their dramatic debuts at the age of nine and eleven, respectively. Angela, too, was destined for lasting fame as a classical actress, and neither was ever again to be out of professional demand for the rest of their long lives. Once established in London, Louise bore one more child, Billy, who took the name Baddeley. Billy's histrionic talents took a different form – he became an Anglican Dean in Australia and later officiated over Wren's little church of St James in Piccadilly.

With the instant fame that *The Likes of 'Er* had brought her, Hermione found that she had become a celebrity. Invitations to the more sophisticated London parties lay thick on the doormat of her mother's genteel boarding house. These were turned down by the protective Louise. However, there came one from the society hostess and fashionable interior designer, Syrie Maugham, wife of Somerset. This was not something Louise felt could be refused. A party was to be held in Argyll House, Syrie's splendid home on the Kings Road, Chelsea, and it was to be given in honour of the Prince of Wales. David Tennant who had by now escaped from Pamela's propinquity by moving in to share Christopher's flat in Sloane Street, was also invited as a matter of course.

Hermione related once more her account of this first strange meeting with David over lunch with the author shortly before her death in 1987. Her voice, familiar to so many for so long, was as fruitily suggestive as ever and laced with idiosyncratic emphasis:

> You see, darling, I had made this sort of *mad* hit, which sometimes is a very worrying thing to do. Too much, too soon. I had far too much, far too *soon* – making this sort of really *blinding* success. Usually in England you have three or four successes and *then* you become a star. I was pushed right up to the front rank at *once*. But my mother would never have let me go to this *very* grown-up party if the Prince of Wales – I always did *rather* love him, you know – wasn't going to be there too. And it *was* a wonderful party and we all danced of course to live music. In those days any hostess worth her *salt* would always hire a band that could play that exciting American music that the Prince of Wales loved so much. And then it was suddenly *midnight* and I was Cinderella – my mother was terribly, *terribly* strict with all her four daughters. So I said good-bye and was half-way down the staircase when there was all this *ringing* on the door-bell and when the footman opened it there was this *man* standing in the hall. He was like a Greek god – very tall and dark. He was the most handsome man I had ever seen. I have never, ever, not in Hollywood, nowhere, have I seen a man with such an air, with such style and grace as David. Then he started coming up the stairs

looking at me *very* hard. In fact he stopped me going *down*. Then he reached up and snatched my Spanish shawl off my shoulders and said: 'You can't go yet! We haven't had a dance.' And he led me back into the ballroom. He had such confidence, you see. I found him irresistible and I always did. Of course I had a little explaining to do when I got home. But I didn't tell Mummy that I had met the man of my life. How could I know it then? I didn't even know his *name*. But he remembered *me*, all right.

Hermione did not mention how irresistibly desirable David certainly found this dynamic and lovely young girl who he was soon to call his 'pocket Venus'. In any case, he lost little time in seeking her out again and inviting her to tea at the flat he shared with Kit, as David always called Christopher. Tea was considered safe and not an occasion requiring a chaperone. As Hermione rather quaintly puts it in her autobiography, not otherwise remarkable for its accuracy, at first there was no hanky-panky at all. But lots of dancing, the next best thing. Those otherwise untouchable, in that non-permissive era, could at least be brought legitimately cheek-to-cheek on the dance floor, as Fred Astaire made manifest for millions. Meanwhile, Louise consulted *Debrett* and certain friends in the know, and cautiously gave the nod to David's request for Hermione to shimmy with him in the Savoy Hotel's ballroom after her performance. But the Cinderella syndrome was still in force – home by midnight. Sometimes they were joined for supper and the dance by Kit and a girl who had greatly taken his fancy, the daughter of family friends from Scotland, the young Elizabeth Bowes-Lyon. David told Hermione that he anticipated a happy conclusion to this budding romance. An engagement ring was duly bought, but when the *moment juste* arrived Christopher either funked it or had a change of heart. Anyway, nothing was said and a tour of naval duty then intervened. Shortly afterwards, Lady Elizabeth became Duchess of York. Had Christopher spoken when he intended to, the British public might have been denied their present Queen Mother.

Little Hermione, her name up in lights in the West End, was working in the theatre every night and, during the day, was rehearsing a new play, while David was, to all intents and purposes, just a playboy. Whether he was goaded by this thought into worthy activity, or whether it was in search of that always elusive mystery, his identity, he now betook himself (and his Cambridge degree) to Coventry, there to start work on the factory floor of Leyland Motors. So keen did he show himself on the production line his work-mates had to urge him to desist, 'Leave off, Dave. Give over, it's yer tea-break.' But the early enthusiasm soon began to pall. He missed London and above all he missed Hermione. There was a paucity of parts for someone of Hermione's tender years if she were to confine herself simply to straight drama as her sister Angela was doing. What was needed was something that would stretch her full range of gifts: her singing, her dancing, her ribald sense of humour, her gift for repartee, her ability to create vivid characterizations. Revue beckoned. And to revue she went, first with *The Co-Optimists*, the most popular variety show in London with Stanley Holloway its principal star. Louise then decided that since her youngest daughter was an undoubted star she had better start being paid like one. She now approached Charles B. Cochran, the producer of London's most elaborate shows. 'Cochran's Young Ladies' were ballyhooed as the 'most beautiful girls in the world'. Cochran made Louise a handsome offer for Hermione's services over a three-year period, rising to £200 a week. Hermione's first Cochran show was to be *On With The Dance*. Noël Coward had been commissioned to write it and this was also to be his first experience of this form of theatrical extravaganza. Cochran always rehearsed his shows in the Poland Rooms in Soho, so Hermione came to be familiar with the area and appreciate it. This was to prove useful. For some time David had been talking about a project he had for opening up his own club. A place where all the rich intellectuals, 'Bloomsberries' and the like, whom he already knew through Pamela, would subsidize the deserving artistic poor, whom he had yet to meet but who held for him some sort of romantic attraction. But foremost, he confided to her, it would be a place for the two of them to dance.

'The idea of owning your own club', Hermione said later,

> all started out, as so many things do, as a sort of *joke*, really. Because, you see, even at the Savoy, there was not enough room for us to do our *wonderful* dancing. And we really *could* dance, you know. I loved it more than anything else. But we really did *mad* dancing and David used to lift me off my feet and *whirl* me around. It took up a lot of room and not everybody liked it. They didn't want a sharp, high heel suddenly full in the face. So David said the only thing to do was open our own place where we could dance the heads off our feet. That was the Gargoyle's first moment of conception.

'Hanky-panky', as well as the energetic courtship ritual on the dance-floor, had been taking place between Hermione and David for some time and both felt keenly, if privately, that it was high time they got down to the real thing. The first memorable occasion took place in the celebrated Adelphi Hotel, Liverpool, after the first try-out night of *On With The Dance*. Hermione's big number was 'Poor Little Rich Girl', a song Noël Coward had written for her and the French star, Alice Delysia. Hermione played the bright young thing whose life was a confusion of drink and drugs and men, Delysia was the lady's-maid preparing her mistress for yet another wild party, while offering up the tuneful advice: 'Poor little rich girl, don't drop a stitch too soon ....' Hermione's dropped stitch that night was not premeditated. David had come over unexpectedly from Coventry. However, the drop was observed. David had forgotten to lock his bedroom door and, inevitably, the anxious mother-hen Louise, on the prowl disturbed the two of them in flagrant delight. 'It was an original experience for us both', Hermione claimed.

A brief reflection is perhaps a permissible digression here, on the sexual mores of the conventionally-educated Englishman, in those days just far enough removed from the war for careless youth to start living again with a guiltless, reckless abandon. There was no equivalent in London of the sexual frenzy that was then erupting in Paris. This was largely Black orientated and initiated by Parisiennes deprived by the war of their fair share of young males. The middle and upper classes in general, of London and England were more decorous, more socially rigid, and more covertly homosexual.

As Cyril Connolly, a contemporary of David's, observed of his own fellow undergraduates: 'We were the last generation of womanless Oxford. Men who liked women were apt to get sent down.' The homosexual world had, in terms of growing up or coming to terms with itself and realizing its own brand of adulthood, a tremendous lead. After all, the apparata of sexual pleasure lay in common ground. There was no dark mysterious cave to be entered holding who knew what castrating dragon in its depths. Once that aspect of yourself had been accepted and terms concluded, you, the invert, were 'away'. And you were encouraged so to be by the public and worldly success of those who had gone before. Boys who had been brought up at public schools in a pervasive climate of homosexuality, however disguised or sublimated, were better able to concentrate upon their work in the comforting knowledge that Jones, major, minor or minimus, was a visible, tactile, if not necessarily obtainable, presence. Confirmed heterosexual boys tended to spend their days in dry dreams of purely imaginary delights, and their nights in wet ones.

To be, as David evidently was, a male virgin of twenty-three, was not rare. To be entirely heterosexual at that age, in spite of Pamela's fixation, but perhaps because of her very insistence on removing him from Sherborne, a likely area of infection, was possibly more so. What is remarkable is the degree to which this innocence and ignorance, at least in regard to the opposite sex, was so widespread in David's world. An example of this oddity, and not necessarily extreme, was to be found in David's own first cousin, Pamela's nephew, Richard (Dick) Wyndham. Dick, the heir to Clouds, was a close friend of David's. He was also six years his senior and was therefore old enough to have fought in the war, been wounded and decorated with the Military Cross for gallantry in the field. For all of these reasons he was very much a man in the eyes of the world. Dick, as a regular soldier, had remained in the army during the immediate post-war years. He had been appointed ADC to Field Marshal Lord French, a friend of Pamela and the Souls, when he was *en poste* in Dublin as Lord-Lieutenant of Ireland. French had a longstanding mistress, a famous beauty called Winifred Bennett, also resident at Phoenix Park. Winifred had a daughter Iris, not as devastating as her mother, but pretty nonetheless. Dutifully, conventionally, Iris and Dick fell in love and, in 1920, were married, to everyone's delight. But then, after three days and three nights, the puzzled newly-weds, virgins both, had still not managed to discover how 'it' was done. Defeated and in despair, they went to consult a Dublin physician. Happily, this good man was able to open the doors of creation for them and a daughter, Joan, was born in due season. An event, however, the marriage was not to survive for very long.

David was more fortunate than Dick in meeting Hermione when he did. Having been trained from early years as a dancer she would have been immune from that agonizing self-consciousness about the body that could have such an inhibiting effect upon potential suitors and which would have been typical of the girls David met under Pamela's guidance. Following the provincial opening of *On With The Dance*, David returned to London highly elated by the delightful turn of events: a triumph reflected in the stormy success of the new revue and in particular in the Baddeley–Delysia rendering of 'Poor Little Rich Girl'. This was to prove the hit song of 1925 and to become a classic.

Hermione had been aware for some time that under an arrogance of manner David lacked a certain confidence. She was delighted at having been able to put to the test her ability to provide the medicine required, which, in the case of poor Dick, the doctor was obliged to order. With David now tucked under her belt, as it were, with the success she had already achieved and with what was now predicted for her when the revue opened in London, the future looked rosy indeed for a girl still only eighteen years old.

As a confirmed spiritualist, Pamela was quick to spot the suspect euphoric aura radiating from David upon his return to London. The long apprehended 'actress' had finally been made manifest: an enchantress into whose thrall she had been obliged to watch her beloved being drawn deeper and deeper. She felt threatened. Her response to this unwelcome disorder in her house was to transmute threat into accusation. 'You realize, don't you, David, that by carrying on like this you are simply putting a pistol to my head?' David had countered with: 'She's not just an ordinary actress. Once you get to know her you'll like her.' Pamela took up the challenge. Invitations were issued for David to bring Hermione down to Wilsford for examination by herself and Lord Grey. The old retainers – cook, governess, nanny and so on, all of whom nursed a special weakness for David – were mustered and expected to close ranks against the outsider.

Hermione seems to have been undaunted by this confrontation. After a number of visits she succeeded in winning the old retainers round to her side. 'You're the one for master David, dear. He needs someone to bring him out of his shell,' they told her. They must have recognized a sympathetic – at least a change from the hoity-toity – personality in this thespian tot. She and Lord Grey also found each other engaging. Pamela masked her feelings and exercised her considerable skills in making the not-so-impressionable young actress feel welcomed and at home in Wiltshire. The fact that Hermione was already a star in her chosen world, and one brilliant enough to impinge upon Pamela's, and that David, although older, still remained relatively unweaned, did not give Pamela a very strong hand. But she knew she still had a card or two up her sleeve.

3

As is the case with many people who feel themselves set apart from the general run of humanity without knowing quite why or in what specific way, David attracted certain individuals who felt bound, if only in self-interest, to shed light upon the shadows of the psyche. 'Undesirables', Pamela might have called them: 'Not to be encouraged'. One such was Harry Walker, now back in David's life. Some ten years older than David, Harry had first been engaged by Pamela as a private tutor to prepare her son for his Cambridge entry exams. He had the necessary academic qualifications, but he had been found wanting in some other particular and did not remain long at Wilsford. Since that time Harry had married and was now looking none too eagerly, for employment. During the intervening years he had taken care not to lose touch with his erstwhile pupil through whom he hoped to penetrate the resistant citadel of Society. David, on renewed acquaintance, had talked expansively about his new ambition, and Harry at once saw how he could make himself useful. He undertook to find suitable premises for the Club.

During his attendance upon Hermione while she was in rehearsal there, David had acquired a taste for the salty side of Soho. There was much to recommend it. As a pungent centre of the restaurant world, the area was ideally situated, its boundaries marching with Bloomsbury, Mayfair and theatre-land – critical aspects of David's past, present and future – and encompassing the heartland of bohemia, the Café Royal itself, within winking distance of Eros's statue in Piccadilly Circus. A part of Soho had once been known as Knave's Acre, today the area is more commonly known as the Square Mile of Vice. But by 1925 the quarter had thrown off much of the ill reputation accorded it by a Police Commission which, in 1913, had reached the conclusion that Soho's Greek Street was 'the worst street in London' from their point of view – one of crime, anarchy and immorality. It had not always been so. Few parts of inner London have not at sometime been fashionable, and in the early eighteenth-century Soho Square was as sought after as is Belgrave Square, or Eaton Square today. George II, when Prince of Wales, had a house there, as did Sir Roger de Coverley, John Evelyn, and the Earl of

Stamford. On the corner was the notorious White House indulgent to gaming, to well-heeled bucks, high-styled courtesans and adventuresses. George, Prince of Wales, 'Old Q' – the Marquis of Queensberry – and the Marquess of Hertford kept the place going then, and it must have had something of the cachet of Annabel's and the Clermont Club housed together in Berkeley Square today.

The explanation for Soho's post-war move up-market was the spread of the thriving film industry in and around Wardour Street, the acute shortage of domestic accommodation in central London, and the prosperity brought to the restaurants and continental shops, by changing social habits and by the floating population of those in whom service overseas had developed a taste for wine and exotic foods. These tastes had first been brought to Soho in the seventeenth century by the Huguenots and enriched by other refugees and craftsmen from Europe and the East ever since. The district also enjoyed a tradition for having harboured the impoverished in the world of the arts, and this seemed to fit ideally into David's grand design. As Harry was able to point out – he was no slouch when a little judicious mugging-up was timely – De Quincey had fainted from starvation on the doorstep of a house in Soho Square where he was befriended by the beautiful Ann, who from that time on became the lost love of his life. Likewise, Lord Mayor Beckford, father of William, opened his house on the corner of Greek Street to the boy-poet Chatterton, who nonetheless managed to starve to death – or was it suicide? – in his own Holborn garret. In the parallel street called Frith – formerly Thrift – William Hazlitt, critic and essayist, had died impecuniously in a lodging house. William Blake, son of an enlightened hosier, was born in Marshall Street and another local boy, John Dryden, Britain's first poet laureate, lived at 43 Gerrard Street.

In 1921 this last address acquired a new and quite different significance when it was taken over by Mrs Kate Meyrick. She achieved renown as night-club hostess to royalty – dispossessed and otherwise – and in that role was herself judged to be queen. The 43, as the Club was called, was already famous when Harry went round to inspect it as a possible site for David's venture. He found the place shut, having recently been raided by the police, and Mrs Meyrick herself detained in Holloway prison at His Majesty's pleasure. The sentence, consequent upon restaurateur 'Brilliant' Chang operating his dope gang from the club, won much sympathy from Mrs Meyrick's distinguished clientele – the Crown Prince of Sweden, Prince Nicolas of Romania, Edna Best, Michael Arlen, Tallulah Bankhead, Jack Buchanan, *et al.*

The choice of becoming a night-club owner as a form of self-expression argued a spirit of revolt in David. Revolt against Pamela, the wilful. 'Night-clubs are man's natural and dignified protest against being overgoverned. They are a sign of robust health which objects to being wet-nursed.' Thus spake the music critic, Edwin Evans, a future Gargoyle member, a friend and promoter of Igor Stravinsky. Evans's target in this case was the puritan wet-nurse Sir William Joynson-Hicks, unlovingly known as 'Jix', who had recently been made Home Secretary and as such chose to appoint himself official spoil-sport. Jix, whose principle it was to be anti-pleasure and thus against the prevailing mood of the times, made ruthless use of DORA, which came within his official remit. The Defence of the Realm Act was passed during the war and gave the government extraordinary powers of interference in public events and private lives, justifying itself at the time as a measure to keep munition workers out of the pubs during factory hours. For Jix it was a weapon with which to prosecute his vendetta against night-clubs – Kate Meyrick being his most notable recent victim.

But David did not feel threatened by Jix or by any of the numerous police raids carried out at the latter's instigation. In the first place, since the gorse-bush incident, he had been brought up by Pamela to be intimidated by nobody – except his own mother. Secondly, there was the implied support of the formidable Margot, between his mother and whom no love was lost, and the qualified support of that most respected establishment figure, Edward Grey. Thirdly, and most importantly, it was not David's intention (still less so, Hermione's) to own the sort of louche establishment run by Mrs Meyrick. (She, in a more refined and less specialized way, filled something of the same social role as the recent 'Madame Sin', Mrs Cynthia Payne.) There would be no question, for instance, of David's club providing 'hostesses' – even for royalty. The author Daphne Fielding (née Vivian, the former Lady Bath) remembers being taken, as quite a young girl and in direct defiance of parental edict, to the 43 shortly before Mrs Meyrick's arrest: 'The jingle of the tinny piano which greeted one on arrival in a dark, smoky atmosphere, and the hostesses waiting to be picked-up at their tables, became intriguing figures of conjecture.'

One of the several possible places nosed out by Harry had struck David with its potential. It consisted of the top three floors of a large and not unhandsome building on the corner of Dean Street and Meard Street, a passage joining the parallel Wardour and Dean Streets. Built in about 1840, on a site where Nell Gwynne reputedly once owned a property, it had later been converted to house a printing works, its walls and floors reinforced to accept the vibration of heavy machinery. High-jinks and heavy-footed dancers the building could take in its stride, but it was going to have to withstand a great deal more than that, as was proved during the next world war, when the immediate area was straddled more than once by German bombs. A parachute-bomb demolished all but the bell-tower of St Anne's lovely seventeenth-century church not two hundred yards from 69 Dean Street, the address which by then had been synonymous with the Gargoyle Club for nearly twenty years.

Available cash emboldened David to reach a quick decision over the property. He was able to secure a fifty-year lease – which he reckoned should 'see him out' comfortably – for a very reasonable sum, proving once again how much easier it is to acquire bargains and live cheaply if you are already well-off.

Builders were already wreaking havoc within the top floors of the building by the time Hermione returned to London and was shown their future playground by David. At first she was dismayed by what she saw. But then David began to unroll the carpet of his dreams. Here, the floor-boards would be cut away to allow for a staircase leading down to the area below, decorated in the most modern style and consecrated entirely to dancing. There, steps would lead up to the flat roof, 350 square yards of it, on which a garden would be created wherein to dine and dance when the moon was up. Where they were standing would be a great 'Tudor' kitchen with open fireplaces of mellow red brick, oak tables, oak rafters, and a vast oak dresser that could be lowered to become a stage. Beyond, on the same floor, was to be the bar of a traditional inn serving real ales. But the entire floor beneath the main dancing-room was reserved as a private apartment with copious wine cellars to supply the club above. Although Hermione was still strictly teetotal – 'We were all having such a lovely time in the beginning nobody seemed to *need* to drink' – David was by now flexing his taste-buds against the challenge of vintage claret and champagne.

While Hermione marvelled at the scope of David's vision, the rickety lift rattled its way to the top floor where they stood amongst the rubble. It brought up with it a form of fly which Hermione soon began to suspect of nursing an ambition to become embalmed in David's desirable ointment. David introduced the fly as 'm'tutor, Harry Walker'. Hermione remembered the unfavourable impression Harry made on her then: 'Not attractive. *No*. Funny little *conceited* man. Not very tall. Rather a sarcastic face.

Quite an *amusing* face, I suppose. Not good-looking, though. And beside David – well....' To her irritation, David continued to address Harry as 'm'tutor' with no hint of mockery. 'M'tutor and I are going to Bordeaux soon to choose suitable clarets', David remarked airily. When Hermione later asked David what Harry's role would be in the club, David replied: 'Oh, I don't know. Manage it, possibly. He knows about these things.' She was not comforted.

Another side to the passive, 'host'-like disposition of David's character was his ability to exercise a charismatic charm that could melt people of both sexes into becoming willing, devoted and humble slaves. Sixty years after they first met, Cynthia, Louise's second daughter always known as 'Ciggie', spoke of David with the deepest admiration and affection:

> I have never known anyone with such charm, such kindness. He was always so helpful. If you were ever ill he was simply wonderful. He would see that you were cared for and he would look after everything. I would always have done anything for him. And did do quite a lot – including dyeing my beautiful black hair an unbeguiling gingery blonde. That was for the Club's opening night. What greater sacrifice....

But the practical help David was now finding invaluable came about through Muriel, eldest of the four Baddeley girls. She, like her mother, had married young, at seventeen. Her husband, Hugh Gee, was also young and a gifted artist working in the theatre as a designer where he was beginning to make a name for himself. Muriel had taken David to Hugh's studio and there had been an immediate rapport. Hugh liked the boldness of David's ideas and David liked Hugh's energy, enthusiasm and technical proficiency. Later, when he began working with Hugh in his studio on the model for his imaginative concept of the club, the whole enterprise excited the engineering and mechanical curiosity David had inherited from The Bart, plus the manual dexterity he had learnt to exercise in the village 'smithy' at Wilsford. Time spent in the studio was delightful play involving a certain creativity that briefly helped to adjust the balance in this aspect of David's relations with Hermione. A conflict over style arose, however. Hugh felt the club should have a consistent expression throughout. But which one? For there to be any point for David in this enterprise the expression of it had to be his own. But his character was one that held many contradictions. There was the dandy's need to startle with his thrust for the avant-garde, for the new, the fresh, the stimulating; and there was the pull of the patrician squire towards established tradition. There was another side to David where perhaps the influence of Pamela was most keenly felt.

This was through her sympathy with and encouragement of the rustic back-to-the-land ethos of William Morris's Arts and Crafts movement. Here patrician wealth and aesthetic whim could meet in the Utopia of a socialist dream, a dream which paradoxically only the rich could afford. The result was compromise. One floor – the point of disembarkation from the Lilliputian lift which shuddered up and down a narrow brick tunnel built on to the back of the building – would incline to this homespun style. The floor below would be sinuous, etiolated. Hidden lighting would bathe the whole in a current of strangeness and mystery. Mystery suffused with a tender eroticism. On the roof a dance-floor would be raised perilously above the level of the surrounding surface which would be screened by trees in pots. Light would be provided by a rosy flow filtering upwards through the frosted glass on the tops of the tables. And – a merry conceit – such neighbouring chimneys as infringed upon the view would all be painted a brilliant red.

Pamela watched these developments from a distance. Her compelling need to maintain dominion over her children had been severely strained over recent years and nothing – not even the spiritual communications with him through the medium of Mrs Osborne Leonard of East Barnet – could compensate her for the loss of Bim. 'All my children are what they are because of *me*', she once had said. The eldest son, Christopher, was 'Lord Sobersides' himself, fully occupied with the family business and making signs of impending marriage. A suitable choice and therefore nothing to be done there. She had shrugged off Clare's challenge to become – if possible – a legendary beauty to outshine her mother. Clare was beautiful enough, as many who trod the country-house hospitality circuit have testified, but Pamela was smarter. She played within the rules; Clare forced herself outside them. The precocious Stephen, at fifteen, had staked a spirited claim to public attention with an exhibition of his drawings and paintings in a London Gallery. It was a sell-out. Princess Victoria, Margot Asquith and Queen Alexandra were among those who snapped up an early Tennant. All this was meet for self-congratulation. Stephen had also succeeded in re-directing Pamela's attention toward himself by developing a fairly mild form of tuberculosis. This required a period of recuperation in Switzerland in company with his new young friend and fellow-student at the Slade, Rex

Whistler. Supervised, or course, by the comings and goings of Pamela, between the parties she gave for them at various hotels. If Stephen was also driven to challenge Pamela in the beauty stakes, with androgynous youth on his side, he won. But the laurel crown was to assume an increasingly grotesque tilt as the years passed after her death.

It was the temper of David's life since taking up with that 'little actress', which was so vexing to Pamela's spirit. And this whole idea of a night-club was deplorable beyond belief. David protested that it wasn't going to be a night-club so much as a rendezvous where people could meet for tea, or come to dine, dance and sup until three. Once again Pamela had to swallow her fury and regurgitate it in the guise of support. By so doing she would at least be able to exert her very considerable influence over the form the venture would take. Her involvement would raise the tone way above mere theatricality, or the jazzmania that currently held dancing youth in thrall. Impulsively, she threw herself behind the Club and alerted the wide range of her friends who might be persuaded to become members. It was one of the disarming contradictions of Pamela's character that beneath the calm and reasonable veneer there lay a pronounced weakness for rips and rakes. Paramount among them was Harry Cust, whom she never ceased to defend, even when, in his unhappy decline, his conduct was not reasonably defensible. Osbert Sitwell, in his autobiography, points up this aspect of her character – the remoteness harnessed to passionate prejudice. 'All her black sheep', he writes, 'as it were, became swans.' Prejudice bristled most fearsomely at the threat of an adventuress within her own manor. Much as she might have liked to cast Hermione in this role, it simply would not fit. If anything, the boot was pinching the other toe. It was Hermione who was launching David into a more vivid and, to him, more attractive world than Pamela was offering – or was able to offer.

Another source of inspiration David tapped while seeking a style for his club was Rosa Lewis, proprietress of the Cavendish Hotel in Jermyn Street, just off Piccadilly. Immortalized – to her undying fury – by Evelyn Waugh's parody of her in *Vile Bodies*, her life was to inspire a television series, *The Duchess of Duke Street*. Rosa has justly been described as one of the most eccentric and formidable women of her age. Some description of Rosa and the Cavendish, as inextricably linked as the Gargoyle was to be with David, is pertinent here, since the cast-lists of the two establishments were to be complementary, often interchangeable, and the flow of traffic between them constant, until the time they were both to go out of business in the same year, Rosa to her death, David to

Spain. For, if the Gargoyle was to have two faces, the Cavendish had two legs: one wrapped in the mouldering tweeds of tradition; the other elegant, high-spirited and high-kicking – when not actually legless.

Modestly-born in a village outside London during the height of mid-Victorian prosperity, Rosa quickly acquired the chirpy repartee of a cockney sparrow disguising a most resourceful and determined nature. She entered domestic service at the age of twelve, for which she was paid one shilling a week. After a period of drudgery, she moved, as under kitchen-maid, into the household of the comte de Paris, exiled head of the House of Bourbon and, in the eyes of the Royalists, rightful king of France. This was a definitive step up her self-made ladder, for it was in this august establishment that she first caught the vagabond eye of the portly Prince of Wales. As the only English member of the vast staff, she was called up one evening from her steaming cauldrons to sing 'God Bless the Prince of Wales' during a dinner party given in his honour. HRH obligingly pressed a golden sovereign into the pink palm of the blue-eyed young wench, the first gesture towards a not disinterested patronage that was to last some thirty years and from which both were to derive signal benefits. Rosa had a Napoleonic instinct about the male stomach; maintaining its gentle swell was to become her prime objective, and command of such a tactical position could secure all her ambitions. There were other focal points of interest, of course, but they could be provided for later.

After being lent by the comte to his uncle the duc d'Aumale to work in the kitchens at Chantilly and thence to his nephew the duc d'Orléans, Rosa's next major break came when Lady Randolph Churchill needed a relief cook. Rosa entered the Churchill household aged twenty and there made friends with the thirteen-year-old son of the house, a morose, unhappy young boy called Winston. This also was to prove a friendship that would be sustained throughout their lifetimes.

Rosa came within the orbit of David's family when some time later she was taken on by Margot Asquith. Margot's force of personality and independent spirit had a strong influence upon Rosa. She began to see what her instinct had been leading her towards: a woman's ability to learn how to dominate and manipulate the social structure. By the time she was thirty Rosa had become a young woman of considerable power. She was the most dependable, imaginative and socially acceptable provisioner, at a time when entertaining was what society was principally about.

It was in this role that she met the man who had the most profound emotional influence upon her of anyone in her long life. This was Lord Ribblesdale, who was later to be the prototype for Professor Higgins in Bernard Shaw's *Pygmalion*. This *grand diable de milord anglais* as the French press chose to describe him, was the epitome of everything to which Rosa aspired. The only man who ever laid claim to her heart, was her own proud claim. So, when he urgently begged her to come and run his kitchens at Epsom on his appointment as Master of the Queen's Buckhounds, she went unhesitatingly.

Queen Victoria died in 1901 and Rosa's old patron at last became monarch. The following year she acquired the lease of the Cavendish Hotel. This stood on the corner of Jermyn and Duke Streets. From the shell of the old hotel ensconced in a quadrangle of Regency houses protecting a central courtyard, Rosa was to create something altogether unique. Under her idiosyncratic reign, spanning two world wars, the Cavendish became known as the most remarkable and, in its quirky way, exclusive hotel in Europe – if not the world. Anyone who did not find favour in Rosa's eyes, or slipped into disfavour, was quite simply excluded.

Apart from the caprice of Rosa's recognition, the Cavendish was entirely unlike any accepted idea of an hotel. In appearance, its furnishing, staffing, style of administration, in its granting, even encouraging, of a certain sexual licence, it was much like one of the Edwardian country houses she had served in as a domestic, only transposed into the fashionable heart of London's West End. 'I didn't want anything hotelly or cheap, or any servants who had ever been in an hotel. I wanted it to be like one's own home. I didn't want a lot of money [Rosa was by now a rich woman]. I like people, and I think if you make a place like the people you like you get the people you like.' So she told Mary Lawton, the American journalist who wrote her biography in 1926. The popularity of the Cavendish thrived with the increasing social freedom of the early twentieth century. Its reputation was racy rather than respectable, and all the more attractive for that. Assignations could be pursued, discretion assumed. Greater privacy was ensured by Rosa having sets of rooms made into suites with their own private dining-rooms and, in some cases, private entrances. One such being reserved for Edward VII.

In the year after King Edward's death, Ribblesdale's wife, Charty, also died after a long illness. That, on top of the death of his son, Thomas, on active service, threw him into black depression. He now sought sanctuary with Rosa in the Cavendish and moved into a private apartment with all his furniture which then overflowed into the public rooms. About the same time another of Rosa's favourites, the choleric and eccentric baronet, Sir William Eden, father of Anthony (later Lord Avon) also settled in at the Cavendish. In originality of style he was a match for Ribblesdale and his own idiosyncrasies more than equalled Rosa's. This note from him gives some flavour of the establishment at that time.

> Dear Mrs Lewis,
> I am coming up crowned in glory on Tuesday. The Hon. Ashley too. Now look 'ere. I shall have a dinner party that night – noblemen, gentlemen, women, ladies, and prize-fighters – and we will box in the dining-room after. See? Tell your *Lord Ribblesdale I want him*, dinner and after, and anyone else you may think of – pretty – either sex – none but the brave deserve the fair. W.E.

Rosa enjoyed her self-appointed role in both men's lives – part mother-earth figure, part lewd nurse and much of her spare time was spent with The Ancestor on shopping expeditions, out to lunch or the theatre.

Another regular at the Cavendish who formed a fast friendship with Rosa was Northcliffe, born Alfred Harmsworth in County Dublin. He liked to stretch his legs under her mahogany in the raffish, aristocratic atmosphere over which she presided while the continual dew from her 'Cherrybums', as she called the Jeroboams of champagne, rose high in the glass. As a pioneer of mass communication – he had launched the *Daily Mail*, owned the *Evening News*, and had recently acquired a national institution, *The Times* – Northcliffe was well placed to celebrate Rosa as 'the most famous woman chef in the world'. Rosa was forty-seven and in the full glory of realized ambition when war erupted on the world. Now, with the first trickle of wounded returning from France, Rosa was to surpass even herself. For many, the Cavendish was to become a brief haven of sanctuary from the horror of trench warfare. Rosa was a great believer in the restorative properties of alcohol and women – or rather, 'good, clean tarts', as she liked to insist. A sufficiency of both always seemed to be on hand even in the war-beleaguered Cavendish. And those returning to the front went laden with provisions from Fortnums all paid for by Rosa. Often she went with the hotel bus to Victoria to bring back anyone on leave with nowhere to go. Whether or not they were able to pay was of no concern. Ninety men were billeted in one part of the hotel and the garage had been made over into a canteen for Belgian rankers. Staff had been cut to the bone. And very old bone at that – Rosa was quick on the draw with a white feather for any remotely eligible man who did not join up.

She continued to cook with very little help. Farewell dinners were given in the Elinor Glyn Room. Among those attending were the politicians Asquith, Lloyd George and Churchill, and the generals Kitchener, Byng, Roberts and Cowans. Crutches now began to pile up among the polo-sticks, the Purdey gun-cases and the abandoned tennis rackets, forcing the theatrical birds of paradise to pick their way with care within the confines of this exotic cage.

Before the war, the younger generation at the Cavendish had largely been composed of people David Tennant would have known as friends, relations or contemporaries of Bim – Charterises, Asquiths, Grenfells, Listers, Herberts. Now, barely into manhood, they were losing their lives at a staggering rate. The grief-haunted Ribblesdale was struck again twice: first, his daughter's husband of a few months was killed in action, then, shortly after, his son Charles died of wounds. Rosa was in despair, her mind, as she later described it, turned with grief. They had become her 'boys', surrogate sons. William Eden died in his bed at the Cavendish with Rosa at his side. The war continued. 'Life', said Rosa, 'had become the war and the war only.' There seemed no reason why it should ever end. Then, when the guns all over Britain announced the glorious news that the end had come at last, euphoria exploded in the Cavendish as everywhere else. But Rosa was almost spent, her indomitable will and spirit drained. 'Since 1914, now that they are all gone, I do not consider anything that I do of any value', she said. Her post-war blues were to be further aggravated by The Ancestor's defection. Ribblesdale had been gradually emerging from his black depression. 'To be a Lord is still a popular thing', he reflected and, to prove the point, he married John Jacob Astor's widow, Ava.

But Rosa's bleak view of life and herself was not to last. With the advent of the 1920s a new charge was once more pumping through the furnaces of the old hotel. The aftermath of war had left a moral and philosophical emptiness and, more obviously, a social vacuum. In his autobiography, Anthony Powell makes a point about the age-gap of the twenties, in that men and women who had grown up before 1914 were not only older, but altogether set apart. A dictum equally applicable to 1939 and the Second World War. Certainly the new life which came to fill the social vacuum in the twenties was happy to disassociate itself from any pre-war behaviour. It was youthful, playful, escapist, wild and, for the most part, well-born. It was breathless for spontaneity and its exploits provided the newspapers with columns of free and easy coverage. In 1924 the *Daily Mail* stamped its exponents with the collective label of the

'Bright Young People'. Numbered in its ranks were Daphne Vivian, Nancy Mitford, Henry Weymouth, Mark Ogilvie Grant, Brian Howard, (the last three still up at Oxford), Lady Eleanor Smith, Martin Wilson (Ribblesdale's grandson), the Jungman sisters, Evan Morgan, Eddie Gathorne-Hardy, Babe Plunket-Greene, Lettice Lygon and, in spite of her marriage to Duff Cooper in 1919, Diana Manners. From a somewhat different, but nonetheless overlapping, milieu was Stephen Tennant, with Cecil Beaton soon high-stepping close behind. 'Fun' was the name of their many inventive games and pastimes and *Vile Bodies*, published in 1930, was to be their satirical memorial.

Now, not for the last time, Rosa and the Cavendish were rediscovered. For some of the BYPs it was like the dream nursery they had never had, presided over by a nanny in turn forbidding and indulgent, ribald and stately, pickled in Edwardiana, peppering them with her fruity vernacular. But with David there was no question of rediscovery. The Cavendish had long been part of his life. He was drawn to it now for reasons quite different from those of the world of BYPs, from whom he in any case chose to keep a certain distance if only because Stephen's star shone so brightly there. And in its vacuous frivolity Hermione might well have felt out of place. David was inventing his own private game and he needed Rosa to help formulate the rules. Rosa had taken a shine to Hermione. She liked her theatrical sauce and she may have seen in her earthy spirit some of the professional dedication which had motivated her own youth. In any case, she was disposed to be helpful. As with the Cavendish, a country-house style would be established in his club, explained David. There would be log fires in the dining-room and only silver with fine bone china and crystal would be used on the tables. The staff, in this somewhat feudal concept, would be loyal and permanent. But one thing he wanted was a French chef. Rosa arranged for him to go and see an old friend of hers, the great Escoffier.

Meanwhile, the transformation within 69 Dean Street was nearing completion. This, in spite of frequent and violent eruptions of artistic temperament from Hugh Gee against the restrictions and interference imposed upon him by the front office, in the person of 'the fly', Harry Walker. Harry, who in protecting David's interests began increasingly to identify them with his own, resented anyone else engaging his patron's attention too closely. And this included Hermione. But he was cagey enough to keep quiet about that. Hugh, on the other hand, had exposed himself by seriously underestimating costs. These, like the skilled workforce for which he was responsible, had grown with the expansion of his own creativity. There was now to be a fountain in the middle of the dance-floor. David balked. Hugh had hit him where it hurt – in the pocket book. Also time was getting short. The Club's opening had already been delayed twice. There was the committee to be convened. A number of resonant names had been canvassed: Compton Mackenzie, who edited *The Gramophone* from parallel Frith Street, Clive Bell, A. P. Herbert and Arnold Bennett among them. David turned his mind to another problem. What to call the place. Hugh had recently dug up from somewhere a number of carved wooden gargoyles from the distorted mouths of which he proposed suspending lanterns to light the upstairs rooms. David became fascinated by them. They may have evoked childhood memories of the gargoyles decorating the mock baronial battlements of Glen. For whatever reason, they seemed an appropriate emblem. The Gargoyle Club it was to be. And Hugh was rewarded with his fountain.

At last the fateful day arrived – Friday, 16th January. Pamela had returned with Lord Grey from Switzerland the day before as an earnest of their support and also in view of the fact that many of those at the opening night would be there at her invitation. The previous night's dress-rehearsal had gone well. The lanterns swung gently from the gaping mouths of the gargoyles. Below, the small band, chosen for the discretion of its beat, played sweet and low, the fountain played in a whisper and the French chef rattled cheerfully on his *batterie de cuisine*. Escoffier had introduced David to a young compatriot, Xavier Boulestin, who was just about to open up a new restaurant in Covent Garden and he, in turn, had recommended a skilled and willing relative for the Club. And, critically, the democratic lift – everyone had equally to wait for it – was transformed from a rusty mouse-trap into a thing of beauty. Brightly shining metal gave it the appearance of a luxury art-nouveau cabin trunk, covering all its ends and sides except for the retractable grille door through which, with the lift in motion, there was an uninterrupted close-up view of the outer brick wall of the building, with two possible stops before the top floor. Into this, four people, if they were thin and had not recently dined or quarrelled, could just fit. And since this newly-furbished article still retained some of its original recalcitrant features a zest of uncertainty was added to the rites of passage.

Tall hats, white silk scarves, fur coats, long dresses, short skirts gathered under the Gargoyle lamp marking the Club's entrance in Meard Street and lapped over into adjacent Dean. It was a mild night. Denizens of Soho and resident prostitutes out for a breath of air or to show a bit of leg would have found nothing surprising in this animated gathering of toffs in toff's togs waiting to be raised up to the latest toff's paradise. Theatre-land was all about them and evening-dress was obligatory throughout the West End for all expensive seats. Drawing its readers' attention to the Club's opening, the *Daily Telegraph* observed that 'the list of members probably contains more famous names in society and the arts than figure on the roll of any other purely social club'. They included Somerset Maugham, Noël Coward, Gladys Cooper, Margaret Bannerman, Michael Arlen, Leon Goossens, Lilian Braithwaite, Gordon Craig, George Grossmith, Virginia Woolf, Duncan Grant, Nancy Cunard, Adèle Astaire, Edwina Mountbatten, Gilbert Frankau, Sibyl Colefax, an obligatory Guinness, Rothschild and Sitwell, a handful of MP's and the odd peer of the realm. Over three hundred members and guests turned up at one time or another on this inaugural night. 'How strange and unreal it seemed to the very unworldly girl I then was', recalls Hermione's sister, Muriel Pearson Gee.

> The lower floor was dark blue, lit from silver stars in a sapphire ceiling. There was a small fountain in the middle of the room and couples moving gently round it in the bluish light. Subdued music was coming from somewhere. 'Tender is the night', suggests the feeling. The other floor was a complete contrast. Homely, with a huge open fireplace on which steaks were spitting. Hermione, then on the wave of a huge theatrical success, was the hostess, of course.

That Hermione was openly, if not brazenly, 'doing the honours' may not have pleased Pamela. But the sense of decorum that prevailed that night probably owed more to Lord Grey's benign patronage of David's venture than to Hermione's first public shot at playing hostess. There was certainly no hint, on that ultra-smart occasion, of David's own professed ambitions to extend his patronage towards the deserving, artistic poor. Even established nonconformists like Augustus John, Epstein, Gaudier-Brzeska, Horace Brodzky and the model Betty 'Tiger Woman' May did not hear – or care to answer – the call of the Gargoyle from their sanctuary in the Café Royal. They would wait and see.

4

Pamela, for her part, found her patience running short. The Club's opening had been an undoubted success. But, on reflection, there was something rather galling for one who had been for so long at the centre of a brilliant and exclusive circle now to find herself upstaged by 'a nobody' and all because of her beloved David's blind and selfish infatuation for just a common little – no, she would not say it again. Nevertheless, that this young girl, not yet even twenty, in her 'teens' still, had been charged by David to act as the official hostess for all these eminent people – some of them, like young Noël Coward, her friends, of course – seemed to be like some sort of public consecration of their involvement with one another. A flaunting of it, even. The time had come, Pamela felt, for her to play her next card.

Shortly after the Gargoyle's chic opening, 'Cocky', the great showman, unveiled *On With The Dance* at the London Pavilion, the principal showplace for musicals. The success anticipated for Noël Coward's first revue and its young star was richly fulfilled. Hermione had become a celebrity. Wherever she went with David where music was playing in restaurants and night-clubs, she would be greeted with her hit number from the show, *Poor Little Rich Girl.* She was therefore not as surprised as she might have been when Louise, with awe in her voice, reported that Lord Beaverbrook's secretary had telephoned to speak to her. Louise had replied that her daughter was asleep and could not be disturbed. An invitation to join the great man for luncheon was duly issued – and accepted. David smelt a rat. The mischievous Canadian wizard had a formidable reputation not only as the Fleet Street dynamo who had become Britain's first Minister of Information, but also as a confirmed and energetic womanizer. Extreme caution should be the order of the day. When that day came, Hermione was collected by a chauffeur and delivered to Max Beaverbrook's private retreat in Fulham, a handsome, well-screened house overlooking Hurlingham Park. Young as she was, Hermione was not so innocent as to ignore what a word from the mighty Press lord to one of his editors could do for a young actress, even for one already acclaimed. The Beaver was as well known for his favourites as he was for his hates – such as, in later years, Dickie Mountbatten.

Hermione described Beaverbrook as having a face rather like a garden gnome which could split suddenly into a broad melon grin when something pleased him – as when she declined the proffered champagne at lunch. He had been well briefed about her career and talked about it enthusiastically, predicting a great future for her with Cochran. Abruptly he stopped pussy-footing around. 'And what about the young man who wants to interfere with all that?' he wanted to know, cocking his head at her. Ah, so that was what he had been working round to. Hermione played possum and said nothing. He leant forward, the concerned older man with a soft spot for nubile youth. 'I want to give you some advice, my dear. Marriage is not for a clever young actress like you. Spoil it all! You keep your mind right there on your career. Don't get married. You hear me?' With his conscience assuaged, Max picked up his knife and fork and prepared to play them boldly over his lunch. Hermione heard herself saying in a small voice that she had no plans to marry and, in any case, none had proposed such a step. And nor had they.

Two versions of this exchange, different only in so far as tact dictated, were reported back to Louise and David. Both were agreed on the one essential – Pamela had been at the bottom of it all. If it had not been a successful machination, in so far as she had been rumbled, at least from Pamela's point of view it had not had the adverse effect of precipitating David into a proposal. He continued to keep quiet about his matrimonial intentions, if, indeed, he had defined them. David and Hermione were both, perhaps, quite happy with the status quo. It was left for Louise to rue the fact that her youngest daughter was not going to be splashed over the front page of tomorrow's *Daily Express*.

The Club, since the opening, had been running smoothly, but rather along the lines laid down by Pamela. That is to say, smart and élitist. This suited Harry 'just swell', as the Prince of Wales was wont to say. In fact, Harry would have liked it smarter – café-society smarter. He had set his sights on luring the dashing young prince to the Gargoyle. That suggestion of unpredictable challenge hinted at by one of the committee members – 'We want the Gargoyle to be a place where the Sitwells will feel at ease, but not perfectly at ease' – was nowhere, except in the *Huis Clos* of the lift, yet apparent. And the founder-owner was not too apparent either.

Insulated by Pamela's hothouse upbringing and Kit's fraternal protection at Cambridge, David had made, as an adult, one or two half-hearted attempts to lead an ordinary life. But the temptation for him to opt out was overwhelming. Cambridge, by virtue of its relative isolation, was more inward-looking, more classically orientated in its homoeroticism than hedonistic Oxford. But it was at Oxford that there had now emerged a dionysiac world of dandies and aesthetes who, on going down from their fantasy world into a real one, were hard-headed and ambitious enough to be the ones to put much of the sparkle in the cultural waters of the metropolis for the next thirty years.

The guiding spirits of this undergraduate world were two cosmopolitan, cultured and flamboyantly defiant homosexuals, part-American by birth, Brian Howard and Harold Acton. They were brilliant and scornful figures whose originality and self-generated intoxication with their lives made a fierce impression on less sophisticated minds at the university, and both of whom would contribute much to the portrait of Anthony Blanche in *Brideshead Revisited.* Among their contemporaries were Cyril Connolly, Peter Quennell (whose languid verse had excited the admiration of Edith Sitwell even before he was to come up to Oxford), Evelyn Waugh, Oliver Messel, Basil Murray and Peter Rodd (the latter two to be joint models for Basil Seal in Waugh's *Black Mischief*), Tom Driberg (later Lord Bradwell), Henry Yorke (who would publish under the name of Henry Green), John Sutro, Patrick Balfour (to inherit the title of Lord Kinross), Anthony Powell, Robert Byron and John Betjeman. All or any of these may have been in literary critic and Oxford professor John Carey's mind when, in an admiring review of Martin Green's *Children of the Sun*, published in 1977, he found that sun shining on '...people whom any person of decent instincts will find loathsome'. Another contemporary of these Oxford *Sonnenkinder*, who was spending this time of his life with the police in Burma, went even further with his 'shrieking little poseurs': Eric Blair, better known as George Orwell. But this observation was to come much later in his life and embraced Cambridge graduates as well as the Left-wing poets of the thirties. Graham Greene and Claud Cockburn (a cousin of Evelyn Waugh's) who had both come up to Oxford a little ahead of Peter Quennell from Berkhamstead School (where Greene's father held the stewardship), ducked out of the dandy/aesthete galère by joining the communist party. It is perhaps fair to think that Carey's scorching lance was principally aimed at the two high-camp priests who aroused such a sense of liberation in their admirers. Some of these bent the knee lower than others. Some, like Powell, Yorke, Connolly, felt, through Etonian familiarity, absolved from the need to genuflect. Still others, like Waugh, were initially obliged to watch from a subordinate distance but, in this case, with hard gooseberry eye fixed in dislike upon Brian Howard. The dons of their day (as would have struck Professor Carey) seemed cowed – if not, as in the case of Roy Harrod, actually deferential – in the face of such exuberant confidence. An exception, perhaps, was the 'dandified sodomite' Maurice Bowra, 'within whose rooms', claimed John Betjeman, 'I met my friends for life.'

All those people mentioned as being at Oxford then, and a great many more besides, were to be drawn at one time or another to the Gargoyle Club. For many it became a habit that they could not, or did not wish to kick. It fulfilled a diversity of purposes which no other place could begin to match. And in that sense, the real world, even if often in disguise, was seen to come to David. But before that happened, radical changes were to be made at the Club.

Harry Walker was proving a perfectly effective manager, as far as he went. But his social ambitions, which the Club was supposed to help realize, were complicated and to some extent compromised by intellectual and critical pretensions. These latter had led him to burn incense at the feet of a guru, who at that time exercised what some regarded as a suspect influence over a school of lost, idle or emotionally dislocated people, youngish and well off in the main, who were in search of 'truth'. He was Matthew Pritchard, a rather remarkable Englishman, sometime Byzantine scholar and putative philosopher, the focus of whose offering was an odd mixture of cult and occult. The cult was for all things Byzantine. Robert Byron was to become a notable interpreter of its art, and the history of its civilization would be written by Steven Runciman. But Pritchard was ahead of public taste in his advocacy of the Byzantine ethic and may have contributed in a small way to its expression.

Peter Quennell will have none of Pritchard or his cult: 'He used to take a group of young people around the National Gallery or the Tate or Wallace Collection and suddenly point to, perhaps, a Giovanni Bellini and say – "Any boot-boy could have done that." And they all agreed. He had been the custodian of a smallish museum in America and he gradually eliminated most of the contents until it was reduced to one battered Byzantine bust. Byzantium was the thing.' Sir Steven Runciman is equally disparaging. As a young Byzantinist he had been invited by Pritchard to lunch at the Charing Cross Hotel, which was where he entertained when in London.

After lunch he presented me with a reproduction Byzantine coin (he had a store of them which he used to dish out to intended disciples). I did not take to him and thought him bogus as a scholar and tried to avoid seeing him again. I remember him talking about the mystical and the occult. But would that make him a philosopher? He probably thought so.

The unflattering view of Pritchard, or Matt, as he liked to be called, held by Runciman and Quennell, who had known him only while young men, is not shared by one who is too young even to have met him. The art historian John Richardson (biographer of Picasso) had, however, known well two of those who had formed part of Matt's circle and had been deeply influenced by the man throughout their adult lives. Willy King and Bertie Landsberg were both in later years his friends. 'The Gargoyle, after all, was such a favourite playground of intellectuals between the wars,' says Richardson, 'that this rather crucial link has to be established and got right. Pritchard preached three things: Byzantium, Mozart and Matisse. These were the three corner-stones of his philosophy. They don't necessarily go together at all – except that Matisse had a passion for Byzantine art and was much influenced by it. Pritchard was also, I gather, the inventor of museology, museum direction as a kind of science.' (As a young man, Pritchard had specialized in Greek archaeology in Boston. He then became employed by its Museum of Fine Arts, But the revolutionary reforms he put into practice there, and which were later to become standard throughout museums in the USA, led to his being given the sack in 1907. After which he then went to Paris where he met Matisse. The painter and tyro-philosopher became friends and Matt remained the Englishman closest to Matisse from then on.)

Richardson finds it interesting that the very different characters of the two men he had known had been largely formed, on their own admission, by Pritchard.

Bertie Landsberg, like David Tennant, was a sort of gentleman aesthete. I think there was a tendency among Pritchard's disciples to talk about life-enhancement; at the same time they were rather sophisticated and world-weary. David would have been about the youngest of this circle and therefore less so. Bertie was the lover of a woman called 'Flames' d'Erlanger, the baronne d'Erlanger. She had bright red hair, was very eccentric and rich, and she was in love with him. She bought him the Villa Malcontenta, where he lived for almost the rest of his life. Unlike some other Palladian villas on the

Brenta, Malcontenta was low-key, not at all tarted-up. Nor were the frescos over-restored. Bertie kept the spirit of 'Pritchardism' going there. It was all very what Cyril Connolly liked to call 'mandarin'. Otherwise he never did anything, didn't publish anything. He was of good family [by birth Brazilian, and in the drawings done by Matisse of his sister Yvonne there is a strong indication of Hapsburg lip to go with the Germanic name], not much money, always slightly [sic] kept by ladies. He was extremely handsome and cultivated. The family must have had some money. Enough anyway to commission that great portrait of Yvonne which is now in the Arensberg collection. That was certainly master-minded by Pritchard. And Willy, whom I knew extremely well, was always talking about Matt. His passion for opera all came from Pritchard. [William Augustus King was a Keeper at the British Museum.] He might have been bogus, as Runciman said. But like a lot of bogus people he obviously had rather a good influence over rather clever people. Certainly, Willy was extremely intelligent and so was Bertie – and so was Georges Duthuit, who I never knew but have read. I should think he [Pritchard] was probably queer, I don't know.

Pritchard did have a wife, however, and Peter Quennell knew her. He said she always appeared discontented – a 'malcontenta', perhaps.

Pritchard may have been encouraged in his metaphysical way of thinking by attendance upon the mysterious genius Yury Gurdjiev at his equally strange establishment near Fontainebleau. Gurdjiev held that everything important was contrived by magic and that he could, if he so wished, lock the front door from his bed by act of will. This, however, was not to be Pritchard's tune. He took his from Gurdjiev's Russian friend Ouspensky, who evolved a systematized form of Gurdjiev's teaching as far removed from the original intuitive inspiration as was St Peter's from that of Christ. Gurdjiev loved to confront the impossible, Ouspensky only recognized the possible. He was committed not to visionary but to practical idealism. And this made a strong appeal to those who could not follow abstract reasoning. From him Pritchard learnt the lesson that there was money to be made from straightening out people's lives. He recognized, also, that the acquisition of the sheen of magus was a helpful ingredient towards achieving this end in the current impressionable market. As with the Byzantine ethic, Central Asian mysticism was new and different.

*

It was not difficult for Harry Walker to tighten his hold over David –

and at the same time ingratiate himself with his guru by introducing him into Pritchard's circle. David's insecurity, alleviated but not completely allayed by his relationship with Hermione – how could it be, given the strength of her own sense of identity – made him a natural target for the gnostic embrace. So he joined the dismissive trudge round the galleries of European art and sat obediently through the early-morning sessions of spiritual input, which for the favoured, as David inevitably soon became, were occasionally held *tête-à-tête*. He was counselled to concentrate his life on the possible and to cast any thought of the impossible out of his mind. He must banish sentimentality and recognize any dependency as absurd. There must be an end to all daydreaming. David was attentive. At last he felt himself subject to a discipline which in a different way would match Hermione's and also finally break his submission to Pamela. A transference, in short. He became a willing discipline of the 'professor' and by pocketing his reproduction Byzantine coin, accepted the King's Shilling.

But Pamela had been doing a spot of thoughtful reflection herself. The reins connecting her to David felt a bit slack. She looked at the Gargoyle, which had now been going for a year and a half, and she was not pleased with what she saw. It was not just that David seemed to have come to regard the club as no more than a hobby – it would have been worse, of course, had he regarded it as a profession – or that Hermione used it to entertain her numerous theatrical friends, free no doubt. The place was becoming too much a reflection of the times; an affectation of callous disillusion. People claimed not to 'give a damn'. For him, for her, for anything. Youth, epitomized by the Prince of Wales, counted above everything. Youth and 'being modern'. This implied cynicism, daring, ruthlessness. The popular press was on the one hand hostile with articles like 'The Modern Girl's Brother' (a 'silken-coated lap-dog', according to the *Daily Express*, 'feminine, bloodless, dolled-up like a girl and exquisite without masculinity') while, on the other, exploiting the activities of such people as Stephen Tennant for their hordes of avid readers. The 'Sisters' went equally far the other way. Hair which had been bobbed after the war had now become shingled and was edging towards the Eton Crop. Chests were flattened, boyish slenderness sought after, with an extravagant amount of silk-stockinged leg on display. That at least was the view of society-watcher Patrick Balfour. 'By 1925', he wrote in what sounds like a spirit of complaint, 'the skirt was so freakishly abbreviated that it almost ended at the knees.' Bi-sexualism was in vogue.

And then there was the dancing. 'This madness' complained a columnist in the *Daily Mail*, 'has seized London and is spreading to the provinces.' The 'madness' in question was specifically the new craze that had arrived from America called the Charleston. The Prince of Wales loved the Charleston at which he was an enthusiastic but indifferent performer. 'The beauty of this new dance', recalled an early exponent, 'was that it could be done solo.' Also popular were the Black Bottom and the Shimmy. The bishops – in the days when their voices could be heard quite loudly – waxed indignant over the sexual significance of this uninhibited indulgence in jazz rhythm. It awakened unholy desires, they said; a return to barbarism they said. A view no doubt emphasized by the fact that it was in the main performed by black, or 'negro', musicians. Not in the Gargoyle, however, where, to Harry's satisfaction, the Prince of Wales had been seen 'cutting a rug' of late. But the BYPs, among them Stephen, were treating the place very much as if it were their own playground and leading it further away from David's original worthy idea. Sometimes they would take the place over completely, as when Allanah Harper, a rich young patron of Cecil Beaton, gave a party there lasting for two days.

The BYPs had not been discomfited by the General Strike of 1926. Many, indeed, as with the middle and upper classes in general, regarded it as a sporting challenge – an attitude from which David distanced himself – and eagerly volunteered to help keep the country's wheels turning. After nine days, the TUC admitted defeat and called off the strike. Once again it was the miners who were to come off worst. People were left feeling somewhat bemused by the manner in which everything appeared to return to normal so easily, with no blood spilt. Nerve and resolution had been stiffened in no small degree by the stance adopted by the BBC. This was firmly behind the Prime Minister, Stanley Baldwin and his Government. The British Broadcasting Company, as it was first called, had been formed in 1922 to provide entertainment programmes from a number of stations. It had only recently been elevated to the dignity of Corporation, by which time it could count on some two million regular wireless listeners. The general manager was John Reith, a pillar of old-fashioned virtues, who saw himself becoming a national figure, a voice of the nation. This was first to become evident with his handling of broadcasts during the General Strike and ending with Baldwin's 'new message to the nation' which he himself had helped to write. He was a headmaster figure who stood firmly against the trends of the times. Pamela now turned to him.

She and John Reith already knew each other and his admiration for her was open. It was not then difficult for her to suggest that David, with his splendid speaking voice, developed since childhood by the reading aloud of verse, would be a desirable acquisition for the BBC. And so it turned out to be. David made no objection to the proposal. It would give him professional status somewhat equivalent to Hermione's and, since he did have a very fine enunciation and effective delivery, it was pleasing to the vanity. Moreover, in those early days the role of announcer was not a very demanding one. Reith, though, was a stickler for upright codes of morality and Christian values among his employees, and he insisted from the beginning on his announcers wearing a dinner-jacket when reading the evening news at 7 p.m. And it was Reith who laid down the standards of 'BBC English'. David thus became one of the pioneer broadcasters of the BBC, along with Stuart Hibberd and John Snagge.

The first permanent studios and headquarters of the BBC (2LO) were at 2 Savoy Hill on the Thames Embankment, next door to the Savoy Hotel. This was convenient for direct relay of the various dance-bands employed by the hotel. The atmosphere at Savoy Hill was, in spite of Reith, relaxed and informal. There had not yet been time for administrative matters to become standardized and all recording and transmission techniques were very much at an experimental stage. David was one of the star voices of 2LO, and soon acquired a considerable following, being described in the press as the 'golden-voiced announcer'. He frequently read the Sunday epilogue and took part in radio plays as well as just straight announcing. Among his listeners was an elderly and wealthy woman who found herself quite seduced by his mellifluous tones. As a mark of her appreciation, and to help lubricate the vocal cords, she had cases of claret and bottles of old brandy sent to him every month. Lance Sieveking, the writer and senior producer at 2LO, became a close friend of David's. He also became a member of the Gargoyle.

Hermione had also made a new friend. She had been named after a waterfall in her native Alabama, Tallulah Falls. This was most apt since through her small person there flowed a ferocious torrent of energy, and speech poured from her in an unrestrained cataract. *Time* magazine observed that 'Tallulah Bankhead can quote readily and at impressive length from Shakespeare, the Bible and the public lavatory wall.' And Beaverbrook was to say that there were only three people instantly recognizable throughout the British Empire – Bernard Shaw, the Prince of Wales and Tallulah Bankhead. So if Hermione was the toast of London, Tallulah was that much 'toastier'. But Tōtie and Tallu, to use their respective nicknames, had much in common. They were roughly the same age, Tallu a bit older, hugely talented and achieving stardom while still very young. As teenagers each had fallen in love with members of the British aristocracy. (In Tallu's case it was with the recklessly wild, bi-sexual Napier, the 3rd Baron Alington – Naps even to those who barely knew him.) Cocky was a catalyst in both girls' professional lives. They were small – barely over five feet – yet both had an enormous stage presence. A Rabelaisian laugh, bawdy wit and a deep and remarkable voice with which to express it was common to both. Each had pledged their single parents to eschew alcohol while under age – Tallu, however, had cheerfully taken to drugs: 'Cocaine isn't habit-forming, darling. And I should know. I've been taking it all my life.' They were both greatly admired as actresses by Tennessee Williams and were to share a deep rapport with him which would bring them into painful professional rivalry. And, in the final act, each might have been seen to have eroded or thrown away their remarkable gifts. Two years before, in 1924, Tallulah had appeared as Iris Storm in a dramatization of Michael Arlen's hugely influential novel *The Green Hat*. Arlen's heroine seemed to epitomize the era and the success Tallulah had with the role was quite phenomenal.

It might therefore be thought that when Tallu, through Hermione, expressed her wish to become a member of the Gargoyle Club, David would have been pleased and flattered. Not so. In fact, he refused to countenance it. 'We really don't want the Club to become too theatrical, you know,' was his argument. 'With people like her' [there were none] 'it'll be jammed every night.' Was he just being haughty and stuffy? Or did he fear that the combination of Tōtie and Tallu might prove too rich a mixture at quarters too close. It might have been that David felt Tallulah's total lack of inhibition and undisguised promiscuity would be a 'bad influence' on Hermione and that he should make a show of putting down a foot.

Tallulah was certainly very sexually self-indulgent, irrespective of gender. But she was a witty woman, particularly in that regard. Some of her *bon mots* have been mis-attributed to Dorothy Parker. Such as, 'There's less to this than meets the eye.' And to Naps Alington, when he failed to acknowledge her while sitting one night with another woman in the Café de Paris, she called out in a loud voice 'What's the matter? Don't you recognize me with my clothes on?' Tallulah did become a member of the Gargoyle, but she had to wait for some time, until David was away in Canada, to do so.

Under the influence of Matthew Pritchard, David began to re-address himself to the problems and responsibilities of the Club. These were aesthetic and ideological rather than purely practical, since the day-to-day running of the place was in the highly capable hands of Miss 'Mossy' O'Neil, the club secretary; overseen, of course, by the ever vigilant Walker. David had, with some trepidation, invited the 'professor' to a private luncheon at the club before the official tea-time opening – there would have been no question of the guru deigning to become just another member. Instantly his hyper-critical eye exposed the obvious flaw of the conflicting decorative styles. David had better realize that the quaintness, the picturesqueness of the Arts and Crafts movement was old-hat, open to mockery and ridicule. Any taint of 'ye oldeness' was at all costs and for ever more to be avoided. Let him be quite clear on that point. As for the downstairs dance-floor, that was theatrical and meretricious. Let him reflect on the merits of Byzantium, to which he was fortunate enough to have been exposed, of how the influence of its art and architecture had been absorbed and spread throughout the Ottoman Empire, by the whole Islamic world. Let his mind dwell upon El Greco. Light penetrated David's mind. Mediterranean light, light from Granada. The Alhambra palace, more precisely, whose splendours Pamela had taken him to see during the long vac from Cambridge. If the Arts and Crafts interiors had to go and the inglenooks be burnt, at least this could be reconciled by the reminder that it was she, Pamela, who had first introduced him to this glory of Moorish (therefore Byzantine) architecture. Hitherto, his most avant-garde idea had been to have the reluctant Ciggie got up with dyed hair as the young woman in Manet's *Bar at the Folies-Bergère* for the Gargoyle's opening night. Henceforth – mosaic all the way.

The other piece of muddled reasoning, Pritchard pointed out, was David's idea of having a swanky club where the rich, who could well afford the stiff yearly subscription of seven guineas, would patronize the Deserving Artistic Poor when they could not. Keep to the possible, banish dreams. Moreover, unless invited, the DAPs could hardly afford to go out in the evening except to the pub. So what was required was a lunch-time opening rather than at tea-time (an hour sacred to gentility), with a good set meal, nursery food, offered at cost. A select number of DAPs should be given honorary membership to get that ball rolling. David enthusiastically agreed to raise the matter – and push it through – at the Club's next committee meeting.

While all this was taking root, things were forming on another front.

As dancer, mime, straight actress, star of revue, Hermione had been on stage, almost without interruption, since the age of twelve. That is to say, for more than eight years. This continuity was about to be threatened, and for a very good reason. Hermione found that she was pregnant.

5

When Tallulah sneezed, that, in those frivolous years, was front page news; when Marie Stopes cleared her throat, this was a warning to the Western Hemisphere to re-think its carnal ways. Tallulah was a symbol of sexual liberation for young women of the urban working classes; the good doctor was the crusader for birth control who opened the flood-gates for all women. The degree of ignorance that still existed in those post-war years about all sexual matters, and particularly female sexuality, was hard to believe. Nor was it restricted to the less privileged as the unfortunate example of David's cousin Dick Wyndham's first marriage bears out. Enlightenment came with the publication of Marie Stopes' *Married Love.* This work formed one of the most sensational and furiously disputed issues of the day.

But all this passed Hermione by. She confessed to never having read Stopes, her own life being too full and too interesting. In any case, she was not married. Disclosure of her predicament was no easy matter. David was told first: in her autobiography, Hermione recalls how this was done:

> David and I had been invited to supper at a house in Knightsbridge; he picked me up in his latest car, a racing Bugatti, and we drove off up Piccadilly and whirled round Hyde Park Corner. The exhaust was being pretty noisy, there was the usual 'vroom-vroom' of the engine, and we wore little leather helmets to keep our hair from blowing away – none of this made it any easier for me to say what I had to say.
>
> 'David!', I shouted to be heard over the din, 'David, can you hear me?'
>
> 'I can', he shouted back. 'What is it?'
>
> 'David, guess what? I think I'm having a baby.'
>
> At that moment an absolutely fantastic Italian car swirled alongside and overtook us. It was an Isotta-Fraschini racing car. 'My God,' cried David. 'That's the car I'm going to get.'
>
> The Bugatti bumped suddenly and I put my hands over my

stomach protectively. 'David! Didn't you hear what I said?'

'Oh yes', he called back, 'what an awful bore!'

It was characteristic of David, an active participant in the optimism of the times which glorified the machine, to take evasive action from this unwelcome disclosure by letting his attention be distracted by such an irrelevant object as the Isotta-Fraschini.

With confirmation that his pocket Venus really was pregnant, David's reaction was unheroic – straight into a nursing-home for an 'appendectomy'. But Hermione balked. This lack of gallantry was hurtful, but there was more to it than that. She broke the news to Louise who expressed outrage. Not on moral grounds, but because of the damaging effect this would have on her career. Hermione thought this nonsense and said so. Her career and her life were intertwined: 'I could no more stop acting, dancing and singing than I could stop breathing.' The fact of the matter was that she liked the idea of having a baby. Louise grudgingly conceded that as a dancer in training her muscles were tight and it probably would not show for some time (so the non-stop career might not have to be interrupted for long). This practical approach helped to stiffen Hermione's resolve against David's suggestion of an abortion. Another solution then struck David. 'I suppose we could get married.' This was volunteered with a marked lack of enthusiasm and no spontaneity at all. Hermione was too proud to respond.

When she began to fear that the strenuous dance routine of the musical she was starring in might solve the problem all too easily, Hermione invoked the 'get-out-clause' on her contract and shortly afterwards went into a nursing home. There she was delivered of a baby girl. David, according to Hermione, was enraptured. But not, evidently, to the point where he felt further commitment was required of him. It is about what happened then that accounts vary. Hermione (in her book), gives a prosaic account of a nanny being employed to look after the infant down in deepest Surrey where 'nobody would know' and to which the proud parents could make discreet weekend sorties. The person at the centre of this domestic drama, the baby in question, now Pauline Rumbold, widow of the 10th Baronet, has a different version, a more romantic one. She was, she says, placed in a baby-farm for adoption – possibly also in Surrey – hidden from the world and not visited by her parents. It was not until a rich and childless couple made an offer to adopt the infant Pauline, that David's nerve broke, or his heart was sufficiently touched to stir him into action. Down he roared in one of his racing cars to where the babe was hid and retrieved his tiny offspring at the eleventh hour. The perils of Pauline had begun.

Hidden from the world the child might have been, but there was one with an all-seeing eye, an eye that David dreaded above all else fastening upon the fact of little Pauline's existence. When it did, Pamela was beside herself; beyond speech but not beyond all reason. The time had surely come to play the one last card in her hand. Appropriately, this card had red hair, was unconventionally pretty – a mobile, expressively humorous face – a bit of a blue-stocking but potentially rich. Her name was Meraud Guinness, the daughter of international banker, Benjamin. Apart from her evident attractions Meraud had a quality about her which was difficult for the English 'quality' to place satisfactorily. So, she was held to be 'rather a fascinator', and it was left at that. But there was much more to her than that. Meraud was fantastical: spirited, reckless, in a way innocent, and avid for experience like some enchanted hippy, a flower-child before her time and at a time when it was still startling and fresh to paint bright flowers all over your car. She was intelligent (contributing monthly articles to American *Vogue*), and she was also a talented artist – she, too, had studied under Henry Tonks at the Slade, in New York under Alexander Archipenko, and then with Francis Picabia, with whom she had a heart-rending affair, in Paris and the South of France. Picabia had written, as an after-thought, above his preface to the catalogue of her first exhibition in Paris: 'She has eyes full of sighs'. She signed all her paintings 'Michael', a name taken from her godfather, the raffish Russian Archduke Michael and which she preferred to the one of Cornish origin with which she had been christened.

It was the unbridled generosity with which Meraud would bestow her affections upon 'undesirables' – there was also the painter Kit Wood to contend with – that was so distressing to Bridget, her mother, and which put her in the same stable as her friend Pamela. Pamela now suggested to Bridget that a possible solution for both their problems might be found if Meraud were to join David and herself for a relaxing holiday in Switzerland, safe from any disturbing influence. This was eagerly seized upon.

David had to break this news to Hermione who received it badly. But there was worse to come: and this was Pamela's proposal, relayed by David, that Pauline and nanny should go and live down at Wilsford. That was one below the belt for Pauline's mother. Not only was Pamela scheming to separate her from David, but the heartless vampire wanted to possess her child as well. Worse still, there was nothing Hermione could do about it. David was paying for the upkeep of nanny and charge and she, at the insistence of Louise, was about to go into new play. It was Hermione's turn to be struck speechless.

When not distracted by the almost constant need to make fine adjustments to the balance between filial, paternal and concupiscent demands, David had been energetically supervising the stylistic metamorphosis of the Gargoyle interior. In this he had been much aided by a friendship struck up with another devotee of the Byzantine achievement and one who also sat at the feet of Matt Pritchard. This was Georges Duthuit, the young writer and critic mentioned by John Richardson, who exercised his talents on both sides of the English Channel. Peter Quennell describes him then as being '... a large handsome man with the chest of a Percheron horse who could seldom resist an invitation to take the floor or, indeed, any kind of social gaiety ... one of those Frenchmen who especially charm the English because they so closely resemble the Anglo-Saxon idea of what a Frenchman ought to be – tempestuous, high-spirited, eloquent, irascible, demonstrative.' He was a natural and, with his pleasure in courtship and the dance, a most willing new recruit to the Club.

Despite his ardent, vigorous nature (he liked, Quennell said, to live at a dramatic pace, plunging headlong into explosive controversies) Georges was deeply devoted to Marguerite, his gentle, patient wife who remained at home in Paris. Marguerite was the eldest daughter of Henri Matisse and thus it came about that David, accompanying Georges on one of his matrimonial retreats, met the great painter and, as a disciple of Matt Pritchard, was made welcome. It was Matisse who then made the suggestion that was to lift the decor of the Club's main room *hors de catégorie* and give the place such a unique flavour. David had explained that he was having an elaborate coffered ceiling, *à la* Alhambra, made for it which was to be painted with twenty-two carat gold leaf. An excellent complement, Matisse suggested, would be to have the walls entirely covered with a mosaic of mirrored tiles. He knew of an eighteenth-century château whose contents were about to be sold. Included were some immensely tall looking-glasses. Doubtless these could be bought very cheaply. When cut into thousands of small squares and set into the walls, these tiles of subtly imperfect glass would produce *un effet éclatant*. David was so elated by this inspired concept, which, moreover, could not but meet with Matt's approval, that he made Matisse an honorary member on the spot. As prophesied, it did produce a stunning effect and one which was to last. This was affirmed by another master painter, Francis Bacon, many years later.

> I didn't go up to the Gargoyle until after the war – about 1947 – and it's true to say that when one arrived quite late most people, including oneself, were generally half drunk. But they looked for a moment like birds of paradise coming down this beautiful gold and silver staircase into what the multiplicity of small mirrors made into a very beautiful room. I've never been a great admirer of Matisse, but this room really worked as a setting.

By the time David left for Switzerland with Meraud and Pamela, the Club had assumed its definitive form. The revamped mouse-trap lift, on reaching its summit, now sprang its passengers into a large panelled reception-room from which all vestiges of 'ye oldeness' had been removed. Identity (usually a formality) was declared and a polite and uniformed member of the staff relieved members of any encumbrances as they signed themselves and guests into the book on the counter. He was called Marks, Anthony Powell remembers, 'quite unusually nice for one holding that sort of office, often far from attractive figures'. From here you made your way to the bar. Guests then found themselves in a room the width of the building with a long mahogany bar behind which were ranged an amazing variety of bottles reflecting the owner's newly acquired and catholic taste in drink, and the barman's skill with the cocktail-shaker. They could then sit on one of the leather-topped stools at the bar or at one of the many low tables facing the banquettes along the walls. Opposite the bar, and to the left of the open arched entry from the reception-room, was the only relic of the original interior design. This space was furnished as a rather fusty country-house sitting-room and was known as the Tudor Room. 'It was,' as Hermione later described it, 'a sort of odd little room that people used to look into.' To the left again of the Tudor Room, was the brilliant mirror-lined staircase leading down into the main L-shaped room now totally transformed by a kaleidoscope of mirrored tiles. Henceforth, this room was always referred to as 'the ballroom' since it was where ballroom dancing was to take place (and much else in years to come), David being resistant to the other expression of the period's optimism, namely jazz. The band and the cockpit-sized dance-floor were at the foot of the L on the right descending; tables, chairs and banquettes, red plush and gold, everywhere else. The kitchen and service area with offices, were under the bar-room; the roof-garden, private flat and cellars remained as before.

The decision to open the Club at lunch-time and the issue of membership to Deserving Artistic Poor (and not so poor) proved a great success. And the infusion of lusty, robust characters from the adjacent territory soon to be known as 'Fitzrovia' took some of the sheen off the Bloomsbury chic that Pamela had introduced.

The DAP and those yet to make their name remained soberly below for an affordable luncheon, while the brighter sparks and those already established in the world became the glow-worms and the fire-flies of the Gargoyle night. 'A luncheon', again the witness is Anthony Powell who had first been taken to the Club by Evelyn Waugh when both their names were still unknown, 'would cost three shillings for three courses: potage or hors d'oeuvre, something like boeuf à la mode, pudding (crème caramel) or cheese. A bottle of hock seven shillings, claret at about four shillings.'

Neither Powell or Waugh, though incomparably perceptive observers of their tangential worlds, could in themselves be thought of as Bright Young People. In the first place, neither could have afforded to be a BYP, and the fact that Waugh was 'definitely *not* one' is explained by Diana Mosley as being due to 'his intense dislike of parties. That's what they were all about, you see.' They both, like so many of their contemporaries, were trying to find their London feet after the slippered ease of life at Oxford. Powell was already in the happy position of being able to help Waugh through his apprenticeship to the publishing house of Duckworth, whose founder, Gerald, was half-brother to Vanessa Bell and Virginia Woolf. Powell introduced Waugh to the firm as a potential author and this resulted in the commissioning of Waugh's first book, *Rossetti: His Life and Works*. Waugh's situation as a future Duckworth author was thus the cause of the modest celebratory Gargoyle luncheon. In his autobiography, Powell describes the occasion, at which they were joined by Inez Holden, very much a figure of High Bohemia, as taking place 'under the large picture by Matisse that hung in the dining-room, lending an air of go-ahead culture to the club.'

This recent acquisition was one of two paintings David had bought from Matisse in Paris. That alluded to by Powell, *The Red Studio*, a large canvas roughly six foot by seven recognized as one of Matisse's most original and daring inventions, and described by the painter as one of his 'all or nothing' works, now hangs in the Museum of Modern Art in New York. The other (now part of the Phillips Collection in Washington), *The Studio, Quai St Michel* caught and held the eye as you descended the main staircase in the club with its subliminated voluptuousness. Lorette, Matisse's favourite model of the period, lies naked on a couch with the spire of the Sainte Chapelle seen through the window across the Seine on the Ile de la Cité.

The art critic, David Sylvester, has remarked to the author on the astonishing achievement of one so young and untutored in the art world having bought two of the most important works of art of the twentieth century. This could not have happened, of course, had it not been for the influence of Pritchard. For it had been he who, before the war, had first introduced David's new friend and cicerone, Georges Duthuit, into the Matisse household. On Matisse's death in 1954, Picasso admitted that the one rival he really recognized had now gone.

The fact that David could hang on the Gargoyle walls paintings he hoped would both *épater* and impress the members, pleased him. It was not just that he had bought the two Matisses for what now seems to be the ludicrously small sum of £600 (a small Renoir – much safer – could then be picked up for about £200) but that his choice, he felt, had been so bold and sure. *The Red Studio* had been painted in 1911, *The Studio, Quai St Michel*, in 1916. Both, except when included in the occasional exhibition, had remained stacked in the Quai St Michel studio, amongst a mass of other canvasses, until liberated by David. Was it David's eye that drew him to choose these two major works, or was it accident? Since his aesthetic coup was never repeated, the answer must lie open.

Through Georges Duthuit, David had met Nina Hamnett, a quirkily tilted pillar of London's Bohemia. She was then in Paris where her work was highly regarded. When not painting in her studio, carousing in the stews of Montparnasse that she had discovered with Modigliani, or being fêted by the Princess Violette Murat (through whom she became intimate with Cocteau and his circle), Nina would sit for hours in the Café du Dôme or the Sélect with Hemingway, one of a number of American writers on the run from prohibition with whom she made friends.

Before David's departure for Switzerland, Nina had returned to London. She found a studio for herself in a house off Fitzroy Square once inhabited by Thackeray. The area, one familiar to her, had long been indulgent to writers and artists such as Walter Sickert who liked, admired, might even have loved Nina. Roger Fry, whose Omega Workshops were established in nearby Fitzroy Street, certainly had. 'You are,' he wrote to her while still smarting from the death of their year-long affair, 'the most fascinating, exciting, tantalizing, elusive, capricious, impulsive, beautiful, exasperating creature in the world. . . .' Exasperating she could be, and worse, to those she had caused to suffer the torments of physical jealousy. She was a confirmed roisterer, uninhibitedly promiscuous, could seldom resist the lure of adventure, particularly in the guise of sailor, boxer or *apache*. Yet her frequent passages of love would be undergone more in the spirit of *camaraderie* than of passion. '*Elle est vraiment putain*', Fry wrote to Vanessa Bell, 'but a very nice one and one ought to accept that as a type of character *comme une autre* and not be amazed by it or demand what it can't give. I suppose I shall learn some philosophy by the time I am impotent.' To avoid the threatening boredom of London, Nina was determined to rediscover the kind of carefree, spontaneous life, in which work and pleasure were not mutually exclusive, that she had known in Paris. But there was no equivalent of the French café – excepting perhaps the ground floor of the Café Royal – nor escape, even there, from the omnipresent and draconian drinking laws. The pub, therefore, would have to play the part of café in her life – a casual meeting-place of no commitment, but lively and inviting to the unexpected. Nina elected the Fitzroy Tavern as the most sympathetic of the several neighbourhood hostelries in which to establish a permanent presence.

The term 'Fitzrovia', which only became current in the late thirties, did not derive, as might be expected, from either the square or the street of that name, but rather from the pub with the high bar-stool near the door which Nina decided to make her own. In so doing she was to become instrumental in helping to give definition to a small polyglot area of London that was neither Soho nor Bloomsbury, but was lapped by the waters of both those wild and calm seas. The Fitzroy Tavern, known locally as 'Kleinfeld's', after its genial Russian-emigré landlord, was bedded into the north-eastern corner where the streets Charlotte and Windmill meet. To the east lies Tottenham Court Road with Bloomsbury beyond, to the south runs Oxford Street, the northern boundary of Soho proper. In the reversed L where these two main roads meet at St Giles' Circus, stands the patch of London in question. Its appeal to the artistic community lay in its traditions, in its proximity to the influential Slade School of Art, in the number of studios around, then, at a very reasonable rent, in the variety of its pubs, and in all its cheap, convivial and cosmopolitan restaurants (and two less cheap but exceptional ones, the Etoile and the Eiffel Tower – now the White Tower), many to be found, as now, in the principal artery of Fitzrovia, Charlotte Street.

Nina padded daily through the sawdust on the floor of the Fitzroy and hitched herself up to perch at the bar, head cocked, long legs crossed, drinking beer in lieu of the unobtainable absinthe. She passed the word to Augustus John and the poet and critic Tommy Earp that she had now established herself at a watering-hole where she expected to rediscover some of the excitement, a sense of the unexpected and the camaraderie of classlessness all three had known in Montparnasse. Both men came and pronounced it good. Soon they were joined by Nina's new friend, Constant Lambert, the young composer whose extraordinary and precocious gifts had recently been recognized by Diaghilev who commissioned him to compose *Romeo and Juliet* for the Ballets Russes when he was not yet twenty. With him came fellow composer, Philip Heseltine (Peter Warlock), whom Nina had known from before the war, and many of the strolling players at Augustus's court. Like Dick Wyndham, who was said to have one foot in White's Club and the other in Bohemia, Nina enjoyed parading from time to time in her glad-rags (usually some grand lady's cast-offs), but she also needed to feel at home in the rich mud of humanity for which she had a certain *nostalgie*. Augustus John did not like to have his feet stuck in any camp. Edging fifty and still a wild magnificent figure, a randy pirate-king, red beard flecked with grey, brass ear-rings, swaying cloak and flashing eye under a black broad-brimmed hat, he preferred, like the gypsy ideal with which he so strongly identified, to be free to roam at will. He had known the area since his Slade days when he shared a flat in Fitzroy Street with his sister and fellow student, Gwen and, later, with his first wife Ida Nettleship. But it was only several years later, as he says in his autobiography, that he first went to the Fitzroy Tavern, taken there by Nina.

A good night for Nina was to be taken to the Eiffel Tower by John or someone else, after the Fitzroy closed. There they might find Naps Alington entertaining some of his favourites in either of the two private rooms upstairs, one decorated in his Vorticist mood by Percy Wyndham Lewis who lived down the road in Percy Street. His guests might include not only Tommy Earp but Nancy Cunard and her fellow ex-Slade student, the poet Iris Tree (with or without her husband Curtis Moffat), Horace de Vere Cole, Michael Arlen, Evan Morgan, Brenda Dean Paul and Brenda's absurd old mother, Lady Dean Paul, a professional pianist. Everyone would then go on to the Gargoyle, which by now had been declared 'in bounds' by the Bohemian leaders, there to dance, for those who were still capable, to talk and drink deeper for those who were not, and amongst the latter Nina could safely be counted. Nina, at this time, was working on a book in collaboration with, and at his invitation, Osbert Sitwell; all three of the Sitwells were her admirers. This was to be *The People's Album of London Statues* (1928), drawings by Nina Hamnett, with an introduction and commentary by Osbert Sitwell. This activity brought her through the doors of Duckworth's where she met the energetic young Anthony Powell. Powell's energies were not totally exhausted by his, no doubt, exacting duties as a tyro-publisher, nor by his somewhat restricted social activities, confined largely to invitations during the Season to debutantes' balls. He had decided (encouraged, perhaps, by his introduction to Inez Holden at the Gargoyle) to cast his fly over what appeared to be the more romantically rewarding waters of Bohemia. The meeting with Nina appeared fortuitous.

The ground floor studio opposite Nina's in Thackeray House was occupied by another, and younger, painter. This was Adrian Daintry and their relationship was marked, at least on Daintry's side, by a certain reserve. 'Nina', he told the author, 'made it her practice to wander into my bedroom in the mornings ostensibly to give me a résumé of her previous night's activities. Her first action was always to look at the ledge of my chimney-piece to see if there was any loose change hanging about. "M'deah", she announced one morning, "I've just met this fellah. He's got a bowlah and an umbrellah. He's an Etonah [sic] and he gave me a fiveah."' (It should be explained that Nina affected an exaggerated upper-class accent.) This 'fellah' turned out to be Anthony Powell with whom Daintry was soon to strike up a close and lifelong friendship.

In his memoirs, Powell touches only briefly and lightly upon his relationship with Nina (he appears not to have liked all the drinking, an absolute condition of its enjoyment). On the other hand, Peter Quennell, his friend from Oxford days, insists that it was a liaison of no small significance in Powell's life. 'Nina was Anthony Powell's first grown-up love affair. He was rather pleased with it at the time. She satisfactorily deprived him of his innocence, which is a thing people were anxious to get rid of in those days. He built her up as a romantic *femme de trente ans*, a Bohemian mistress.' And since Nina did a drawing of Powell in her studio at the time, opportunity for bohemian abandon with erotic instruction at first hand thrown in, was there for the asking. Nina played her part, too, in other ways. Not only did she introduce Powell to Adrian Daintry, but also to Constant Lambert, likewise to become a valued friend (and recognizable as Hugh Moreland in *Dance to the Music of Time*). The occasion was when she took them both to the Cavendish Hotel, where Nina was *persona grata* with Rosa. Powell, on his own admission, did not feel entirely at home in the Cavendish, detecting there a '... tense, menacing atmosphere. ...' And later, '... all question of sentimentality', he sternly reminds one, 'should be rigorously excluded from any account of Rosa Lewis and her hotel, both apt to become blurred with nostalgia over the years. An aroma of toughness permeated the place; the fact never forgotten that dissipation must be paid for.' If the Cavendish could appear alarming to impecunious youth, David's more relaxed concept of the Gargoyle's purpose allowed it to become common ground for all the principals in this Fitzrovian comedy, although not without attracting acerbic comment in later years from Constant Lambert. And when dissipation arose there, a not infrequent occurrence in those later years, it was certainly not always paid for in coin of the realm. Much to David's displeasure.

6

The first few weeks in the New Year of 1928 were a particularly testing time for Hermione. There was the emotional split with her infant incarcerated at Wilsford on the one hand and her lover, its father, loose in Switzerland on the other. Communication with David had been sparse. Postcards from St Moritz with views but no news. That is to say, no hint as to where the coursing heart might veer; or whether it was just, as Pamela intended, laying siege to her captive, Meraud. But some comfort was to be found at the centre, where her professional being lay.

A new farce, *Lord Babs*, in which Hermione had a leading role, had just opened at the Vaudeville. She had now forsaken the straight theatre, which had held out so much promise, in favour of the very much more financially rewarding field of comedy, musical and revue, where she was among the most refulgent of the young stars. This was also no small comfort to the chronically impecunious Louise with whom Hermione still lived. Louise's other theatrical daughter, the married Angela, then playing Lady Teazle in *School for Scandal*, was building up a lasting reputation in classical roles for which she would be lucky to earn as much as twenty pounds a week.

Not only was Hermione having a success in *Lord Babs*, but word had now reached her that MGM were seeking likely talent from Britain to be processed by Hollywood for stardom. The age of the talkies was about to dawn and they were anxious not to be wrong-footed. The Brooklyn squawk of their biggest star, Clara Bow, was a secret best kept from the public, whereas Garbo's disinclination to try and improve her diction caused dismay and vexation within bald studio heads. An ambassador from the dream city was even now in London and his predatory gaze had fallen upon young Hermione. She had diverse talents, he reported back, could sing and dance, was intelligible and, above all, had 'SA' (sex appeal). That was all Louis B. Mayer, despotic ruler of MGM, wanted to hear. But what did it profit her having sex-appeal if fateful Pamela was preventing it being trained upon the one and only object of its desire. All the balm of knowing that she was being head-hunted by Hollywood could not disguise the bitterness and frustration Hermione felt.

Then once more the wheel turned and spun David into her lap, or rather at her feet in the theatre. She was making up to go on stage when he 'burst into my dressing-room and plonked down on his knees before me,' she recalled.

> He didn't look sun-tanned and rested, he looked strained and bad-tempered. The first thing he said to me was: 'I hated every moment. It was the most ghastly mistake.'
>
> 'What about poor Merrod [sic] Guinness?'
>
> 'I hated her, too. Darling', said David earnestly, 'don't let's wait any longer. Let's get married at once before someone else tries to interfere and spoil things for us. Marry me, please?'
>
> 'Do you want to marry me desperately?'
>
> 'Of course', said David.

So Pamela had again muffed her attempt to determine the course of David's life. She also seems to have seriously mis-read the character of Miss Guinness, who opted shortly after this débâcle for the life of a painter. She would then herself marry a painter, Chili Guevara, one who at the time of David's rather desperate and belated proposal, was enjoying the double distinction of putting the finishing touches to his portrait of Rosa in the Cavendish and being drawn (one of many efforts) by Nina Hamnett.

Hermione and David were both agreed that their marriage ceremony was to be a very low-key affair and to be performed in a Register Office. She had been in enough farces not to wish to perpetrate her own – garbed all in white at the altar steps. Although it was made clear to all concerned that they were very much 'together', they felt it better to say nothing of their intentions to anyone until all arrangements were securely in place. There was one person, however, who got to the heart of the matter very directly and that was Louis B. Mayer of Hollywood.

Hermione had confessed to David the overtures she had received from the MGM talent-scout. An appointment to come and examine matters of mutual interest had been issued from MGM's West End office. David, with his newly acquired sense of responsible ownership decided he should come too. On arrival they were both surprised to find the man himself, Louis B. Mayer, there in the London office to conduct the interview. The first hurdle over the correct way to pronounce her name safely negotiated, the shrewd eye was turned to David.

> 'Is this guy your agent, Herm-*eye*-on-ee?'
>
> 'Certainly *not*!' David replied loftily.

Hermione decided to defuse a potentially tricky situation and explain his presence. The beaky nose looked beakier.

'A bride, huh.' The prospect did not appear to have much appeal. Nor did what he then went on to propose have much appeal for David – a seven-year contract. He laughed the idea out of court. Not the sort of response the MGM tycoon was used to.

'You don't want your bride to be rich – to be a famous international movie star?'

'Not particularly', David replied.

'Perhaps, darling, we *should* involve an agent. They know how to sort these things out,' David said as they left. Hermione knew whom he had in mind. It was Christopher Mann, young, inexperienced but clever and ambitious. Much of his ginger derived, then, from an unrequited passion for a radiantly beautiful girl with whom he had fallen in love when they were both up at Birmingham University. This was the half-French, half-Irish actress, Madeleine Carroll who, represented by Mann, was about to land her first starring role in British films. David had come to know Mann through Madeleine, who had once had a severe crush on David, and they both came to the Gargoyle quite frequently. 'She used to put her arms around his neck,' Hermione recounts, 'catch my eye, and say "I'm going to weave my web around you." It didn't bother me – any web that Madeleine could weave I could unravel quite easily.'

The movie mogul is often a more sensitive creature than appearance or behaviour might suggest. When confronted with the calibre of arrogance that David could so easily dispense, the response within the hard shell is liable to be that of the oyster on receiving its preliminary squirt of lemon juice. But after the initial shock a black pearl of fury can easily form. It was not therefore surprising that Christopher Mann, entrusted by David to negotiate Hermione's contract, was unable to make any progress with MGM before the departure of Louis B. Mayer for the States. The prospect of Baddeley's forthcoming marriage was not welcomed, he was told. Postponement was counselled. Also, Mann was informed, the three-year contract he was suggesting was too short. The Studio had to protect itself – seven years, no less. Impasse. David airily dismissed the whole matter as being of little importance. Hermione felt twinges of regret. The prospect of international stardom had a powerful allure.

In the event (the event itself taking place in April of that same year), elements of farce were not to be denied attendance upon David's and Hermione's wedding. Hermione had timed her preparations with professional skill so as to make her entrance at the Strand Register Office at noon, the hour revised from the original 11 a.m. appointed by David. This arrangement, however, turned out not to suit the Registrar, so the ceremony reverted to the original time of eleven. A change of which, for some reason, Hermione and the close friends she had invited, remained blithely unaware. Then, driving down the Kings Road in good time, she chanced to see her sister Angela's husband, the stage director Stephen Thomas, sloping down the street with what she rightly judged to be the absconder's suitcase in hand. Not a good omen. Angela, for one, would not now be there.

On arriving at Henrietta Street, off the Strand, Hermione was surprised to see a small crowd waiting outside the register office, including many of the company of *Lord Babs* which she had just left, and a rather unexpectedly larger one inside including a tight-lipped David.

> 'We're supposed to be getting married, you know. Do you realize you're an hour late? We've all been waiting here since eleven.'
>
> 'Darling, you told me twelve o'clock. And it's just twelve. Look.'
>
> 'Yes, but he can't *do it* at twelve! Everybody was told.'
>
> 'Nobody told *me*. One might think I would be the first. So *now* what?'
>
> 'We'll just have to wait until he comes back. What a bore.'

One who had been there since eleven and let it be felt was Pamela. Likewise her two sons, Kit Glenconner and Stephen, faultless in morning-dress while her third, David, incongruously, just wore a casual but well-cut suit with a sloppy pullover. Finally the Registrar returned from his pressing engagement and they could get down to the business of the day, recorded by gentlemen of the press with cameras. Despite the intrusion of a farcical element, it appears to have been rather a grim affair, the ratty overtones duly caught in the published photographs. Pamela, eyes lowered, looks as if she had just been shot, or at least mortally wounded, which indeed she may have been since she was to die in that same year. Stephen has found his best profile for the cameras, David looks bemused, stiff and uncomfortable, his mother's hand hanging loose through his arm. Louise stares mournfully ahead in jowly resignation – she had been heard for some time muttering darkly about 'bad Tennant blood'. Only Hermione, kiss-curls peeking out from under her tight-fitting hat, seems to know exactly what she is doing and to be doing it with steely determination – signing the marriage register with well-aimed pen.

Things livened up later at the Gargoyle for the reception organized by Harry Walker, a crowded and rather mixed affair of the grand, the gifted and the fair. This, Hermione claimed, was where and when she drank champagne for the first time. As good an introduction to alcohol as one might wish. There was a splendid array of wedding presents, and some less splendid such as the book from Bertrand Russell entitled *How to Remain Happily Married.* A volume he may not have studied too closely himself since he separated from his wife shortly after this occasion. Something even less splendid but invaluable to Hermione at this moment was offered by Mrs Patrick Campbell who had created the role of Eliza in Shaw's *Pygmalion*, but had now rather run to fat. 'Oh dear', she muttered as she made her way through to Hermione, 'I didn't have time to buy you a wedding present.' Hermione patted her hand. 'You mustn't think of such a thing.' 'Oh, but I must.' She rustled about inside her handbag. 'Let me see now....' Triumphantly she pulled out a rather grubby chiffon hankie. She shook it and a cloud of face-powder floated over her dark dress. Within the hankie was a grey-looking swansdown powder-puff and it was this uninviting object she now pressed upon Hermione. 'Just a little remembrance, darling.'

Hermione had discovered that in the excitement of getting married she had left her own compact behind. Gratefully she went to the ladies room and started putting the 'little remembrance' to good use. She was followed in by her new mother-in-law. Pamela embraced her affectionately, slipping into her hand a pearl, emerald and diamond ring. 'This is something very precious from me to you', she said. 'The first man I ever loved gave it to me.'

David's own wedding present to Hermione showed finesse in the grand manner. It started with the purchase of a crocodile dressing case from Asprey's in Bond Street inside which were numerous compartments. David filled these compartments with objects acquired through walking up Bond Street on one side and then down the other buying what took his fancy as he went.

Hermione emerged with freshly powdered nose and newly be-ringed fingers to be met with a rather different response to her new status from Harry. 'Congratulations', he said to her with a crooked smile. 'You won.' Hermione was not totally taken aback. She had long suspected him of having a malign influence over David and knew well he was very jealous of her, 'but this was really a bit much,' she said later. 'Holding out his hand as if we were *boxers* or something ridiculous.'

If Hermione's family were a little thin on the ground at the reception, through Angela's domestic crisis and the falling out between David and Muriel's husband Hugh Gee, her supporters from the theatrical fraternity were out in force. Of the Tennants only Clare was predictably absent. Stephen's emergence from what had now become his customary winter retreat in Switzerland was possibly at Pamela's insistence. But he also had his own reasons for wishing to return. In the summer he had met Siegfried Sassoon for the first time. Mutual attraction developed and Stephen had persuaded this austere and aloof man, some twenty years his senior, to take part in some frolicsome activities he had organized at Wilsford involving the Sitwells and such BYPs as Rex Whistler, Cecil Beaton, the Jungman sisters and the Sitwell protégé, William Walton. The war-scarred poet 'didn't *quite* like all that dressing-up' at Wilsford, but this did not deflect his growing infatuation with Stephen. As a mark of favour, he took him to see the ageing Thomas Hardy at Max Gate. After observing his young guest's eager approach, Hardy told his wife that Stephen Tennant was the only person he had ever known with a walk like Swinburne's.

With the reception in full swing, David had the car loaded with their honeymoon luggage and the two of them 'vroomed off' for Dover, for Paris and thence to the South of France. Their return through Paris, where they had intended to spend a week, was unexpectedly interrupted on their first day. They were sitting in the bright spring sunshine outside the Café de la Paix peacefully taking their morning apéritif – Hermione had proved a very quick student where the pleasures of the social drink were concerned, an appreciation that she was never to lose – when a voice behind them called out: 'Hermione! Haven't you heard? They've sent an SOS for you over the wireless!' This startling testimony to her renown proved to have its origin in relatively small beer. A message had been broadcast by the BBC, whose servant David still was, asking Miss Hermione Baddeley to get in touch urgently with a certain important theatrical impresario. A new play was about to start rehearsal and its leading lady was missing somewhere in France.

David was not pleased at this interruption. Still less that the world of the theatre appeared to have stronger claims on his wife than he did. Hermione explained that this would be the first time that the young John Gielgud would have his name up in lights in the West End (in fact he had taken over from Noël Coward in *The Vortex*). He was a very close friend of Angela's and she would never be forgiven by her sister if she let him and the rest of the company down. So they set off for home again.

7

'Home' was a capacious flat that David had rented on the first floor of a porticoed house in Adelphi Terrace, whose eighteenth-century elegance has been sacrificed long since to the developers. Tall windows provided an uninterrupted view south across the Thames, bisected only by Cleopatra's Needle rising from the Embankment in the foreground. They were on the perimeter of theatre-land, a short stroll away was the BBC's Savoy Hill Studios, while a quick 'vroom' up to Soho was all it took to measure the Bugatti's considerable length outside the Gargoyle.

All seemed set fair. God would appear to have done for David what the Glenconner family motto – *Deus Dabit Vela* – required of Him. He had filled the sails. A vividly attractive young wife, money-spinning and sexy; a bold and successful enterprise; personal recognition as the 'golden-voiced' news-reader for the rapidly increasing number of wireless listeners; beauty, health, careless wealth and a little daughter he found quite captivating; all these benisons blew David's proud ship confidently through untroubled waters.

Although there was room enough for both Nanny and Pauline in the new flat, it suddenly became, through the social demands presently made upon David and Hermione's joint and several selves, more convenient for them to continue to remain down at Wilsford and visited (sometimes) at weekends, or 'Saturday to Mondays' as they were known in Pamela's world. Pamela, who had once been quite guarded in her response to the 'little actress', now welcomed her warmly into the fold; one of Pamela's friends going so far as to say: 'David and Hermione are inevitable to each other.' Young upper-crusters, from whom David tended to hold himself aloof and on that account had been envied and admired by them, found their renewed overtures welcomed and encouraged by Hermione; subject always to the prior demands of the theatre. Their lives were separated only by nightly attendance at the theatre on the one hand and news-reading at Savoy Hill on the other, the hours being roughly coincidental. Reunion took place when David picked Hermione up after her show when she was, as she said, always on a 'high' and 'the deep, deep peace of the double bed' was not yet on her mind. He would then take her dancing at the Savoy before a late supper at the Gargoyle. If he was caught up at the Club, the chauffeur would be sent to bring her there instead.

On one such occasion she joined Harry Walker at the bar while waiting for David to come up from below. The Fly, not one to parade fidelity to the wife whose style he did not consider to come up to Gargoyle standards, had a new mistress. She was Brenda Dean Paul and she was sitting beside him. Hermione makes the point in her autobiography that 'Brenda Dean Paul was going to be one of the most notorious women in England. She was perhaps the first woman in London that the media picked up and helped to destroy by splashing her picture across the front pages, and by hounding her every time she appeared in court.' There is some exaggeration here. Brenda was the only daughter of a baronet but she shared Tallulah's penchant for cocaine. This combined with a certain carelessness in her dealings with private people in public places – and, vice versa – frequently led her into the courts and to the attention of the more sensational newspapers such as the *News of the World* and *The People*. Hermione had been fascinated by her from their first meeting, '... a voluptuous girl who has plenty of sex-appeal and lets every man within eye-catching distance get the message'. Oddly, she saw her as the epitome of the role she herself had played in *On With the Dance*, Noël Coward's 'Poor Little Rich Girl'. Peter Quennell, who knew Brenda from much the same time, remembers her as looking like 'a Lely portrait of Nell Gwynne, *very like*. She was a nice, affectionate, drunken, amorous girl who took to drugs like her awful brother, "Napper".' A contemporary and fellow baronet-to-be, Michael Russell, complained that 'I knew much more about Napper's anatomy than I did about Brenda's, more's the pity. He was such a fearful fellow, he was always being de-bagged at parties, you see.'

Brenda leaned over the Gargoyle bar and held out her cigarette case to Hermione, tantalizingly. 'Look at it. Don't you think it's divine?' Hermione looked. She weighed it in her hand. It was heavy and it was gold and on it were Brenda's initials pricked out in diamonds. She glanced from one to the other of them. Harry gave her one of his strange half-smiles. He always reminded her, Hermione said, of one of those dark secret men in medieval Venetian paintings whispering in the ear of the Doge. 'It's a present from Harry', Brenda sighed, leaning over and kissing him. She looked triumphantly up at Hermione through pupils dilated with cocaine.

Hermione raised the matter with David, backing up her suspicions of

Harry with what she considered to be rather tangible evidence. It was well known that The Fly had no money other than the salary David paid him. This was generous enough but by no means enough to enable him to splash out on very expensive *bibelots*. David responded angrily. There could be some perfectly rational explanation – a win on the horses, whatever. In any case, he did not want to hear any more about it. So much for that. But Hermione continued to brood over the matter and the vehemence of David's defence of Walker against her intuitive instincts. Before long her misgivings would prove to be well-founded.

The hectic life David and Hermione were now tempted to lead was very much a reflection of those times. 1928 – the year immediately preceding the Wall Street Crash – was a climactic period for parties and party-goers. 'Oh, Nina, *what a lot of parties* . . .' a character in *Vile Bodies* (1930) was to lament. 'Masked parties, Savage parties, Victorian parties, Greek parties, Russian parties, Circus parties, parties where one had to dress up as somebody else, almost naked parties in St John's Wood, parties in flats and studios and houses and hotels, in Windmills and Swimming-baths . . . .' These doings and those who did them were captured for the popular press.

Not to be outdone, David and Hermione threw what they felt was their own quintessentially original pyjama and bottle party in Adelphi Terrace. 'We'll get the girls out of their suspender belts and silk stockings', David mused in anticipation. They did, and it was described thus by the *Daily News*:

> The hundreds of guests came in pyjamas the colours of which might be the envy of the foremost futurist artist of the day. The first arrival was a pretty flaxen-haired girl of about nineteen, wearing pyjamas of salmon-pink, blue, red, green, orange and white. Her contribution was a bottle of 1840 champagne which was immediately consumed. The host and hostess were attired in sleeping suits of orange. Many of the men's pyjamas were trimmed with lace. The bottles of refreshments the guests were expected to bring provided an amusing diversion. The second bottle was gin; the third, hair-restorer; the fourth, health-salts; and other bottles included distilled water, beer, ink, petrol, ethyl, smelling salts, Thames water, Jordan water, cabbage water, and water from a pool alive with tadpoles . . . . All the while, in another room, the orchestra was playing dreamy music.

Perhaps it was the 'dreamy music' that brought their neighbour,

J. M. Barrie, to knock on their front door and ask wistfully if he might be allowed in to join the fun. Or possibly it was because he had caught a glimpse of Dick Wyndham's future wife, Grethe Wulfsberg from Norway. With her Eton crop and bright eyes, she had a distinct look of Peter Pan, he later told her. The description of the event in the *Daily News* certainly does not read like a barrel of laughs, although the guests may have 'been thoroughly enjoying themselves'.

*

On a Sunday in the third week of November, David and Hermione drove back to London after lunching in the country. They went to the Gargoyle before going home. Harry was drinking with Brenda at the bar upstairs. On seeing them he looked grave. 'David', he said, coming over, 'I'm afraid I have bad news.' 'Bad news?' 'The butler telephoned from Wilsford. Lady Grey has been taken ill.' There was a silence. 'Is she dead?' David then asked quietly. Walker nodded. Pamela had played her last card. They drove straight down to Wilsford where they were met by Kit. Their mother had died suddenly from a heart attack. It was very quick and she had not suffered. Stephen had been contacted in Paris and was now on his way back. Lord Grey was coming down from the North by train.

A room had been prepared for David and Hermione across the landing from where Pamela lay. David went in to be alone with his mother. When he came out he seemed very calm. He told Hermione to go in and kiss Pamela good-night. This was her first encounter with death and she felt quite uneasy. But once inside the bedroom uneasiness left her. Pamela lay there still and beautiful. 'She looked asleep and completely at peace. There was not a line to be seen on her face and her profile was noble.' Hermione's warm heart remembered her suddenly with affection and even gratitude. She bent over and kissed her cheek. Not, however, sharing the views on spiritualism which Pamela had passed on to David, she thought it prudent to substitute a whispered 'good-bye' for the suggested 'good-night'. Neither was able to sleep for a while, but David was the first to go. Listening to his even breathing she, too, closed her eyes. The headlights of a car coming up the drive made her open them again. Stephen must have come over from Paris by aeroplane, was her first thought. She began to doze off.

And then

> 'I heard the door open gently. Someone came in and walked over to David's side of the bed. 'Is that you, Stephen?' I whispered. No one

answered. There was complete quietness in the room. I sat up terrified. No one was in the room. 'David,' I said hoarsely, 'someone's been in here.' My heart was thumping. 'There's someone in the room.' David roused himself. 'What are you saying? Someone's here?' 'They've gone', I whispered, 'whoever it was bent over you.' David lay back. 'Don't worry, darling', he said sleepily, 'it must have been Mummy coming in to wish us goodnight.'

So much for Hermione's whispered 'goodbye'.

The next morning, the three Tennants were sitting around the table having a late breakfast, when a car bowled up the drive bringing neither the expected Stephen, nor Lord Grey but the quite unexpected Harry Walker with Brenda Dean Paul. They had come to cheer them up, was Harry's curious explanation for their presence. Over coffee Hermione guilelessly related her strange experience of the night before. This appeared to interest the psychic curiosity of Harry greatly. The next day a highly exaggerated account of what Hermione had disclosed at the breakfast table appeared in a morning paper: 'Actress, daughter-in-law of Lady Grey reveals her terrifying experience with the other world....' Stephen telephoned indignant and upset. Hermione, recognizing the sly hand of The Fly behind all this, was hard put to persuade him she was not the culprit.

Pamela was buried at the village church of St Michael's, Wilsford, where, in due course she would be joined by David, Stephen and Hermione. In her will, Pamela left Wilsford and all its contents to David. She also left David the tidy unencumbered sum of £90,000, the approximate equivalent today of £1,650,000. From being just a rich young man David now became extremely rich. But with the additional riches came also cares, even moral responsibilities – such as what to do with Wilsford. He needed guidance and for this he turned to his old friend, Matt Pritchard. David's attendance at his circle had recently dropped sharply, what with one thing and another. But Pritchard responded swiftly to David's plea. He ruled out any possibility of David going to live down at Wilsford. 'It would be like wearing your mother's old clothes', he said. He was quite firm on this point. David found himself rather relieved. But the problem remained and with it the obligation to all the people, inside the house and out, who worked there. 'Let Stephen have it', advised Pritchard. 'That way it remains in the family and the retainers can be retained.' And so in time it came to pass, more or less. The house and all its contents were bought for Stephen by his trustees for £30,000

(£550,000). No snip. But when both came under Sotheby's hammer in 1988, they fetched £3 million.

Hermione at first was dismayed at David's decision to sell Wilsford to Stephen, although she could hardly have imagined that the shoes of its previous *châtelaine* would have fitted her. But there was comfort in being awarded a maid of her own to live in at Adelphi Terrace. Gwen was a calm, soft-voiced girl from Wales. A jolly cockney lady came in daily to do the 'rough', and, with her help, Hermione prepared for the arrival of Nanny and Pauline. David's chauffeur-valet lived out.

The death of Pamela came as a profound release for David. But the form this took caused Hermione to feel justifiably apprehensive. She began to realize that his mother's strong personality and extreme possessiveness had also served as a restraining influence on David's excesses. His extravagant dandyism, yoked to an almost puritan search for perfection, became noticeably more pronounced. As did the quest for sensation. A new death-tease in the form of a Leyland-Thomas racing car was delivered to the Terrace. With this superb machine, David was determined to break and hold the track record at Brooklands. And, for a time, so he did.

He had also recently been taking flying lessons, a skill which he mastered very quickly. Equipped with his pilot's certificate, the next step was to buy a Gypsy Moth, the two-seater aircraft favoured by the Prince of Wales and his brothers, Prince Henry of Gloucester, and Prince George of Kent. The royal princes did much to make private flying seem a most desirable pursuit for those with the time, the money and the dash. Private flying became an enviably casual and carefree habit. 'Flying in the twenties', said the Duke of Richmond, 'was great fun and very relaxed. You saw a nice pub and a handy field beside it, so down you went.' David, making no sartorial concession to flying, other than the leather helmet he normally drove in, thought nothing of touching down near the country road he might be following to check his whereabouts from the road sign.

Many of David's sorties were with Hermione to Paris, to visit various couturiers, Paul Poiret among them. (Hermione had poor dress sense and David was happy to repair that failing.) If there were three of them Paris bound by air, as was often the case, David would be obliged by the authorities at Lympne Aerodrome, their point of departure, to leave one behind and then shuttle back for him. Frequent companions on these sorties were either Martin Wilson or Brian Howard. Wilson, known to David as 'Mother', the eldest son of the horse-racing enthusiast Sir

Matthew 'Scatters' Wilson, had made something of a reputation for himself at BYP's fancy-dress parties for his female representations – Queen Mary in yachting costume circa 1911 was remarked on as being particularly successful. On one of their Paris trips Hermione remembers looking down as they soared into the air 'to see one of the funniest sights of my life: poor Martin sitting on the deserted runway disconsolately dabbing his nose with an enormous powder puff!'

Brian Howard also had been made briefly to abandon aircraft at Lympne. He wrote a highly-charged account of one of these Paris expeditions included in *Brian Howard, a Portrait of a Failure*, edited by Marie-Jacqueline Lancaster. In it he sees David as having the godlike authority of Von Möltke, then as Nietzsche, finally as the new Satan, with Brian and David spouting Milton to each other down the speaking tube as the plane whizzed along at 120 m.p.h.

In order to take part in all these revels, Hermione decided, at the end of the year, to put her career to one side. This was regarded with much disapproval by Angela who thought it a terrible waste – 'I have talent but Hermione has a touch of genius' – and much dismay by Louise who saw her hard-earned meal-ticket vanishing. Now that she was no longer earning her large salary – after all, she did want to be a proper wife and mother – Hermione asked David to take over her responsibilities to her own mother. David baulked. An unhappy compromise was eventually reached, lodging the thought with Hermione that David had a distinctly mean stripe.

The tempo of their lives since marriage had increased so suddenly and so dramatically that overheating looked inevitable. And it was. The result, a fierce blaze of marital discord. Accusation and counter accusation, with sexual jealousy central to the argument. It had all been provoked by some remark made by Brenda Dean Paul. Harry Walker had mischievously been encouraging the amorous Brenda, his own acclaimed mistress, to 'console' David at the Gargoyle when, for whatever reason, Hermione was not there. A frequent reason being that Hermione was always 'lit up' after her show and would want to go on to parties that would not appeal to David, in which case, she would be escorted on the arm of another – Christopher de Bathe, Lillie Langtry's son, often being the one. Hermione was aware of Brenda's powers of consolation but as far as she and David were concerned 'I didn't bother. People on drugs, as Brenda was much of the time, are usually not very interested in sex.' Nevertheless, she felt that the apparently artless Brenda was basically a trouble-maker.

This was borne out when one of her barbs had been brought back to her by David. Hermione retaliated by accusing Brenda of being a 'bad influence'. That touched a sensitive spot, because what David was trying to be was a 'good influence' on Brenda. 'Mr David Tennant is an eager student of Philosophy', wrote gossip columnist Lady Eleanor Smith at the time. 'One of the greatest triumphs of his philosophy is that he has persuaded the laziest young girl of my acquaintance to rise at eight o'clock each day to join him in his philosophical researches.' Surprisingly, Hermione had no idea that David was taking Brenda to receive the wisdom of Matt Pritchard (connived at, of course, by Walker). But then she was a late riser. Perhaps Brenda had an appeal for David that Hermione lacked. She needed help. Hermione did not.

In any event, David, who had always held that 'marriage is not a strait-jacket', now fired the de Bathe shot at Hermione. She, at bed-level, blameless, provocatively capped this with the Lords Donegall, Hastings and others. What seemed to start as just a tiff ended in David's abrupt and enraged exit to the Savoy Hotel. Hermione's emotional resilience was proved when the next sign of life that David made was to inform her through his solicitors that he was intending to sue for divorce citing all the admirers she had claimed. It was now February 1929. They had been married less than a year. Within a week Hermione was back in the theatre rehearsing a new show called *The Five O'Clock Girl*, in which the young John Mills was appearing as a chorus boy. When the show went on tour, Louise went too, overjoyed to be back on the road again and having Hermione all to herself just like the old times. Meanwhile Pauline remained with Nanny and Gwen at the otherwise deserted Adelphi Terrace. On the surface, Hermione, too, rejoiced at being back in the fun and camaraderie of the theatre where she felt so at home. But she wanted David back – badly. She felt somehow confident that it would not be too long before that happened.

In March, David announced his resignation from the BBC, to take effect from the end of the month. This was a piece of news he did not read himself but it was nevertheless picked up by all major papers. It was not, therefore, news to Hermione when he later telephoned her in Birmingham, where her show was, prior to opening in London the following week.

'I'm off to Canada,' he said. 'I'm going to Vancouver to open a factory.'

'Oh!' replied Hermione, busily calculating how soon she could go out and join him. 'What do I wish you? Bon voyage?'

'Oh, I'm sure it will be a good voyage', he said with what she thought was rather an odd emphasis. 'By the way', a slight pause – what was coming next? 'By the way – I'm taking Brenda Dean Paul with me.' Lothario's box was now open.

8

On 29 March, 1929, David and Brenda embarked at Southampton on SS *Berengaria* (sister ship to the *Mauretania*) bound for New York. Sailing on the same vessel was a young man going to the New World to seek his fortune (he found it and is now a very comfortably retired merchant banker). He became infatuated by the dazzling Brenda and was encouraged in this by remarking that she and David did not behave together as lovers and, of course, had separate cabins. Bumping into him one morning on deck, she took compassion on the young man's evident adoration and said, 'David's giving a cocktail party to-night, do come.' The Cunard line was very accommodating about such matters: they would provide stateroom, stewards, bar and barmen; you would foot the bill at the end of the voyage. The young hopeful was one of the last to leave the party. He noticed Brenda picking up a handbag someone had left behind. There was nothing inside except two lipsticks. 'Don't touch that', warned David. 'You might get the pox.' But she did, and she would.

David's decision to take Brenda Dean Paul to Canada was a confusion of pique, jealousy and rage and an histrionic way of showing Hermione who was in control. David may, indeed, not have had any precise idea of what he was actually going to do in Canada – the Press had variously described him as going out to run a farm in British Colombia; as becoming involved in the timber industry; or even becoming a rancher. He would certainly not have been so wild as to compromise a large share of recently inherited capital without consulting his sensible elder brother. In fact, Kit must have approved the factory acquisition, or steered him into it a bit later, for he himself took a stake in the enterprise. Kit, however, would not have so happily sanctioned Brenda Dean Paul. But again she might just have been a last minute addition to David's travelling baggage.

The manner of David's departure now gave Hermione all the grounds she might wish, had she so wished, to press for divorce herself. And with the prospect of a whopping financial settlement to boot. Perhaps that was the bold risk David was taking, deliberately putting her to that test. It was not her way, of course, as David must have known; Hermione's way was to soldier on in her profession. And, with David and Brenda Dean Paul somewhere in British Colombia, this was what she was now doing at the London Hippodrome, while at the same time trying to fend off the curiosity of the Press.

Brenda, as it happened, did not remain very long with David in Canada. Perhaps Hermione had been right in supposing that her cocaine habit made her 'not very interested in sex'. In all events, she was given the same treatment as David had once meted out to the Mercedes Benz he had ordered from Germany to try out at Brooklands: 'Tried and found wanting. Send it back!' he crisply ordered his chauffeur. So, amorous or not, Brenda was returned alone by boat. Hermione, scrupulously avoiding the Gargoyle and those who went there, knew nothing of this. Then, out of the blue, a call from Kit came to the Scala Theatre where she was in *The Shanghai Gesture*. Kit had received a telegram from David asking him to do what he could to persuade Hermione to come and join him in Canada bringing Pauline. Innocent of false pride, Hermione did not hesitate. She arranged her release the next day and, after serving the obligatory three weeks' notice, set off with Nanny and child for Vancouver in early July.

*

The people who did go to the Gargoyle were at all times various, but in the dying years of the twenties the emphasis leaned towards highbrows and away from the BYPs, whose own time was in any case in decline. The intellectual power so often then assembled at the Club was quite remarkable. And not just for staid luncheon. It would fill the place at night, using it as a social and sexual gymnasium – the work-out on the dance floor followed by the cold shower of penetrating and significant exchange. In her autobiography, Juliette Huxley remembers that she and Julian often joined H. G. Wells at meetings of 'The Realist' together with Bertrand Russell and intellectuals such as Major Church, Richard Gregory, Herbert Read, Alec Carr-Saunders, Malinowski, Gerald Heard, Naomi Mitchison, Eileen and Rhoda Power, Hilda Matheson and others. After the meeting they might go on to the Gargoyle. 'I was always delighted to see B.R. [Russell] again', she writes in her diary for 1929, 'remembering my platonic passion for his electrifying mind. We danced together at the Gargoyle Club, not dangerously, but curiously umbilically. And Malinowski', she goes on, 'did an odd Charleston which Eileen Power called "the sexual dance of the savages – as strange as if one were dancing with a tassel."' (The Polish-born anthropologist had only recently published what was regarded as an important work, *Sex and Repression in Savage Society*.)

Many writers and artists enjoy the experience of sexuality being cognate with creativity. Wells, with his vanity, his high-pitched voice and glittering reputation, was no exception. He would have liked 'to fecundate England' in the view of Anthony Burgess. But 'H.G. only danced on compulsion', Lady Huxley told her diary, 'and promenaded Hilda Matheson round the floor.' On any evening, disposed about the Club, there might also be Gilbert Murray, William Beveridge and Arnold Bennett, whom Hermione remembered playing racing demon in the Tudor Room. Among the younger intellectuals, Cyril Connolly, as relatively impoverished as his friends the lunch-time Gargoylers, Waugh, Powell and Quennell, now took to patronizing the Club at night.

A fresh but shrewdly observant eye was also fastened on the Gargoyle at the decade's end. It belonged to the novelist Stella Benson, who had come from about as distant a place as could be found – the Customs barriers of outer Manchuria. Stella's husband, Seamus Anderson, was an employee of the Imperial Chinese Maritime Customs Service, charged with discouraging foreigners from importing opium, while collecting taxes on other necessities. Stella's return to England after two years exile was a coincidence of home-leave due to Seamus and her most recent novel, *Goodbye, Stranger*, having been short-listed for the Femina-Vie Heureuse literary prize.

Stella and Seamus came to the 'crude, material universe' of London with high expectations. Rumours had reached them even in the 'distant planet' of Manchuria that there was abroad 'a new, anything-goes style of London social life'. Stella found it 'roaring, confused, but enchanting'. Shortly after their arrival they were taken to the Gargoyle which pleased them enough for them to fork out what they felt was the high membership fee. And they enjoyed dancing 'to a whispering band which left most of the beats to the imagination', Stella's deafness not helping here. Often they went to the club with their new friends, Cuthbert and Lady Eileen Orde, both of whom were painters. Eileen Orde had the appalling handicap of multiple sclerosis which necessitated her painting with brush held in mouth. But they were witty, *mondaine*, sexually outspoken and lived a very convivial life, and though Eileen had to navigate the tables of the Gargoyle 'quivering and shaking on her escort's arm', it was their chosen place, as it came to be for the Andersons.

In spite of her supposed dread of highbrows, Stella encountered a great many in that hectic London year, among them Aldous Huxley, whom she was determined to hate, having recoiled in horror from the cynicism of *Those Barren Leaves*. When met at the Gargoyle he turned out to be human after all – vulnerable, frail, nearly blind: 'I could only be very gentle, and contented myself with saying I couldn't bear his books, and took it for granted that he couldn't mine.' As a reward for this plain speaking, the Andersons were immediately asked to stay with the Huxleys in Italy. She found Vita Sackville-West easier to be with '... since she seems better bred [than most highbrows] and not so busy being clever at all costs.' Her husband, Harold Nicolson, on the other hand, '... has a very glittering picture of himself as a very cultured cosmopolitan, and so can't be calm ... he likes to show off ... but none of it *quite* gets across....' Arthur Waley fares better '... a kind of Bloomsbury Saint – he lives in a cloudy ecstasy of cleverness.' He made, however, a rather unsaintly remark to her about Virginia Woolf's brother-in-law, Clive Bell. 'He was a buffoon,' he said, who had 'got by mistake into a highbrow Bloomsbury world – he was really a 'country gentleman'. Stella did not believe him. E. M. Forster is a 'very crooked, gentle-looking man...', but the man who comes off best, perhaps, in Stella's diaries is Walter de la Mare whose verse she already loved. A luncheon was arranged at the Gargoyle for the Andersons to meet the de la Mares, the poet being fifty-five at the time. Stella found him '... very gentle and honest – I should say not at home in the grown-up world, but rather calm and tranquil and therefore not afraid of that world.' In her biography of Stella, Joy Grant remarks of this occasion that 'The conversation went deeper than at the average luncheon party: people asked not merely what each other's opinions or convictions were, but *why*.' As a description of an average Gargoyle luncheon this could not have been better put.

On a less euphoric note, the Armenian literary wizard, Michael Arlen, is described by Stella as '... an ugly underbred-looking little man and a great poseur'. But most disarmingly, when they met later in the year with some of the Ordes' Riviera cronies in Antibes, Arlen said: 'I must tell you right away that I am a cad; I should be kicked out of any club in London [the Gargoyle excepted] – and rightly so, for I am a born cad. All this time I have been writing cads' books for money, but now that I have got money, I thought I would begin to write books from my heart. But I find I have only a cad's heart to write from!' This was recounted in a letter to Virginia Woolf and Stella adds: 'The poor lamb was, of course, a little binjed [sic] at the time.'

Surprisingly – and no-one would have been more surprised than David – he and Hermione became the targets for one of the most waspish entries in her diary for that year. 'David Tennant', she wrote on 17 December, 1928, 'has an inhuman, fairy-like – mask-like – face – and can't really be so vulgar as he pretends to be. Perhaps he feels he has to keep pace with his Hermione – who certainly looks more like a bar-maid than anyone ever did who wasn't.' Perhaps Stella's view of the dancing Tennants had been soured by her own sexually tormented marriage, a condition remarked upon by Virginia Woolf.

Stella's acerbic view of some of the people she met was not generally shared. Christina Foyle was much younger than Stella but they both went to the Gargoyle at much the same time. And at much the same time they both met the writer William Gerhardie. Gerhardie's father, a businessman in Russia until the Revolution, was fortunate in having his name mis-read by the Bolsheviks as 'Keir Hardie' and was thus given *carte blanche* to return home with young William. He became a close friend of Katherine Mansfield, and Stella had much admired his two novels, *Futility* and *The Polyglots*. A '... bulbous-browed delicate looking young man, pink-eyed looking about nineteen', was how he struck her during that year in London. But to the impressionable Miss Foyle he was 'Handsome, debonair, utterly cosmopolitan and a great flirt'. She met him through her own initiative: 'I began my literary luncheons before I was twenty years old at the very end of the twenties. Being young and pretty, I soon discovered that it was far easier to persuade famous writers to come and speak if I called upon them, instead of just writing to them. One of the first writers I visited was William Gerhardie. He lived in Hallam Street, off Portland Place. He was charming to me. He said he would love to come to my luncheon, but on one condition – that I should dine with him at the Gargoyle Club that night. So I did. I remember the tiny lift – the mirrored walls, and the other ladies who all looked like Gertrude Lawrence. William Gerhardie told me that I was pretty, that my dress was pretty, but that I wore my hair too forward. "You should have a little on the forehead and the sides combed back behind the ears." He reached across our table and showed me how to do it. And I wore it like that for several years. He bought me my first dry martini – and for me it was a glamorous night.

'It was a very attractive club with the clientele a good deal above the other Soho clubs of the time, like the Hambone and the Tatty Bogle which attracted types like Nina Hamnett downwards. I went to the Gargoyle many times over the years, and among the curious characters I used to go there with were A. P. Herbert, Aleister Crowley and Epstein.'

The last three were fair representatives of the dionysian factor (diabolic in Crowley's case) as the Gargoyle moved into the thirties. To whose number could be added – not quite at random since they were all close friends – David's cousin Dick Wyndham; the South African poet Roy Campbell; Constant Lambert, composer son of a leading Australian painter (Constant's brother, Maurice, had sculpted a bronze bust of Stephen in 1928, as had Epstein the previous year); Freddy Mayor, *bon viveur* and pioneer from the art world; the actor Robert Newton who had founded the Shilling Theatre (that was the entrance fee) in Fulham; Curtis Moffat, American photographer, designer, raconteur and husband of the wayward Iris Tree; and, of course, Augustus John.

The coterie of brilliant and beautiful heartbreakers at the Gargoyle, and of whom Nancy Cunard, who had given Aldous Huxley, Michael Arlen and many others such a hard time in the early twenties, was the archetype, included also Diana Cooper, Iris Tree, Sybil Hart-Davis, Marie Beerbohm and less frequently Dora Carrington and Dorothy Brett. The penalty for the 'femme fatale' dealing hardly with brilliant novelists was, as Nancy Cunard soon learnt, that she was likely to find herself excoriated in print. Nancy appeared recognizably, and far from flatteringly, as Marjorie Carling in Huxley's *Point Counter Point* and more acceptably as Iris Storm in Arlen's *The Green Hat*. The latter was not only a huge bestseller but was adapted for the stage and made into a film. So Nancy acquired considerable renown. All the heartbreakers were close (when not intimate) friends, most of them were ex-pupils of the Slade who had been drawn or painted by John, and many of them he had pleasured. They included, also, John's daughters, Vivien and Poppet. (Like his friend and contemporary, the sculptor Eric Gill, Augustus did not regard consanguinity as necessarily an insurmountable barrier to the gratification of desire.)

Ruthven Todd had a story which nicely caught the lusty vigour drifting in with the tide from Fitzrovia. Sickert and John were walking down Charlotte Street together and passed a shop with its window full of plumber's supplies. 'Augustus, my boy,' said Sickert and laid his hand on the younger man's shoulder. Augustus waited for the pearls of wisdom from the voice of experience. 'Augustus, my boy', Sickert's voice was serious, 'I *wish* I had a *brass* cock.' When, many years later, the first extract of John's autobiography, *Chiaroscuro*, appeared in Cyril Connolly's magazine, *Horizon*, Ruthven asked him if he would put this in. 'Won't fit', was the reply.

John and Epstein were the pre-eminent figures in their world and they looked at each other above the heads of their contemporaries with respect and guarded friendship. The reserve, which on occasion took paranoid form, was largely on Epstein's side, John showing a more open and generous spirit in their dealings. Discord had erupted during the First World War. Early in 1917 Epstein did a somewhat saturnine portrait-head of John about which the latter had certain misgivings. 'I wanted to capture a certain wildness, an untamed quality that is the essence of the man', Epstein explained in his memoir *Let There Be Sculpture.*

David's cousin Dick Wyndham's homage to Epstein took a practical form. In 1928, Dick gave all the proceeds of an exhibition he was holding of his own paintings towards a subscription for the Tate Gallery to buy Epstein's 'The Visitation', completed two years earlier. The exhibition itself marked the recognition of a sea-change in Dick's life. While quite a young man he had inherited Clouds the massive house his grandparents had built in Wiltshire. Clouds had assumed an almost talismanic significance for the Souls and the many born in their shadow, as in lesser degree had Wilsford. But with the upkeep of all its land and tenanted farm buildings it was a large inheritance, and a large post-war responsibility. After the fiasco of his marriage, with subsequent divorce in 1925, Dick broke from the upper-class mould into which he had been poured at birth and sought to embrace a wider world where his muffled artistic talents might find expression. He came to live in London in pursuit of its bohemian elements, and at the same time bought himself a studio in Paris. Clouds he visited infrequently and when there only occupied what had once been the housekeeper's rooms. Patches on the William Morris wallpaper began to appear where the large collection of Pre-Raphaelite and other valuable paintings had once hung – to the satisfaction of the sale-rooms.

In London, Dick, too, found the need of a guru. But whereas David's had manipulated and helped to liberate, Dick's new mentor was to instruct, as required, in the movement of modern art and in its relevant application, but was then to bite savagely, in satirical prose. His name, now almost forgotten, had a marked resonance between the wars. As a modern prophet no less important than Eliot, Pound and Joyce, Percy Wyndham Lewis, avant-garde painter, critic, writer first made public impact through launching the Vorticist art-movement in January 1914, with the poet Ezra Pound. They brought out a sensational high-brow periodical named *Blast* with typography and layout suitably aggressive. Through this they would lob grenades of scalding sarcasm at the 'Fry-ites', at the hated 'Bloomsbuggers'.

Dick and Lewis had first met in Venice. It was in 1922, the year of Mussolini's celebrated march on Rome. Lewis was staying in Lady Cunard's palazzo for the purpose of painting Nancy's portrait. Nancy, 'the modern girl supreme', in Brian Howard's words, was not only an artistic muse but herself a poet and later publisher. Every day they would gather at Florian's in St Mark's Square – Nancy, the Sitwells, Lewis, Hugo Rumbold and other itinerants, ignoring the political events fomenting around them. On one occasion a very tall figure, otherwise unknown, had been standing over the group talking to Hugo Rumbold. As he sauntered off, Lewis asked who he was. He had remarked on his dimpled chin and fine blue eyes like 'those of a big child who looked out upon a nice but annoying world'. 'Oh, he's the boy who's got Clouds', explained Rumbold. 'What I liked about Dick Wyndham', Lewis wrote some years later, 'was the attractive candour and absence of vulgarity which made him seem almost like a nice workman among all those "clever" people.' Dick, the outwardly simple soldier, and the truculent Lewis made friends, the latter teaching him the art of sketching Venetian palaces set on their malodorous lagoons – 'the fingers of one hand grasping the pencil, the fingers of the other grasping the nose' – and thereby, he claimed, sowing the seeds of the artist who would later emerge.

The friendship was resumed when Dick metamorphosed from gentleman-soldier into bohemian artist. Lewis assumed the mantle of mentor and drawing-master with lively expectancy. But the roles of master and pupil failed to chime. The root cause was money, of which Dick, on account of Clouds, was thought to have bags, and of which Lewis was acutely and perennially short. Lewis saw in his well-heeled disciple a potential patron, a function Dick, then seeking only honest artistic recognition for himself, was most reluctant to fulfil. Lewis's constant demands to be subsidized with Dick's gold were excessive and far outpaced the frequent evenings at the Gargoyle for which Dick was happy to pick up the bill. When Dick jibbed, Lewis turned nasty. He emptied his poison-sacs into *The Apes of God*, a satirical work which lampooned not only Dick but also the Sitwells and others. Two chapters were devoted to the ridiculing of a pernicious dilettante known as Richard Whiddingdon, or just 'Dick', with what Peter Quennell described as a display of 'Hogarthian comic verve'. The second chapter Lewis subtitled 'Ape Flagellant'. This was far too near the knuckle for comfort. Among the cognoscenti Dick was often, and quite without malice, referred to as 'Dick Whippington'. This on account of certain 'leanings' he had toward the infliction of corporal punishment on acquiescent girls in his search for sexual solace. When *Apes* appeared in 1930, a reviewer declared that the key to the identity of the *dramatis personae* was easily turned. Dick was enraged and, normally unvindictive, he threatened to bring legal action against critic and paper. This brought forth an apology, but there ended the friendship.

*

Since the moment of her arrival, Hermione decided that Canada pleased her very well. There was no threat of being upstaged here. On the contrary, she was centre-stage as the Honourable Mrs David Tennant playing hostess to the local swells, and on one occasion entertaining the prime minister, Mackenzie King, in their rented house. The Tennants went yachting and deep-sea fishing, motoring, climbing, socialized and drank, and generally led the life of graceful careless ease so matchlessly drawn by Scott Fitzgerald, different only in so far as Hermione here being determined to recapture innocence lost.

Loss of innocence – of a sort – was just on the point of becoming a widespread condition. In the spring of 1929 a second British Labour Government under Ramsay MacDonald had taken office with the Liberals holding the balance of power. The trade union leader J. H. Thomas had been sent to Canada to promote Labour's concern for the Empire. The last British troops were withdrawn from the Rhine, a popular move, and Aristide Briand, the French premier, was proposing a plan for the United States of Europe, an unpopular move with the many isolationists in Britain. Ramsay MacDonald arrived in New York to siren salutes and showers of ticker-tape on a visit to President Hoover. All seemed well with the world and the prospect of a lasting peace appeared hopeful. But by October's end the prosperity boom in North America also came to a sudden end when the Wall Street stock-market collapsed, as it were, overnight. Banks closed and millions found themselves redundant, unemployed or ruined. A rash of suicides spread over the continent.

Kit Glenconner was staying with his brother in Canada when the crash happened. He had come out to check on how the steel container factory was going (at the time far from well). He may have been privy to rumours of an impending world depression, for when the signal appeared on Wall Street he remained calm. Hermione seems to remember that he had to cancel a new aeroplane, otherwise the Tennant empire remained cradled and unrocked in his hands. Great Britain itself was not immediately much affected by the crash. As was noted in London, repercussions from Wall Street 'broke few windows in the City'.

But more than windows were broken in David's Canadian enterprise. He and Kit decided there was nothing for it but to close the factory down. David took it badly, feeling, illogically on the face of things, that he was in some broad way responsible. However, the collapse of Wall Street coincided with confirmation of Hermione's second pregnancy. All the more reason for their return.

9

The practical consideration of new quarters arose for David and small family on their return – a temporary soft landing had been made at the Savoy with the acquisition of a relatively modest (Canadian losses having to be taken into consideration) house in Canning Place, off Palace Gate, handy for Nanny and Pauline with Kensington Gardens and the Round Pond nearby. And since the Gargoyle Club posed no problem at the moment, David felt free to set about planning his social rehabilitation which pride demanded. Lothario's box had been opened; then let Lothario himself appear. And how better than in the form of Don Giovanni.

The post-war passion among the *jeunesse dorée* for dressing-up had in no way diminished. This particular bug had caught Stephen when he was very young and, Siegfried Sassoon notwithstanding, never left him. 'How do bad people look like good people?' he once innocently asked Pamela as they left the congregation hand in hand after church. 'Do they dress up?' Fancy-dress provided almost unlimited opportunity for effecting instant change, for alter-egos to inflate, for the escapist's balloon to take the air and go with the winds of fantasy. For David, launching a Mozart extravaganza would satisfy all the dandy's delight in dressing-up coupled with the need for style and perfection in so doing; and allow him also to strike a significant aesthetic pose. Ravishment to the eye, then, would be provided by evoking the high style of the eighteenth century, but the eye must be subordinate to the ear. Mozart's 'divine' music would have to be 'divinely' played. David enthusiastically began to weave this golden concept into shape.

29 April was the auspicious day – chosen to honour the occasion of a visit by Mozart to London in 1764. Hermione by then would be in her ninth month of pregnancy. It now became a question as to whose creature would be born first. But whereas Hermione was content to let nature dictate its course even if this meant delivery on the concert platform, C. B. Cochran himself could not have been more painstaking than David in the supervision of every small detail of his production. Not only the orchestra but all visible and attendant staff were to be dressed in full eighteenth-century rig. Guests were to be met in the New Burlington

Street Galleries in the West End by eighteenth-century runners and shown into lifts with operators likewise clad.

Pageboys in brilliant red and white would pepper the reception rooms and dining hall, and squat on cushions in front of the audience in the concert room. The silver, china and crystal would conform to period. The guests, seated round the horse-shoe dining-table, would be suffused in the warm glow of candlelight. For his own turn-out as Don Giovanni David had a theatrical costumier create something 'too beautiful' in velvet frothing with lace; while Hermione, on account of her pronounced bulge, was allowed a little period licence as a crinolined Donna Elvira.

To take five or six hundred diverse people, to persuade them to put on costumes which are decorative rather than comfortable (and unlikely to be found in their bottom drawer), to provide them with a full-length concert of classical music and then – and this was David's daring move – to then transform all that as if by magic, but with the help of a lively jazz band, into a gay informal frolic is something of an achievement.

Only a few shirked the effort of dressing-up. As Tom Driberg, anonymous under his cloak as 'The Dragoman' of the *Daily Express*, wrote: 'Never in recent years can there have been such efflorescence of cotton-wool wigs in a London ballroom.' Among the shirkers were Madeleine Carroll and the silent film star Lya da Putti. They may have felt that for them to don costume was the taking of coals to Newcastle. Another shirker was Dick's sister Olivia. Dick, like Stephen an incorrigible dresser-up, made a striking impression as the Pasha Selim from *Il Seraglio*. Olivia had the excuse of only arriving from America on the morning of the fête, having been married to a young American on the day she sailed. He, Howland Spencer, failed to make the voyage; but Dick made the gallant gesture of flying his aeroplane from Paris to Southampton in order to sprinkle rice on his sister from the air as she stepped down the gangway.

The evening was a notable success. For everyone, that is, except for the particular Don Giovanni responsible. In Hermione's version the host's collapse was as the opening bars of the concert proper sounded under Barbirolli's baton. The Don himself flown with exaltation and wine had to be carried out through the party – on a bier.

'Nobody seemed to mind', said Hermione. 'The party went very well.' Even allowing for theatrical hyperbole in Hermione's description it now strikes their daughter Pauline as consistent with the father she loved: 'The opening bars – tragical. The story of his life. Dream life – the whole concept was there. But the nerves proved too terrible. He could put his secret dreams into action and then couldn't bear to be there to witness them. The field of the cloth of gold. "I've put it out for you, now you can cavort."' Meanwhile he had other dreams to dream. Which is one way, perhaps, of describing passing out in full fancy dress – on cue to the opening bars of music.

If indeed he had surrendered so soon to a surfeit of nectar and ambrosia his seconds must have got to work on him in the dressing room because, by the time the jazz band had picked up the beat, David was back in the social ring dancing the night away. 'I slipped away very late last night without saying good-bye', wrote Clive Bell the next day from Gordon Square in the heart of Bloomsbury. 'You were dancing and I couldn't see Hermione.'

Of the many letters of thanks and congratulations David received, his was the most fulsome:

> Even without Mozart, your dinner and dance would have been a delightful evening. Mozart made it one of the most delightful of my life. I don't think I have ever heard a more delicious concert of music. If dog-like devotion entitles one to the honourable style of 'Mozartian', a Mozartian I am. And when a Mozartian says that he never heard the master to greater advantage it should mean something – and perhaps it does.

And so on. Very gratifying. The shortest and most formally, even curtly, signed came from Aunt Margot of Berkeley Square, 'Wonderful, wonderful, wonderful. I can't tell you how much I enjoyed myself. Yours, Margot.'

The most down to earth, if somewhat time-warped, came from Rosa Lewis on a post-card but in telegraphese: 'Dearest David. A billion thanks. The old times renewed. Greatest pleasure to all kinds and all sorts. Rosa Lewis.'

Then, an afterthought on a second post-card firmly marked 'Private':

> My dear David
> If it comes to more than you can afford let me know as it is the best and nicest pleasure I have had for years and I know how costly this (may) have been. Private.
> Old Rosa.

And from an appreciative John Barbirolli:

> It was a delightful experience. Can we meet sometime and discuss a project for some concerts. I would be willing to give my services for a start to see how things went. In fact as far as possible make it a collaboration of effort.

Nothing came of this. David was already into his next secret dream.

The social columns of the press went to town and made a meal of it there. 'As Mozart's transcends other music, so did the provision of Mr. Tennant's munificence surpass that of other men.' 'Such a brilliant party has surely never been given in London before....' 'For loveliness of costume and imagination in the details there has surely been no more remarkable party for years.' 'Altogether', reported *Echoes of the Town*, 'it was a wonderful spectacle, and the supper, with quail and strawberries and cream in profusion (the latter had been sent from Clouds), was one of the best I have ever eaten.' *Echoes of the Town* had not been invited to the dinner, at which peacock, more often seen gracing the English lawn than the table, was the element of surprise provided by Monsieur Boulestin.

By a consensus of opinion the belle of this night's ball was Barbara, the daughter of Rosa's old flame, Ribblesdale, the wife of Sir 'Scatters' Wilson and thereby the mother of 'Mother' or Martin. In spite of her second son, Anthony, competing with painted naked torso and silvered hair as Mithras, Persian god of light, Barbara's '*grande dame* profile, her exquisite features and her proud Edwardian bearing' took the night. Euphoria from the night spilled over into the day with a number of wags from the party larking about among early-morning road menders in Piccadilly. They stand looking on with bemused tolerance as John Sutro, quizzing glass held to eye, studies the efforts of a fellow reveller to operate a pneumatic drill while Patrick Balfour exhorts from the barricades for the benefit of a press photographer.

Hermione wisely left the party before the night grew too old. She was driven back to Canning Place where Welsh Gwen, whom she had retrieved on her return from Canada, anxiously awaited her. Ten days later, Little David, as he was to be known, was born in a London nursing home.

*

The next three years were a time of relative happiness for David and Hermione – indeed, Hermione remembered this as the best season of their marriage. The strains and satisfactions of their life were composed in the domestic key and measured by comfort and mobility – the cars were back in play and so was the Gypsy Moth. There were lengthy stays up at

Glen with Kit, now married some five years, and his family; there were visits to friends in Wiltshire like the sportive Robin Mount, who was married to Frank Pakenham's sister Julia. Best of all were the times when they rented (*prix de famille*) Dick Wyndham's magical retreat near Blackboys in Sussex, Tickeridge Mill. Dick had bought Tickeridge in 1926, encouraged to do so by the painter Edward Wadsworth, onetime Vorticist whom he had met through Lewis and who had just moved nearby. Tickeridge was to play a part in the lives of many a Gargoyle member, to the extent that it became not only a refuge from mundane reality but almost an extension of the Club itself.

Cyril Connolly, an eager if somewhat later recruit to this group of friends, described Dick's idyll in *The Unquiet Grave*:

> The Mill where I sometimes stay is another perfect cure for Angst; the red lane down through the Spanish chestnut wood, the apple trees on the lawn, bees in the roof, geese on the pond, the black sun-lit marsh marigolds, the crackling wood fires, low bedrooms, creak of the cellar door, and the monotonies of the silver-whispering weir – what could be more womb-like or reassuring? Yet always the anxious owner is flying from it as if from the scene of a crime.

Hermione liked nothing better than 'playing house' at Tickeridge. The gardener and other retainers always referred to Dick as 'The Captain' she noted approvingly.

But the Captain, though admired and widely liked, was extravagant and feckless with money and frequently short of it. In 1932 he put Clouds House and the estate up for sale. The original estate, bought by Percy Wyndham in 1876, was well over four thousand acres. Some outlying farms with attendant acres had since been sold but there still remained, with the 'dignified stone-built mansion and beautifully placed residential property', over three thousand acres. But Dick only managed to sell fifty-eight of them, mostly attached to cottages. Poor Dick. Unlike Madame Ranevsky, he was only too willing to see his Cherry Orchard dismembered and the land turned over to building development. But there was no Lopakhin to interfere in his sad comedy.

David and Hermione went to Switzerland to get their first experience of skiing that winter of their return. St Moritz was the chosen place but unfortunately they had arrived during the preparations for the European Winter Sports Championship. So no Palace Hotel. Instead they were obliged to 'slum it' in a place where many of the competitors were lodged. This was to have a happy outcome. As a consequence of Hermione's gregarious nature they made friends with the English bobsleigh team, whose leader asked David if he would like a trial run with them. He proved a success and took to the sport with enthusiasm. David was physically very strong and fit, with a dancer's instinctive sense of timing and balance. As Ivan Moffat, son of Curtis and Iris Tree, noted: 'His close friend Robin Mount, in a somewhat curious phrase, said, "David's just about the strongest member of the upper classes."' But the balance and the fitness – he had chopped a lot of trees in Canada – were the vital elements in St Moritz. These were unexpectedly called upon when, on their big day, one of the English bobsleigh team fell sick and David was asked to sit in for him. The team won and David picked up a gold medal. Then the Belgian team had similar trouble in a different event. David was called upon again – the rules of national representation must have been elastic – and again he was in the winning team. More gold. David came to be regarded as a bringer of fortune with teams competing to get him on their sleigh. Twice more he raced, winning a third gold and then a bronze.

They returned to London bronzed but without having put foot to ski. Nevertheless there were the medals of triumph which Hermione then had made into a bracelet. She sported them for the first time when they both went to the Savoy for supper. Noël Coward came over to greet them. Hermione flashed her wrist. 'Medals I see, my dear', said Coward. 'Did you win them, might one ask?' 'Not win exactly. David just decided to give me a medal for each lover I had on holiday.' Noël fingered the bronze medal. 'Congratulations, darling. I see you've had Paul Robeson.'

*

The early thirties were marked by two deaths among Gargoyle members which particularly affected many of those who remained. The first was the suicide, in December 1930, of Nina Hamnett's young drinking companion, the composer Peter Warlock. The second was the death of David's step-father, Lord Grey, at seventy-one. Whether or not he was David's real father was never resolved, although there were times when David chose to believe it was so. Initially bullied into it by Pamela, Grey had given unswerving support to the Club in his late years and by so doing had bestowed upon it a distinction that was none the less welcome for being slightly out of the Club's character.

In lighter vein, a much welcomed event was the early release from Holloway prison in 1930, on good behaviour, of Mrs Kate Meyrick. This was her second stretch for which she had been awarded fifteen months hard labour (prison laundry) for involvement in a police bribery scandal. She was befriended by the remarkable 'Colonel Barker' – one of the earliest British Fascists – who was inside with her and who, on inspection, had turned out to be a woman. Her loyal clients – to whom were now to be added the Boxing Champion of the World, Primo Carnera, and the flying hero Jim Mollison – waited up all night in evening dress in the '43' to help her break her fast with champagne. The popular Sunday newspaper *The People*, of all papers, took great exception to this demonstration of solidarity for what it called 'one of the most dangerous women in London . . . .' David and Hermione were happy to show their own solidarity by going there again on Kate's return. They liked the '43' because it was something the Gargoyle never tried to be – a 'proper' night-club.

In the following year (1931) Oswald Mosley formed his New Party with John Strachey as his principal lieutenant. In the previous nine years Mosley had encompassed a broad spectrum of political life by successively having been a Conservative, an Independent, a Liberal, a Socialist, and now a New Party Man, which was assumed to be loosely Left-wing. With his personal bravura, owing something to Nietzsche, he dominated such intellectuals as Harold Nicolson, Strachey and Osbert Sitwell. They were attracted by the Party's manifesto pledging itself to dynamic 'Action'. A publication of that name, edited by Harold Nicolson, with Peter Quennell, Alan Pryce-Jones and Raymond Mortimer among the contributors, was launched and a rally for the party, given by the Sitwells, was held at Renishaw.

When, in October 1931, a National Coalition Government, involving representatives from all major parties with Ramsay MacDonald at its head, was elected with a massive majority, Mosley temporarily, the New Party permanently, were run out of business and *Action* discontinued publication. A fresh wind of national dedication and rebirth came to blow away the mood of anxiety and depression consequent upon, in the view of Evelyn's brother Alec Waugh, Great Britain having gone off the gold standard (September 1931). That was for the middle classes; for the majority the cause lay in the shackles of poverty and unemployment from which there was no apparent release.

All this did not engage David too deeply. His inclinations were to the Left, but at this time they were still in the closet and he had remained untouched by the political passions that affected the young men who were up at Cambridge not long after he had gone down.

What did concern him now was that Hermione felt the need once again to answer the call of the footlights. There, in front of them and her audience, she was at least a star. The star at Canning Place was unquestionably Pauline.

10

Hermione's return to the boards took a predictable, and at least to Angela, a disappointing form. The dramatic talent which had once emerged so strikingly was once again passed over in favour of something she could do on her head, and occasionally did: revue, light comedy and musicals. From January 1932 there were four shows in a row, none lasting more than three months (as was normal at that time for the genre), and ending with the musical *Ballyhoo* for which Frederick Ashton did the choreography. In the cast with Hermione were Walter Crisham and George Sanders. Young Sanders was yet to go to Hollywood and make his name as a major movie star. He had been engaged for *Ballyhoo* on the strength of height, looks and an excellent singing voice. But his stage presence proved so agonizingly awkward that the stage itself was pronounced forbidden territory to him and he was required to sing his role unseen from the wings. On arrival in Hollywood, George stepped boldly out of the wings by marrying Zsa Zsa Gabor.

There seemed no reason why demand for Hermione and the run of shows should ever dry up. This caused David to reach down deep for another secret dream. He found one. China. That was where he really needed to go. Why? Well, China was far distant, mandarin, mysterious. It was an unknown continent. No one of David's age and background had 'done' China. Nobody, that is, except the one-time Gargoyler, the dandy-aesthete, Harold Acton. And he was doing it as it had seldom, if ever, been done by an Englishman before. There were, of course, Guinnesses – even in China. But these were a crop of evangelical preachers and missionaries descended from and inspired by the Bible prophet Henry Gratton Guinness, and their time was wholly taken up in providing Christian service for the heathen – wherever to be found. No danger of distraction from that quarter.

Matt, to whom David still deferred in matters of the psyche, was not insensible to the arrival of Chinese philosophical influence in the West. Confucius, his opponent Lao-tze, and Taoism, the system of understanding inspired by his teaching, these were now words to be conjured with. Sensibilities in Britain had been stirred by the unencumbered beauty of the translations of Chinese poetry by Arthur Waley. The lofty detachment of these classics from contemporary events, their endorsement of the green bamboo virtue of bending before the storm, held an immediate appeal (in translation) to Westerners conditioned to the ethos of competition and confrontation – not that David had been much exposed to either. But it was Waley who unlocked for the Western world the mystique of this most ancient and alien civilization. He was that rare combination of scholar and poet, with, in addition, a quality of genius which reawakened in people an interest in China that had lain dormant since the eighteenth century.

When David's dream of China became apparent to Hermione, she was far from pleased. She had always accepted, she claimed, that if David wanted to do something, he did it no matter what chaos he left behind. The rich were like that and he, with too much money and no settled job, was no different. She recognized, also, that David, as well as being rich, was many things that she liked: he was young, energetic, charming, beautiful, bright, but – and this went to the heart of the matter – David could become all too easily bored. Furthermore, he was without ambition, of which the boredom was a consequence.

So if David wanted to go to China, then to China he had better go, and he embarked at Tilbury on the P&O Line bound for the Far East. Before leaving, he had the grace to say to Hermione that he wished she was coming too. For a moment she felt tempted to abandon theatre, children and all responsibilities just to pack a bag and join him. That, for David, might have been quite in order. But the invitation did not sound as if it came from the heart. And, in any case, it had come a little late. She shook her head. 'If you change your mind, come out and join me', was his vale. At least, this time, he was not travelling with any excess baggage.

With David gone, and for how long neither of them had any clear idea – it would take six weeks at least to get there – Hermione's thoughts, as with many a young colonial wife abandoned in the name of far flung Imperial duty, turned to the consolations of hedonism. David, true to form, had imposed no verbal restraint on her. She had the removable bonnet and there were windmills a-plenty. Freddy Childs was a champagne salesman, a ladies man and a dab hand on a piano. Hermione had met him staying with her new young friend, Nina Seafield, on her vast estates in Scotland. Nina had inherited the title of Countess and with it great wealth when she was only nine. She had recently married and was now persuading her husband that he enjoyed providing lavish entertainment for her friends as much as she did. Freddy eyed Hermione appreciatively. He caressed a chord with one dab hand, twitched his little moustache with the other. 'I'm after you, Hermione', he said. So were many others. When, in 1986, Hermione's obituary appeared in *The Times* it claimed that so socially fashionable did she become in her heyday that someone adapted to her Kipling's line, 'I am Town; I am all that ever went with evening dress.' This, then, was the beginning of her social heyday.

Freddy, who, as Hermione said, 'had such a way with him', did not find the seduction of this self-assured but sexually relatively inexperienced young woman a difficult task. And Hermione, for her part, was pleased to find in Freddy the champagne salesman a skilful and attentive lover: attentive, that was his great point. She did not love him but he became a most acceptable *cavaliere servente*, courtly in manner and handy about the house. Down at Tickeridge Mill, he would carve the Sunday joint and walk the dogs and amuse the children, and, in London, he would mix the cocktails for Hermione's friends and escort her to parties in his Bentley.

Word came from David in China to the effect that he had arrived and settled in Peking where he had been made welcome by Harold Acton. Since they had come down from Oxford the ways of Harold and Brian Howard, the one-time inseparable duo, had tended to drift ever further apart. 'Harold no longer understands us', Brian wrote to a friend. 'I foresee him passing out of our lives.' Harold was, in any case, far less part of the London scene than Brian and spent much of his time – before leaving for China – between Florence, Venice and Paris. His novels *Cornelian* and *Humdrum*, both published in 1928, were not well received (except, in the case of the former, by Gertrude Stein). Neither was his next book *The Last Medici*. Most readers, he reported on the re-issue of this book in 1958, had been shocked by the 'moral detachment' they read into his historical account of the scandalous Florentine prince, Gian Castone. *Humdrum* had appeared simultaneously with Waugh's *Decline and Fall*, dedicated in homage and affection to the very Acton, who, overall, had had a benign influence on the young Waugh. Except for the one unfortunate occasion when a criticism he had passed on a novel, in the throes of being written, had driven Waugh to attempt suicide. Cyril Connolly, a friend of both authors, reviewed the two novels together in *The New Statesman*. He chose to demolish *Humdrum* quite savagely, the better to eulogize the merits of *Decline*. Acton, it appeared, knew as much about English people as a Chinese might who had picked up his information from the back numbers of *Punch*.

David was not a man at peace. Intuition may have led David to seek from China the spiritual peace, the essential oneness and harmony of man with the universe (something of which a side of David's nature was at least conscious), that the culture of the country appeared to offer. But it is doubtful if he ever managed to get far outside that expatriate society in Peking which Acton found to be very similar to the one that he had known in Florence. Acton himself certainly did not think so: 'I suppose David Tennant came to Peking as a tourist. Though I doubt if it influenced him in any way. He seemed a fish out of water there. A polite and elegant fish.' To bring the fish a drop of comfort, Acton's welcome to David in Peking included the customary provision, for the 'Travelling Man,' of a Chinese concubine – 'on the house', as it were. This accommodating creature would, when not in use, repose on a mat outside the door of David's hotel bedroom. Otherwise, nothing more is known of David's sojourn in China.

*

The vivacious mouse left behind in Canning Place grew ever more playful during the long absence of the cat. Apart from Champagne Freddy, there were two other men in Hermione's life. First was an old friend, the actor Robert Newton. Bobby was the son of the Cornish landscape painter, Algernon Newton. But Bobby's passion was for the theatre and for that he was happy to sacrifice anything or anybody. Early in 1933 he acquired a lease on the old Fulham Grand, once the home of musical comedy where Gertie Miller had made her debut. He renamed it the Shilling Theatre (the better to serve the low rent neighbourhood) and intended that it should now be consecrated to straight drama, presenting plays tried and untried. Both his sisters Joy and Pauline willingly lent their energies as scene painters and shifters to help support it. They were even resourceful enough to set up as pavement artists to help raise initial funds to get the theatre going and chose the broad flagstones outside the Ritz Hotel as their pitch. It was a shrewdly selected site since they, or their husbands, respectively Igor Vinogradoff and Basil Murray, were well known to many of those who used the Ritz bars as their regular watering holes.

The play that Bobby now offered Hermione was something Hermione had denied herself ever since her early success – straight drama. Or rather, in this case, straight comedy. There were two splendid parts in it which were made for her and Angela. The play was called *The Greeks Had A Word For It* by Zoë Atkins and it was going to have its première in his Shilling Theatre. Hermione was somewhat wary on account of Bobby now, as quite often, being drunk. But his drinking was not then so bad that managements thought twice before employing him. Bobby had a beautiful, persuasive voice, striking looks with dark hair tumbling into large expressive eyes, and he was highly regarded in the profession for his talent and theatrical flair. So Hermione promised to read the play, little thinking that embedded in its wine-stained pages was the part which, in her words, was going to put her right back at the top of her profession.

The second man of the hour was altogether different, but no less exceptional. Hermione had first met him casually sometime before at the Gargoyle. He had gone there because of his identical and virtually inseparable twin brother, and *he* was there because of Poppet John who had been a frequenter of the club since the time Augustus used her, at quite a young age, as a prop to get him round the Gargoyle dance floor. These were the Jackson twins, Derek, and Hermione's new admirer, Vivian. They were young, extremely rich and extremely clever. Derek, somewhat to the disgust of Augustus – he referred to him as 'that repulsive little swine' – had married Poppet when she was nineteen. The Jackson twins were born in 1906. Their parents both died when they were still at school at Rugby, whereupon Lord Riddell, a newspaper magnate, became their guardian. They then went separately to Oxford and Cambridge where each achieved the expected First. Derek, who had been at Cambridge, was swiftly recruited by 'The Prof.', Professor Lindemann (later Lord Cherwell) for the Clarendon Laboratory at Oxford. There, at the age of twenty-two, he pioneered a brilliantly original break-through in the field of spectroscopy which earned him a lasting place in the world of science. Vivian, less celebrated than his twin, nevertheless, on coming down from Oxford, held an important place at London University, working as an astrophysicist. Alike in so many ways, they shared the same passion for science and horses. They were smallish, neat, finely proportioned and fearless; assets which stood them well when hunting, racing and steeplechasing. Derek was particularly successful at the latter and twice rode in the Grand National. They were also both impulsive, impetuous and impatient. Qualities which were to make Derek, in particular, extremely unpopular with persons in authority as, for instance, race-course stewards and senior Air Force officers during the war; and, in Vivian's case, these qualities were to be directly responsible for his accidental death at the early age of thirty.

But that would not be for three years. Now, in 1933, Vivian was ardently pursuing Hermione. The twins shared one other determining characteristic, a sexual one. As Derek said of himself, in racecourse terminology, 'I ride under both rules.' But this was not something that was ever to cause Hermione any loss of sleep. She was flattered and intrigued by the attentions of this most original and attractive-looking man. She liked his boldness, his iconoclastic disdain for convention and his furious energy. He used this to pursue Hermione up until the very moment of David's return. By now David had had enough of China. He had spent about four months out there before deciding to return, again by boat. But his patience ran out during the long sea voyage, and by the time the liner reached Malta, he jumped ship. He crossed to Italy and took a train to Rome. From there he telephoned Hermione to say he would be flying back via Paris.

This intelligence was communicated to Freddy, the *cavaliere servente*, and also to the ardent wooer to whose riding tactics she was far more drawn. Hermione later gave the author her version of how the events developed: 'You see, darling, when I was left behind there I was with all these chaps around me and Vivian Jackson thought he had fallen *violently* in love with me, tried to persuade me to leave David and run away with *him*. Even when I was getting ready to meet David at the airport he was ringing me up from the Savoy. "Listen to that aeroplane", he said. "Can't you hear the propeller going round?" – they were mad of course, he and Derek – "Run away with me before your husband lands. Do it. Do it!" All this went on. The only way to shut him up was to say: "Have dinner with David and myself this evening because I know he'll like you and be amused by you." So David got back and I told him I had a new friend and I'd like us all to have dinner together. So Vivian joined us at the Savoy and in the middle of dinner I *suddenly* saw Vivian Jackson's hand on David's knee.' Hermione enjoyed the memory of this. 'He found David *very* attractive, was enchanted by him. And David liked him *tremendously*. We became very good friends of both of them. Though Vivian was much the nicer of the twins. He was sweet. Derek was *quite* unkind to Poppet John.'

David's return made a dramatic impact on his daughter Pauline. 'He looked like Sinbad,' she remembered delightedly. 'He was very brown and had this great black beard. Piratical – too marvellous.' There was also great excitment when the many cabin trunks were finally delivered to Canning Place, unlocked and allowed to explode their contents all over the house: Chinese scrolls, porcelain, earthenware horses and military men, wooden toys, bamboo toys, little gowns, embroidered silks, precious stones, jade and jewellery – plunder from the Orient. But before this exploration of exotic gifts could be enjoyed, there was also the problem posed by Champagne Freddy to be aired. Freddy had carelessly or deliberately left his spoor, in the form of bottles of the 'Boy', all over the house. David, smooth chinned again now the pleasing effect of Sinbad's beard had worn off, correctly and dismissively diagnosed the source of the many bottles by the brand (a rather inferior one), but he quickly became irritated by the constant telephone calls.

'What's the matter with the man?' David wanted to know. 'He thinks he's in love with me', replied Hermione with a casual delivery that Noël Coward would have appreciated. 'Oh, everybody's in love with you. Has he been a bore?' No worse social sin in David's book. There was a silence, a long and uncomfortable one. David looked at Hermione keenly.

'You're not in love with him are you?' This was asked in such a manner as to expect the answer No. He was perfectly right, of course. Hermione was not. But she had no intention of letting David off too lightly. At the same time she was going to have to come clean about something – before anyone else did. So she avoided answering David's question but admitted that she had been seeing a lot of Freddy and that, yes, as it so happened he was in fact her lover. There. How was he going to take that? After all, David had been unfaithful to her and more than once, she suspected. And they had known each other as lovers for nearly ten years now. So it was not *so* bad. David took it on his newly shaved chin. 'It must stop', he said quietly and firmly. 'I'll get over it', Hermione said, allowing the implication to register of an entanglement rather more serious than that which she actually felt. 'Just give me a little time and I know I'll get over it', she went on, careless of the risks involved in playing games with the heart. 'Find some way to tell him that it must stop', David insisted. Hermione gave way – just enough. 'I promise. Just give me a little time.' 'Very well.' David seemed quite calm. 'If that's what you want.' Then he added the familiar refrain: 'Don't let's be dreary about it.' And there was nothing more 'dreary' than jealousy, as everyone knew.

Hermione's confession of infidelity had bitten deeper and harder into David's *amour propre* than she had anticipated. The shameful jealousy, forbidden to show itself outright, festered within. And this was exacerbated by having to behave normally when encountering the ubiquitous Freddy's hovering presence on their frequent social sorties. In public he was discreet enough to remain in the background and as a reward was allowed, on the brief occasion, back into Hermione's personal foreground. But Hermione kept her promise by making it clear that the affair would inevitably have to end. David was far more possessive than she had supposed. In time Hermione came to have painful regrets over dissembling the truth to David about her feelings for Freddy. But by then, of course, it was too late.

The initial expansive mood of David's return was to receive another disagreeable rebuff. This was when he opened his wardrobe only to find some of his best suits missing. Champagne Freddy? No, he was the wrong shape. In any case, he wouldn't dare. Hermione needed to come up with an answer rather quickly. She did and it had the advantage of being truthful. 'Bobby must have borrowed them', she said. She elucidated this by explaining that during the rehearsal period of *The Greeks Had A Word For It* Bobby needed somewhere to live as he was going through one of his frequent periods of domestic upheaval. Since they were working together it made sense for her to put him up in the house. He probably helped himself then as he was banned from his marital dwelling and therefore could not get at his own. David decided to let this drift for the time being.

The Greeks Had A Word For It had opened at the Shilling Theatre in November 1933. Though only booked for a short run, it was an immediate hit. A transfer to the Duke of York's in the West End was arranged for the following year with the same excellent cast. Apart from Bobby and the two Baddeley sisters this included Margaret Rawlings and Clive Morton. But the most gratifying thing for Hermione was the delight she and Angela experienced in working together for the first time since they were children. Although the play had to be taken out of the Shilling Theatre and the cast laid off, when it did re-open in the West End, it was to run without a break for over two years. But in the circumstances it turned out to be a good thing, in the short run, from David's point of view that Hermione was not working at the time of his return. The marriage was threatened and he had a clear idea of how it could be saved.

11

David's romantic nature, which when harnessed to his tellurian skills had such an irresistible appeal for Hermione, now reasserted itself. And the proof of it lay quietly down at Wilsford. This was a horse-drawn wooden caravan which David had built himself, aided only by the anvil of the Wilsford smithy. It was friendly, functional and unadorned. The pervasive spirit of Pamela impregnated it with memories of childhood spent in her own gypsy caravans – the smells of grilling bacon on the primus stove, of the oil lamps and the sound of her guitar to which she sang softly and whimsically. The time was now ripe to get his masterpiece out of mothballs. The best chance, David felt, of reviving his marriage lay in settling himself and family in a home in the country. He was drawn to the West Country where he had spent such an idyllic youth. So he cast about, asking agents and friends in the area – the Johns, the Mounts and many others – for guidance in what he was looking for. In the end he found it himself. Unsurprisingly, it was a manor house not unlike Wilsford, built of the same grey stone with a stream running through it down to a lake. It sat well back from the road in the tiny village of Teffont-Evias and had a little church in its grounds. But the foundations of this house were laid in the fifteenth century and modernization took place in the eighteenth. The embarrassment to David's planned occupation lay in the fact that it was already inhabited and that its owners had no intention of selling. David put in an agent to undermine this resolve. The man succeeded in so far as an invitation to tea, and therefore a view of the interior, was extended by the owners, a retired tea-planter and his wife.

David planned his approach with care. It was to be made by caravan, preliminary reconnaissance having already been made by motor car. They would harness-up and set off from Wilsford with Robin Mount on horseback as their outrider, make camp for the night on Salisbury Plain, rise with the dawn as the first rays of the sun struck the altar stone at Stonehenge, break their fast on grilled bacon then proceed at a leisurely pace to Teffont Manor. David would bring his guitar. There would be none of Pamela's lullabies but raucous, ribald stuff such as he liked to play and sing with Nina Hamnett in the Gargoyle – her salty version of

'Nautical William' being a particular favourite. All this interspersed, perhaps, with the haunting refrain of Scottish ballads. And a sacrificial salute might even be improvised for the great Henge at dawn.

They arrived in orderly fashion for tea at the Manor. They were all somewhat dismayed by the interior of the house, as faded as its owners. There would be no possibility of them selling the Manor, they said. It had to remain in the family. But David refused to be dismayed or put off by their intractability. He was under the spell of the house and continued to press his suit for its possession. In the end a compromise was reached. The owners would be prepared to lease them the house subject to certain improvements being carried out. David was triumphant, but Hermione had misgivings. She felt, and continued to feel, that it was not a lucky house, however much David might try to enthuse her with all the things she would be able to do with the interior to dispel the gloom. On their return to Canning Place, news reached them that Louise, who had been living quietly in the country, might be seriously ill. Certainly she could not be left by herself in her cottage. So David and Hermione moved her first into the London house and then, when matters did not improve, they found a nursing home in Sloane Square where she could be visited by at least one member of her family every day. That was the theory. Not so easy in practice. Ciggie and Muriel were married with growing families. Bill, the younger half-brother, had taken his cloth to Australia where he was soon to be made a Dean. So the undertaking largely rested on Angela and Hermione – David not counting himself as one of Louise's family.

Meanwhile the enlarging of the rooms in Teffont Manor, the revitalisation of their decoration and the installation of plumbing proceeded. David and Hermione felt safe in taking a holiday in the South of France. While they were there, Louise discreetly passed away in the nursing home. Hermione was to derive comfort from the belief that 'the evening of her life was filled with happiness'.

*

David was now unexpectedly presented with a distinctly ticklish situation in the Gargoyle. He was advised by the loyal secretary, Miss 'Mossy' O'Neil, that Harry Walker planned treachery. Using David's frequent and prolonged absentee stewardship of the Club as the excuse, Harry planned to table a motion at the next committee meeting which would effectively lose him control. Forewarned, David turned up at a meeting he might otherwise have skipped and forestalled the Machiavellian plot. He was then prompted to take an uncharacteristically close look at how Harry exercised his own managerial responsibilities. He came back one evening to Canning Place and said to Hermione: 'I've had a tremendous shock today. I've discovered that Harry has been augmenting his salary (David's gentlemanly way of describing 'fingers in the till') for a long, long time ... and also he recently tried to ...' He then described the attempted skullduggery. 'I think it was such a *strange* thing for Harry to do', Hermione later commented, 'because he was doing rather well out of David being silly.' Harry would have to go, of course. Hermione could have told David that a long time ago. But this came at a rather inconvenient time since Harry's responsibilities now devolved upon David, until a suitable replacement could be found. And just when he was hoping to make the move down to Wiltshire.

Teffont Manor was a manageable house to run. Manageable, that is, if you had a cook, butler, kitchen maid, parlour maid, two house maids, ladies maid (Welsh Gwen) and boots to help you run it – as David and Hermione had. There was also a governess, a nanny and a chauffeur. David only had four cars at the beginning although there was, invitingly, garage space for six. And two gardeners, of course, one doubling as a groom for the horses stabled there from time to time. For Dick Wyndham, David's manor became a place of sanctuary at a time when he was still smarting from the wounds inflicted by Lewis's ferocious caricature of him in *The Apes of God*. He found solace at Teffont. Solace too, from nearby Clouds, increasingly assuming the form of an Edwardian white elephant bled the whiter by the imposition of double death duties. He found solace, too, from the effects of the bizarre life-style he had imposed on his second marriage. His insistence on a separate dwelling for his wife (and their daughter) persuaded the susceptible London troubadours that the deliciously appetizing Grethe was fair game for amateurs at the courts of love.

Dick would come to stay at Teffont for days on end, setting up his easel in the grounds to paint, often watched by the silently squatting seven-year-old Pauline. The razor-sharp line that Wyndham Lewis had taught him to cultivate had not cured him of his early affection for the English nineteenth-century landscape-painters.

Dick had all that Iris Tree found most appealing in men: 'rip, grip, smash and dash'. His influence on David, as the older man, and the more accomplished, began increasingly to be felt. He became his social cicerone, taking over that role from Matt. This was just as well since Matt's powers had gone into a sharp decline. Not in his own eyes, however. If anything the reverse. Matt had recently become convinced that he could control the weather. On one occasion, while trailing his court of young disciples round Kew Gardens, he was heard to turn to the nearest follower and say: 'Would you mind taking charge of the weather, old chap. I would like to sit down and read for a bit.'

Dick, sometimes reserved and brusque in manner and speech, was not shy. He was tougher than David and made friends more easily and with more interesting people. He introduced them into David's life and to the Gargoyle. Old stalwarts such as Freddy Mayor, Curtis Moffat, Constant Lambert and Tom Driberg apart, there was the painter Matthew Smith who had studied with Matisse in Paris but had kept well clear of Matt's esoteric philosophies on returning to London. Oscar Wilde's son, Vyvyan Holland was another. Vyvyan had for some years known and liked well the irrepressibly gregarious A. J. A. Symons, dandy, gourmet, bibliophile and wag. AJ, the name he had taken for himself, was someone who dearly needed to make his way in the world. He longed, his brother Julian has stated, for a fame which would be both social and literary. As a move in this direction AJ, in his very early twenties, had founded The First Edition Club just after the war. This duly attracted the attention of the Foyle brothers, Christina's father and uncle, who had diligently been building up their thriving business selling books. They became AJ's business partners and, for a time, his present, if not his future, was secured. It was at The First Edition Club that Vyvyan Holland first met AJ, his own interest in first editions being of a very specialized nature, namely pornography.

It was when the FEC began to slide gently into decline that Vyvyan introduced AJ to Dick and Dick in turn brought AJ into David's life. The three became, and remained over many years, boon companions sharing many tastes – poetry, conversation, walking tours, the art of good living, food and wine. Interest in the latter proved an instant bond between David and AJ. In 1931, 'London's most exclusive club', a small dining club limited to a membership of fifty, had been formed to redeem from neglect the ageing Professor George Saintsbury, author of the classic *Notes on a Cellar Book*, and much else of a pedantic nature. AJ was in his favourite position as secretary and Vyvyan Holland sat on the committee. It was the success of this (although the Professor himself wanted small part of it) that led, in 1931, to The Wine and Food Society; President, André Simon, Secretary, A. J. A. Symons. It was a bold step to take in the shadow of the Depression where so many people still stood, and it got a mixed reception from the Press with a notably ironic piece in the *Manchester Guardian*. But it was just there, in the enlightened middle class, that the appeal of the Society was most keenly felt and its success assured.

The bond of discriminating gluttony aside, David and AJ were well suited; the later was a skilful dispenser of admiration, the former an appreciative recipient. AJ remarked David's '... height, elegance, dark long locks and film-star good looks ... his zest for personal pleasure, philosophic speculation and mannered voice'. 'David's chief characteristic', he declared, was his '... carefree charm, his absorption in the moment, his overflowing impulse to please and be pleased.' David for his part admired the wit and eloquence of this negligently flamboyant personality, skating recklessly over thin ice with a dandy's disdain for his own chronic shortage of money. But AJ was also intermittently industrious. He had recently delivered to his publisher, Desmond Flower at Cassells, a manuscript on which he had been furiously working the last few months. This now left him free to go down to Wiltshire to join Dick and David on their walking tours. The rules were strict: twenty-two miles a day, no midday break, no girls. For, like Dick and David, AJ was an ardent believer in girls. And he, too, was married, although his wife, Gladys, was never much in evidence. Fondness for this form of recreation, the long country ramble, was characteristic of the period – a search for a new virility. But though often earnest, the British way tended to be homespun, private and innocent. A marked contrast to the hiking hordes of exultant youth stomping about the emergent Nazi Germany seeking a mystical idyllic past to forge into a new system and chanting with messianic fervor 'Heavenly grace gave us the Führer!'

In his biography of AJ, his brother, Julian Symons, describes one such walk through unknown country undertaken by the three friends. Setting out from Great Yews, on the top of Whitsbury Down south of Salisbury, 'They planned to follow the ridge which stretches through Dorset, and to strike the sea at Weymouth. AJ, who loved oddly-named villages, "cherished a secret desire to visit an obscure village of which I knew (and know) only that it has the romantic and improbable name of Rime Intrinseca", and he observed that "Dorset challenges my favourite Essex in the charm and quaintness of its place names, with Toller Porcorum to set against Shellow Bowells, Cricket Malherbie against High Easter or Wendens Ambo". At the end of a day's walking, appetite sharpened by lack of lunch, he remarked on the excellence of the meal they obtained for two shillings each, "Rabbits swimming in an appetising half-stew-half-sauce, garnished with good carrots and floury potatoes", followed by English cheddar, fresh lettuce and household bread. On the next day he viewed with sceptical interest the products of anthropological research in the local Pitt-Rivers museum, and remarked on the beauty of the Benin bronzes whose "Impressive, V-lipped, broad-nostrilled faces look beyond the visitors to the surrounding English landscape, so demure, safe and parklike, and call up another land of torrid sun and dangerous, thoughtless life".'

When Cassell published what was to be AJ's major work in 1934 it received immediate recognition from such discerning critics as Graham Greene, Desmond MacCarthy and Peter Quennell. *The Quest For Corvo* was seen then, and is still seen, as one of the more successful and unorthodox essays in biography ever written. As Desmond Flower himself claimed, it was a masterpiece. The book brought AJ what he had always wanted, literary recognition. For five years after publication that most acerbic of critics James Agate had avoided reading the book. When he was finally persuaded to do so (by AJ) he wrote to him as follows:

> Dear Symons,
>
> I have now finished *Quest for Corvo*. The book's existence at all is a miracle. First there was the right kind of curiosity to be aroused, second it had to be aroused in the right person, and third there had to be the original Corvo. Well, the hat trick came off....

*

Hermione complained of David's rich-man's restlessness, but she was no less afflicted; and particularly so when not working. The lure of country life, however seigneurial, quickly began to pall. Whenever she held the siren sea-shell to her ear it was the creak of the boards she heard calling her back. There, in the theatre, amongst theatre folk, was the place she felt truly at home. Although due to re-join Angela and Bobby Newton for the West End opening of *The Greeks Had a Word For It* at the end of 1934, she allowed herself to be tempted by the offer of a new farce at the Vaudeville in August. David was not pleased. His answer was to revive his own interest in the Gargoyle from which he had absented himself for long periods and which had therefore grown somewhat stale. He planned to mount an occasional zestful event at the Club, something to bring a little drama into the place and stir everybody's stumps a bit. Inspired by Dick's example of giving the entire proceeds from an exhibition of his painting to help the Tate Gallery buy one of Epstein's works, David decided to hold an auction of paintings in the Gargoyle in aid of charity, donations of their works to be canvassed from artists amongst the members. Included was a Teffont landscape by Dick, works by Adrian Daintry, Matthew Smith, C. R. W. Nevinson, Curtis Moffat (drawing), Paul (4th Baron) Methuen, Augustus John, Gordon Craig (theatrical design), George Belcher (cartoon), Edward Wadsworth and others. The evening was a great success. Everything was sold and sold to fellow members or their guests. This was in no small degree due to Freddy Mayor whose advice and support David had sought.

Convivial, a notable trencherman, devotee of good claret, Freddy, like Henry Fielding, was a great believer in 'the Benefit of Laughing'. His brown hair contrasted oddly with rich ginger side-whiskers, as if he had applied to each nostril with an over emphatic flourish the snuff to which he also was addicted. Freddy looked and dressed as if he would be more at home on the Turf than as the owner-director of one of the outstanding modern art galleries in London, showing such painters as Picasso, Rouault, Juan Gris, Miró, De Chirico and, particularly, Paul Klee. Both activities suited him well. They had in common an appeal to the gambler, an energetic force in Freddy's temperament. He was not only perfectly at home in his gallery off Bond Street, but he induced in those who came there that very same sense.

Another of David's ideas to promote the Gargoyle – and it did seem clever at the time – was to present an exhibition of fencing at the Club, the proceeds of the evening once again to be reserved for charity. The master of ceremonies chosen for this occasion was Sir Oswald Mosley. Mosley, in spite of a pronounced limp which required him to wear a surgical shoe, was very athletic and a member of the British Fencing Team. He was also the leader of the British Union of Fascists which he had founded in 1932. Up until this time, 1935, Fascism had still not generally been seen to be the monstrous portent it was fast becoming in the hands of the Nazis with their mounting and horrendous persecution of Jews, their introduction of conscription and a massive rearmament programme. Mosley was not yet beyond the pale, but he had lost the respectable intellectual support he had once enjoyed with the New Party. If Mosley was to incur censure amongst his peers, it was more likely to be on account of his persistent philandering which some held to have contributed to his wife Cimmie's early and unhappy death in 1933. Lady Cynthia (Cimmie) was the daughter of Lord Curzon by his first wife Mary, herself the daughter of the rich American manufacturer, Levi Leiter. Cimmie was a particular and close friend of Dick's – they had Soulish connections in common – and he would do what he could to bring wisdom and comfort when she confided in him her distress at her husband's marital transgressions. The most aggravating one, perhaps because the most serious, was the relationship he had formed, in what was to be the last year of Cimmie's life, with Diana, wife of Bryan Guinness, and one of the Mitford sisters.

Mosley enthusiastically lent himself to David's cause and assembled a group of swordsmen of the highest calibre to fence at the Club. There was a full house on the night and all was going famously except for one discordant note. This was struck by the Jackson twins who had a ring-side table on the edge of the dance-floor which served as the fencing ground. A sporting contest was afoot and they were not part of it. The truculent school-boy which lay not far beneath the brilliant and sophisticated surface emerged in both. They began to make uncomplimentary remarks in loud sarcastic voices about the performers – who were after all demonstrating their skills freely for charity. Egging each other on as they always did – 'Horse' and 'Old Horse', as they called each other – they began to heckle, then to barrack. So far Mosley had been very restrained, only asking them please to keep quiet. Now he came over to them and told them to shut up or get out. The twins' double dander was up. They both turned on Mosley. Poppet John thinks she remembers that a political argument developed. This is unlikely. It is more likely to have been simply personal. A challenge to a fight was issued. Mosley accepted. The matter now became formalized. Clearly a fight in the ballroom, or anywhere else in the packed club, was impractical. The fracas would have to take place in Meard Street. David attempted to calm the situation but there was nothing to be done. The three marched solemnly to the lift and squeezed inside. At once their difference in height became exaggerated by unwelcome proximity. The twins looked up from five foot eight at Mosley's six foot two. A fierce harlequin face stared contemptuously down at them. Derek grunted. 'You're too *big*', he said. The lift bumped to the ground. Through the grille they could see David's strained smile there to greet them. Like Mercury, he had hurled himself down the emergency staircase to reach the ground first. The message he brought was in a bottle of champagne. 'If not oil, then let wine be poured!' he declaimed. The situation was defused. From then on the three antagonists became the firmest of friends. Or so history relates.

David did not always manage to endear himself with his ready quips. There was an evening when Freddy Mayor's young and pretty wife, Pamela, brought a rich merchant from the East End to the Club. He had expressed a tentative interest in modern art which Freddy sought to encourage. As they eased out of the lift into the foyer, there was David in the role of 'greeter'. He was wearing a certain smile which the experienced had grown to learn did not always bode well.

'Oh, David', said inexperienced Pam. 'May I introduce Mr Behar.' David looked at her guest hardly. 'Get thee Behar me!' he boomed. In time the rich merchant grew richer yet. But David was neither forgiven nor forgotten.

The Gargoyle had proved a catalyst in Pam's life, as in so many others. A first cousin of Robin Mount, whom she adored for what she saw as his Regency buck qualities, she was brought up in horsey country in Berkshire where her father was a Justice of the Peace. Tiring of the hunting field and hunt balls, longing for London and the world of the arts she persuaded her parents to let her go there, aged nineteen, with a living allowance of one pound a week. For a reasonably attractive girl, who could expect to be taken out, fed and wined thrice a week, it was just possible to get by on such a sum. But Pam was rather more than reasonably attractive. She was tall, dark, slender and graceful. To augment her allowance she took to modelling clothes (at Liberty) and working in films as an extra. Extras got paid extra if they could provide their own evening clothes. Pam had one long evening dress and frequently appeared in this on film as the dancing partner of Stewart Granger (then Jimmy Stewart) in swanky night-club scenes. One day Robin telephoned Pam to say that one of the models for a dress show being given by Maison Worth at the Gargoyle had been taken ill and could she please step in. It would be a sort of cabaret and a fee of £2 was on offer. Her idea of the world of the arts was not sweating in evening dress under studio lights at nine o'clock in the morning and in the arms of Jimmy Stewart – no matter how famous he was confident of becoming. Could this be a dash into another world? With some trepidation, she agreed. In any case she could do with the money – which, in the event, she remembers having the greatest difficulty in obtaining out of anyone. On arrival at the club, Pam was greatly reassured to be taken in hand and given a stiff swig from her flask by the beautiful and greatly more experienced Marcelle, Peter Quennell's first wife. Having successfully 'strutted her stuff' on the ballroom floor, she was beckoned over by Robin to a long table where he, David and a few others were sitting having dinner. Pam was instantly seized upon by the noted libertine and scribbler, Simon Harcourt-Smith. Freddy Mayor was placed at the other end of the table near David. 'Who's that girl with Simon?' he asked. 'If he's got hold of her she must be a bit of all right.' 'Robin's cousin. Talk to him,' David replied. Freddy did. An introduction was effected. After a shaky start – Freddy asked her to lunch the next day but when she turned up at the gallery on time he failed to recognize her – courtship commenced, and this was to result in a lasting marriage. As far as is known, theirs were the only wedding banns to be given out from the Cavendish Hotel.

Robin and David enjoyed each other's company. Too much Pam thinks, reflecting on the damage that drink was to do to Robin. David, she feels, 'led darling old Robin astray. Not very difficult.' There was one celebrated occasion on which David and Robin did over-encourage each other. It brought out what Peter Quennell has called David's 'Squire Mytton' side in high relief. (Squire Mytton, it may be remembered, when a mere boy, just after the turn of the nineteenth century, had written to his legal guardian, the then Lord Chancellor, to protest that the sum, a large one, which he had been awarded as yearly allowance was totally inadequate – particularly as he was about to be married. He was then aged fourteen. Lord Eldon's reply was laconic, brief and to the point: 'Sir, if you cannot live on your allowance, you may starve; and, if you marry, I shall commit you to prison.' The *Dictionary of National Biography* describes Mytton as 'a man of great physical strength and foolhardy courage, with an inordinate love of conviviality and a strongly developed taste for practical joking. He was a daring horseman and a splendid shot....')

It was the 'splendid shot' aspect of Mytton in David that was pinpointed on the occasion in question. There was the usual week-end house-party at Teffont to which a recently married couple named Dugdale had been invited. David had known Carol Dugdale, previously married to Oswald Mosley's youngest brother, quite well: her new and very well-off husband, Eric, much less so. Quennell says of them that 'they were the sort of people that were rather made fun of, because if there was a party they wouldn't want to miss it and arrive before anyone else and leave after anyone else. They were eager for occasions – smart Bohemian occasions.'

As far as the Dugdales were concerned the weekend house-party had not been an unqualified success. Perhaps because Eric was not insensible of the fact that for some years Carol had nourished a sentimental tenderness for David. David himself was certainly not insensible of it. 'So', Quennell goes on, 'they left on Sunday afternoon not entirely unlamented. And David and Robin decided to see their departure off with what I believe is called a "feu de joie". So they took out their shot-guns and fired their "feu de joie" over the back of the retreating car. Then they thought it would be amusing to try the back tyres, which they did. One or other of them then chose to fire through the back window of the car severely peppering Mrs Dugdale.' Poor Carol got it in the neck and would carry the scars to her grave. Good Squire Mytton stuff. When the astounded Eric Dugdale managed to turn his car around in the drive in order to confront his host, it was Robin who was caught with smoking gun in hand. 'We were only trying to stop you leaving', he said lamely. Meantime David had beaten a strategic retreat in order to call the doctor.

*

Some months before this disgraceful event there had been another 'happening' – and not one of his own devising – which was to have a profound and long-lasting influence on David's life. This took place on an autumn Sunday in the little town hall of Fordingbridge on the edge of the New Forest and not one mile from the Johns' home at Fryern Court. It was to be an entertainment consisting of sketches and numbers entirely devised and performed by John's many children, born on no matter which side of the blanket. The title it had been given was *Wild Oats* in celebration of all that John had sown. The youngest seed there, however, was not on stage since he was still in the arms of his mother, Mavis de Vere Cole.

One of the participants was Gwyneth Johnstone then at the Slade School in London. She had invited her close friend there, the eighteen-year-old Virginia Parsons, daughter of the late Alan Parsons and his wife Viola, to be in the audience. Viola had been the most favoured daughter of Sir Herbert Beerbohm Tree, and also a great favourite of Squiffy Asquith, likewise of Ribblesdale. She was a singer and an actress, often playing with her father, and when quite young had been sent to the Royal Academy of Dramatic Art which Tree had founded in 1904. Alan Parsons died in 1933 whereupon Viola continued in the theatre in order to bring up her children, playing on tour up until a month before she herself died.

Shy and not wishing to sit alone, Virginia had persuaded Ivan Moffat to come with her. The closest of her cousins, a year younger than herself, Ivan was the only son of Curtis and Viola's sister, Iris. Although still a schoolboy, he was intellectually and socially very precocious, with a charm well laced with Iris's impish wit, her self-mocking merriment. Iris, rich in so much else, was short on maternal impulse. Moreover, she had divorced Curtis in the year Alan Parsons died and was now living in California married to the magnificent-looking horseman, Count Friedrich Ledebur, a penniless Austrian nobleman. Consequently, Ivan had spent much of his young life with his grandmother, Lady Tree, or with Viola and her family, before being sent to the progressive co-educational school Dartington Hall. He and Virginia, since their earliest days, had always been very thick.

When the curtain parted in Fordingbridge Town Hall it disclosed Poppet (the ex-Mrs Jackson) about to break into a little gypsy dance number and half revealing charmingly provocative naked breasts. Her performance was interrupted by the late arrival of a couple, one of whom, the woman, was making a great deal of noise, calling out greetings to friends and generally drawing attention to herself. Virginia turned to Ivan. 'That's the best looking man I've ever seen in my life. Who is he?' Ivan, who had previously met him with Curtis, his father, replied: 'That's David Tennant. And *that* is his wife, Hermione.'

After it was all over, audience and players repaired to Fryern Court where preparations had been made for feasting and dancing. As the agonizingly shy Virginia was also surpassingly beautiful – tall and graceful with a fall of golden hair half hiding her heart-shaped face – it was not therefore surprising that with the unfolding of the evening David's keen eye should fall upon her and be well pleased by where it landed. Virginia, the young aspiring artist, screened by her hairfall, had hardly taken her eyes off David since his arrival with Hermione. When he came up and asked her to dance she instantly realized that he would be irresistible to her.

12

The Gargoyle had been in existence now for rather more than ten years. The country was making a slow recovery from the Depression which at one point had led to nearly three million being unemployed. In most countries affected by the economic crisis the result had been, generally, to lower the standard of living. But spirits of the country as a whole had been raised by the Silver Jubilee in 1935 celebrating the twenty-fifth anniversary of King George v's accession to the throne. By no means popular on his coronation, the King had endeared himself to the British by his very ordinariness, by his modesty and his evident quiet decency. The Jubilee euphoria had briefly carpeted over a deep social malaise, a restless confusion which provoked ardent spirits in Britain to cross dangerous frontiers; frontiers of class, sex and political ideology.

Ivan Moffat, who came to know David well and to like him well, makes the point of his 'very irrelevance to his times'. One effect of this was to keep him buoyant, a buoyancy which was reflected in his Club. The unique thing about the Gargoyle and the recruiting of its members was that there were no denominations that were excluded. Everybody was potentially acceptable so long as they were acceptable to David. But here his quirky side would often emerge unexpectedly. One of the world's most desirable social figures had recently applied for membership and been turned down. This was the Aly Khan. Hermione was extremely upset. She was star-bedazzled by Aly – the most wonderful person to be a member of the Club, she felt. 'Don't you realize he's a *Prince*', she said. 'I've got nothing against Indian [sic] Princes', David answered, 'but we just don't want to start that kind of – fashion.' Pauline Rumbold explains this: 'My father was the only person I've met in my life without a scintilla of snobbishness. He felt he had created an atmosphere in the Gargoyle where everybody could be themselves, if they had a self to be. He wanted people to be excellent, to excel themselves. And if they weren't excellent, provided they achieved what they were capable of, that was all right.'

The conceit that the Club should be 'a place where the Sitwells would not be ill at ease and not perfectly at ease' still held. But many of Pamela's old friends and contemporaries were less evident now that she was no longer there and some had dropped away altogether. Bloomsbury had been watered down with deaths and departures. The BYPs had dimmed, finding the demands of career, wedlock or the fiscal drag too exacting to leave much time for the pursuit of pleasure. The Prince of Wales, under the influence of Wallis Simpson, sought places of diversion that were grander, flashier, more palatial, like The Embassy Club; and his set followed suit. So, although Edwina Mountbatten still often came to the Gargoyle, Dickie did less so.

At lunch-time the place was usually full because of its proximity to the temples of influence and because of its ambience, its professional service and the excellence of the wine and food (the fare more elaborate than when Anthony Powell first went there) all at reasonable prices. But at night the patronage was less consistent. The theatre crowd, led by Hermione, were usually well-represented. John and his court were constant. The old guard, like Dick Wyndham and his friends, still used the place frequently. But the ideal of establishing a meeting place for the Arts and Society, where the gilded pollen of the latter might rub against the bare pistils of the former, became less and less achievable. The times were not propitious.

If David was aware of this he was too distracted by thoughts of Virginia's Titania-like beauty for it to be of much immediate consequence. He felt disenchanted. His life was turning sour. And then – behold! – this new and unsought encounter. Years later, under the baleful influence of the dark war years, he was to write, for Virginia, an account in verse of the effect that first meeting in Fordingbridge had on him.

When I first saw your face, at the party
I was tired; tired of the effort of ten years
To drown the nagging conscience of boyhood –
A conscience I despised, but which ruled me by reverse compulsion.
I, as yet, knew not free-est choice
And struggled unruly against a phantom:
My beckoning star being freedom, freedom to disdain.
When I first saw your face, I thought of it as a charm
A charm given me – gratis – the right to love again,
So long denied. The fume of empty bottles,
And the carrion guests, could now be renounced
Or chosen when I wished.
When first I saw your face, pale cheeks and aureole hair,
Angel eyes and sensuous mouth, fine waist, and floating breasts

It seemed that this was my escape, my human solution.
Who would not recant, to be fired by a glory such as this.
Flattering my vanity: after much sin; what a prize.
Now could I unloose the flood of my emotion
Many years in prison, waiting for release.
Now here was nascent love, a whirlwind in a girl's form.
A promise of new life, a human pair of skates
To glide over the sparkling ice of the future.
Yours was an unwitting star, a light prisoned
In a chalice that threw strange patterns of
Assurance and diffidence on the tablet of your mind
. . . .

The 'fume of empty bottles, And the carrion guests . . .' of which he complained in the poem were those to be found in his own home at Teffont rather than in the Gargoyle. He had grown sick of playing a welcoming Hamlet to the crowd of mummers brought down by Hermione on week-ends, distinguished though many of them were. Amongst them was Laurence Olivier who had just made his first big impact as Romeo at the New Theatre (now the Albery). 'He presented', wrote Sir Alec Guinness after his death, 'a beautiful, graceful, Italianate youth; gentle, passionate, highly strung and desperate with love.'

'Desperate with love' was what David now felt himself to be. But the pursuit of it was a ticklish matter. Virginia was so young – fifteen years younger than himself. And since he was, in spite of all, still married, courtship could not reasonably be made open. Therefore discreet chaperones had to be pressed into service bringing her casually at first into his old conscience-ridden life.

Hermione first became aware of these manoeuvres when Virginia was brought over to Teffont for a small dinner party by a man she did not recognize. It turned out to be a larger occasion than expected. They went in to dinner where a large rack of lamb was laid out on the table. 'Oh', Hermione reports Virginia as having said, 'I've never seen such a big lamp chop.' Hermione noticed that David seemed to find this very funny and laughed immoderately. Too immoderately, she felt.

*

David moved his family up to London for Christmas 1935 and the New Year. There were numerous festivities to be attended including a children's party at the Gargoyle which had now become an annual event. David wanted Pauline to wear something quite special for this. He loved dressing people up (a Tennant trait?) and always ordered all

Hermione's clothes. The day before the party he took Pauline, aged nine, into a dress shop in Bond Street. 'I want something in El Greco green for my daughter,' he told a bemused assistant. Then there was the Chelsea Arts Club Ball traditionally held in the Albert Hall. In those days the Ball was not conducted by mob rule but had some of the formality of a Roman Circus, the patricians secure in their champagne-fortified boxes watching the plebs indulge in their bacchanal on the floor below, and everyone in proper – sometimes improper – fancy dress. Pauline remembers Hermione coming into her bedroom before leaving 'shimmering all over with sequins and with this amazing pink skirt with wire round it, her legs bare and this tiny little monkey sitting on her shoulder. I said "What have you got the monkey for, Mummy?" And she said "Well, I *am* the ring-master's wife."' And let no-one forget it.

But the ring-master himself did seem a little forgetful about it now and then. There was the New Year party given at the Gargoyle with a cabaret, in which Hermione performed with Wally Crisham, who had appeared with her in *Ballyhoo* at the Comedy. The evening itself was very lively with David and Hermione the focus of affectionate attention and much exchange of hugs and kisses. 'Fruity' (Major Edward) Metcalfe, equerry to the Prince of Wales, was being judiciously indiscreet about the powerful grip in which Mrs Simpson held his royal boss when Hermione suddenly became aware that David was no longer listening. His eyes were on a young couple who had just come down the mirrored stairs. The girl was instantly recognizable by the fair hair which almost completely obscured her face. She pushed it aside as David got up to welcome them. He and Virginia kissed each other affectionately then, detaching her from her escort, he led her onto the cock-pit dance-floor. As Hermione watched them dance she felt a stirring of unease. They did not dance as she and David had always danced, with fire and brilliance, exciting onlookers to applaud their brio, but, their heights being compatible, they held each other close moving gently to Alexander's ragtime band. Hermione remembered how necessary dance had been to them both from the time they had fallen in love. She felt threatened.

Since the Champagne Freddy affair, and due also to the fact that, except for weekends, the theatre kept Hermione in London while David remained with their children at their supposedly marriage-saving home in the country, there had evolved a mutual acceptance that each was free to go out with other people. A *mariage complaisant*, in short. David had recently let it drop to Hermione that he had taken Virginia out once or twice. So although Hermione felt this pang of apprehension on seeing the easy intimacy between the two of them on the dance floor, she reminded herself of how often David had told her that it was she he had chosen to marry and no one else. And as for her, there could never seriously be anyone else but David.

*

During Dick's absence abroad, Clouds house was once more put on the market with about 3,000 acres. 'This important mansion', ran the advertisement, 'is for sale at a sacrificial price or', came the threat, 'will be sold later for demolition.' In the end Clouds shared both these fates being sold at a 'sacrificial price' to two property speculators who disposed of it with forty acres to Mrs Elisabeth Houghton-Brown for £3,300. There is a certain irony in that this once so proud mansion, a citadel of the Souls, subsequently became a Church of England refuge for down and outs and is now owned by the Life-Anew Trust, who run it as an Alcoholism and Addictive Disease Treatment Centre, and in such guise is known to have been patronized by descendants of the very Souls.

David meanwhile was ardently wooing his young beloved, Virginia from the Slade. For the pursuit of this courtship one of the places they liked best to go to was the Eiffel Tower, the most favoured restaurant amongst London's Bohemia. Often there at the same time, and set upon a somewhat similar course, were Freddy Mayor and Pam Colledge. The encounter of the two couples would be an embarrassment to Freddy since he was particularly fond of Hermione and it was clear that David's infatuation for the beautiful girl was of a rather different order than the more familiar careless love. There were also dinners at the Jardin des Gourmets in Soho and at Boulestin in Covent Garden, and there were drives during the day down to Kew Gardens. David also drove Virginia down to Teffont where, amongst all else, he kept a powerful motor bike. 'He drove at 95 m.p.h.,' remembers Virginia, 'with me on the pillion – too vain to sit astride, as being ungainly, so I sat dangerously side saddle.' Apart from the Bugatti, the Isotta-Fraschini, the Leyland Thomas in which he had broken the lap record at Brooklands 'all else' also included a Terraplane.

His obsession for Virginia helped to make David somewhat inattentive to the political thunders which were raging over Europe: German troops goose-stepping into the Rhineland; Mussolini establishing an Italian empire in Abyssinia; more pertinently, the outbreak of the Spanish Civil War. In England, Mosley was to be seen in his true colour – black. There were two events in 1936 which briefly stopped David in his Lothario tracks: one, not totally unexpected, was the death at a good age of Matt

Pritchard, whose influence on David's life had been, Pamela excepted, more keenly felt than any other; the second was the early death, brought literally on his own head, of Vivian Jackson. This came about when, in order to demonstrate his skill to the sweetheart of the moment whom he was taking for a spin in the snow, he arrogantly seized the reins from a protesting sleigh driver in St Moritz, turned the vehicle over and broke his neck. The driver fell onto soft snow and was unhurt and the sweetheart got away with a broken leg. From their first meeting Vivian had transferred the main charge of his affection for Hermione on to David. Loving horses as he did, he always saw that David was provided with a good mount at Teffont. The accident was very much in character, but David was nonetheless greatly shocked by its wasteful absurdity. When trying to explain to Virginia in the Gargoyle the effect this death had upon him he was reduced to tears.

In that same year, the Mayor Gallery acquired a new recruit to join Buster Crabb its permanent staff of one. This was the young Scots poet Ruthven Todd, son of a hard-drinking Edinburgh architect. He had been encouraged to try his luck in London by Louis MacNeice, whose own reputation had been firmly cemented by Faber and Faber's publication of his poems the previous year. Ruthven was first brought into the Mayor Gallery by the painter John Piper for whom he had been doing a spot of gardening and proof-reading. Freddy liked the cut (necessarily rather austere) of Ruthven's jib. He offered no money but told him he could work in the Gallery on commission. Ruthven had started his artistic life as a painter, so in that sense it was rewarding to be working in that ambience. Although he greatly enjoyed living amongst pictures and seeing new works coming in, he could not afford to remain. He parted from Freddy on the best of terms, astutely choosing a morning when Freddy's bookmaker's monthly statement had come in with a sizeable cheque made out in his favour.

13

Although Champagne Freddy had long been demoted from ardent lover to *cavaliere servente*, he continued to serve Hermione cheerfully in this less heroic role. And in the circumstances of David's prolonged and increasingly open courtship of Virginia this was a considerable comfort. It allowed her to pursue the active social life her professional status demanded and helped to take the curse off an unhappy and somewhat embarrassing situation. But Virginia was not being quite as amenable as David might have wished. David had taken her on a cruise to Madeira (separate cabins) and they had driven, in his newly-acquired American Cord racing car, down to Positano on the Italian coast (separate bedrooms all the way). Today this strict observance of separate rooms on a romantic holiday might seem unlikely if not absurd, but times then were very different, and if they were not, then Virginia certainly was and Viola, despite maternal misgivings, knew it and trusted her daughter. Also, she rather loved David. Given the openness of David's rapturous pursuit of Virginia it seems a little odd that he should have taken exception to Freddy's attendance upon Hermione. But he did.

'I heard a note in your voice when you spoke to him on the telephone once,' David complained. 'It was one I recognized. You used that note in your voice when you were in love with me. It upset me very much to hear you use it to another man.' Why was he telling her this now, Hermione wondered. Why had he not said so at the time if he was so upset? She knew that he had always thought he owned her and that even if he did not she would never fall in love with another man. But still....

'But this was always the kind of marriage you wanted,' Hermione protested. 'With nothing ever hidden between us.'

'Perhaps I was wrong,' David replied.

So why, Hermione wondered, was he bringing up Freddy Childs now? Ah, of course. David needed to justify something he was about to tell her. Something she knew she did not want to hear.

'Virginia and I want to get married.'

That was exactly what Hermione did not want to hear and until it was said she had no idea just how deep it would cut.

Instead of bending with the wind until its direction changed, Hermione's reaction was to stiffen up and reach, this time, for her solicitor. A socializing solicitor, moreover, who smacked his lips over the prospect of a juicy society divorce. He painted their marriage in the bleakest of colours and assured her he would find the quickest way to end it. In fact, David had dissembled the truth in telling Hermione that it was Virginia's idea to get married. It was not. 'I'm afraid I was a horrid tease,' says Virginia, 'and rather enjoyed keeping him on a string, and although I adored him I did not want to settle down quite yet.' Not only young, beautiful and talented, Virgina was 'nervous' in the sense that a 'nervous horse', in racing parlance, is a horse in fine fettle. She was also nervous in the sense Pope gave to the word which was to mean someone who was resolute and steely. This factor in her psychological make-up had been recognized by her cousin Ivan who saw the screen of golden hair as concealing more than just part of her physical presence – 'paradoxically it disguised a strong underlying personality and will.' Certainly, her 'nervous' nature all went to make David highly nervous in a more contemporary sense.

Twirling on the end of Virginia's string was exasperating in the extreme for David and an embarrassment to his pride. Her dilly-dallying also made him indecisive. Hermione moved with Welsh Gwen into a two-bedroom mews house in Bayswater. David disposed of the house in Canning Place and moved in too. Warned by her solicitor that this was an absurd situation which could only prolong and complicate matters, Hermione told David that if he wanted a divorce they would have to separate and the sooner the better.

'I'm going to move – eventually,' said David. The intention was that he should move into the flat under the ballroom in the Gargoyle once inhabited by Harry Walker. The immediate problem was that he could not find his suitcases. 'I will find your suitcases. Gwen will pack them for you. I am then going out to lunch. I expect to be back by two. And I expect you by then to have left,' said Hermione, surprised to find how much iron had entered her soul with the pain. Hermione lunched at some length with a sympathetic girlfriend, afterwards driving back in her open sports car. Feeling sure David would have left, Hermione asked the solidarity sister in for coffee. But no, there was David's head sticking out of the bedroom window. 'I can't find my binoculars', he yelled. 'Any idea where they are?'

The protracted evacuation went on for weeks, the prevarication provoked, surely, by Virginia's reluctance to commit her unblemished youth to such a dangerously attractive man – and a still married one, to boot. Nevertheless, she knew that, whether she was to like it or not, sooner or later she would marry him. Later, counselled Viola. And if it was to be so, then she had better go to Paris to become better educated and learn French. Accordingly, Virginia was despatched to France and enrolled in the White Russian Princess Machesky's Académie pour Jeunes Filles in Auteuil – something Viola could ill-afford.

Never at a loss for a Gypsy Moth, David would fly over most weekends to take her out. 'We had romantic times walking in the Bois du Boulogne, dining at a lovely restaurant La Belle Aurore and going to the wonderful exhibition open that year built around the Eiffel Tower,' said Virginia. 'We *loved* the Romanian Tent. There was a man there who played the Pipes of Pan, wild, passionate, gipsy music which made David dash away tears.' David was a success with the *jeunes filles* at the Académie and with their *préceptrices*. '*On peut dire c'est un vrai Lord Byron*', they declared. '*Il est si beau*.' It is true that when David went to Paris, chauvinist pride required that he should affect the true-blue *milord anglais* look, but when at Teffont, the appearance of a rather different David had already begun to emerge. Ivan Moffat's comment about David's irrelevance to his times was conspicuous in his disdainful, arrogant indifference to his own (unassailable) good looks. The dandy had become carelessly dressed, unashamedly unshaven very much like the film star of today.

But whatever the state of his deportment, he always, as Virginia says, 'managed to smell so good. I remember when he went to sea during the war I kept one of his old shirts by me. When depressed I would inhale it and was greatly comforted. I remember, too, Iris saying to me before we were married, "I like David. He smells so nice." I was rather cross at the time.' Personal smell – an often overlooked factor in sexual selection.

On the London home front, Hermione kept on arranging for David to leave and she kept on returning – at the time she was appearing in *To and Fro* at the Comedy – to find him still in residence. One afternoon she came back to find David removing all the paintings from what she rather grandiosely described as the 'drawing room walls' of the mews house. 'But some of those were given to us *both*!' she protested. 'Well, I'm going to leave you the furniture instead,' David replied firmly. Hermione was beginning to feel that this was a very one-sided divorce. Their farewell, as he left the mews, this time for good, was cool.

Shortly after this David wrote to Hermione asking for a meeting. It was decided it should be on neutral ground, a hard bench in Hyde Park.

They chatted about her solicitors and his solicitors, about the children and about their respective romantic interests – Hermione's ostensibly still being Champagne Freddy. Then it transpired that David was getting cold feet about the divorce and what he was now seeking from Hermione – the purpose of their meeting in short – was comfort and soothing advice on this very matter. He did not want to give up Virginia and he did not (apparently) want to give up Hermione. 'No man,' he said ungallantly, but in the measured delivery of the Comédie Française, 'in his right mind ever wants to get married.'

'Look here,' Hermione said severely, grasping the wrong end of the stick, 'you've been dragging this wretched girl around for ages, giving her expectations, leading her to suppose . . . you can't possibly give her up now and you can't keep on hedging your bets. I was a little sixteen-year-old when I fell in love with you and now I am a grown woman with two children and a career of my own. I *like* my independence.' Hermione admitted later that several times over the years she wanted to kick herself for being, as she saw it, so proud and noble. The wrong end of the stick that Hermione had grasped lay in the fact, and one which David was not prepared to acknowledge – certainly not to Hermione – that he was still in the humiliating position of rotating at the end of Virginia's string. As Virginia said, David wrote her many letters at this time, some euphoric, some despairing at her refusal to give her commitment to a marriage once he was legally free to ask for her hand.

David and Hermione were duly divorced and a modest settlement (£50 a month by deed of covenant) was made on the offended party. But the streak of meanness Hermione had off and on noticed in David raised its obdurate head over the matter of the children's education. He could not afford to pay any school fees, David assured her. Little David had been put down for Eton and was about to go to a preparatory school; Pauline was bound for a co-educational college in Kent. Hermione, David went on, was earning very good money in the theatre. She had the children, she could and should afford to pay for them. Hermione was flabbergasted. But, as Ivan Moffat has noted, David had a marked ambiguity in his nature when it came to money. 'He could veer,' says Ivan, 'between great generosity and what my father, who liked him vastly, had described as "psychological retentiveness". My father had had financial exigencies of his own, which had gained him a keen sense of any latent "psychological retentiveness" on the part of richer friends.'

Pauline without much, if any, parental supervision, was rapidly developing independence of character and qualities of leadership. She became 'leader of the gang' at Teffont; her gang of village kids, and with *droit de seigneur* she braved its only pub in order to buy her faithful followers forbidden fags and bottles of cider. Virginia, when David brought her down to Teffont, was gentle, sweet and at ease with the children, who did not seem all that much younger than she – certainly not the adventurous Pauline. 'I liked her very much,' remembers Pauline. 'I never thought of her as an interloper, I thought she was wonderful. I used to see her sitting in the grass with her hair hanging down over her eyes and I thought she was like a magical fairy.' Virginia's sensibility and delicacy made an indelible impression on the young Pauline. 'I remember driving with them both in the country and Virginia made David stop the car. She shot out and ran fifty yards into the woods and disappeared. I said "Daddy, has she gone to pee?". And he said "*No.* Just to blow her nose." I said "But she can't mind about that!" He said, "She's a fairy and she doesn't want to do any of these acts." Of course that is why he loved her. The first present Virginia ever gave my father was when she was aged twenty and he thirty-three. She came down to Teffont bringing for his birthday a basket full of coloured ribbons. I was about ten and Daddy showed me proudly these coloured ribbons. And I said "Daddy what on earth are you going to do with those?" He said "Oh, but don't you see, it's the most wonderful present because it's what she would have most liked to have been given herself." The principle of present giving being that you must, if you possibly can, give what you long to possess yourself.'

With Little David, Virginia would go walking stealthily along the hedgerows beside the cornfields, small boy's hand held in maiden's, looking for wildflowers and butterflies. Although she was David's beloved and none tried to hide it, she still preserved her 'amateur status'; consequently there was none of that contaminating spirit of guilt that can adhere to the *maîtresse en titre*. If anything, it was Hermione who had lost caste in the eyes of the two children who saw a mother more interested in herself than in them.

The prolonged courtship was for Virginia 'a passionate idyll just skirting complete possession'; but for David, now that he was free honourably to seek her in marriage, it was at times a nightmare of torment, uncertainty and frustration. At the beginning of 1938 Virginia went back to Paris for one last term. David's pining for some sort of rationalization of his condition was reflected in his bilious attitude to the Gargoyle which had slid into a decline; a result, David thought, of the 'threat of war depression'. Hermione, who was aware of the bad time the Gargoyle was going through, simply attributed it to the fact that, in her view, the principal attraction of the Club had always been the united presence there of the two of them and once this was severed it was inevitable that the rot should have set in.

In April David wrote to Virginia, 'The trouble about the Gargoyle is that I feel I ought to entertain different groups of friends in order to advertise it to them but don't feel able to stand the strain of talking to people – someone with a different personality could do it much better.' Pauline has always said of her father that he hated social life. This seems odd in one who chose to experiment with the creation of his own social world. Was it then initially just a self-indulgent whim? A form of escape from Pamela? The second view is the one Pauline would uphold: 'The whole of my father's life was a breaking away from his mother's domination. And all that self-regarding quality of the Souls. Of course they were very beautiful, very intelligent, but they were a clique and my father hated cliques. So the Gargoyle was a complete breakaway from the beautiful and talented, the exquisite and the élite – those aristocrats grouped together and admiring one another.' That may have been the intention but in the event it was nothing of the sort. And at no time was it without rather more than its fair share of the beautiful and talented. In spite of the anxieties that he expressed to Virginia and the dark depressions which could take such a savage hold, David was justly proud of the Gargoyle. There was the story Robin Mount used to tell of David and Dick on a train together going up to London from Wiltshire. Dick suddenly leant forward in his seat and said:

'Look here David, you really haven't done much with your life have you.'

'What do you mean, Dick?'

'I mean, let's compare what we've done. *I've* written two books. I've taken some very *good* photographs. I'm a journalist and I've painted quite a few rather respectable pictures. What have you done?'

'Look here, Dick, this isn't the sort of conversation I enjoy on a train.'

'Well, David, really.'

David's brows creased.

'I can tear a telephone book in half!'

Pause.

'I've crossed the Sahara. I can pilot an aeroplane.'

'Well, I'm a pilot, too, so that doesn't count.'

David felt he was getting a bit near the bottom of the barrel.

'I run a club. The Gargoyle. Favoured meeting place for literary and artistic minds.'

Dick grunted dismissively. David thought he was not winning, so he sat up very straight and played his last trump.

'*And*, I'm an Honourable.'

Dick's piloting of aircraft was notoriously susceptible to hazard. His daughter Joan remembers being taken up in his plane for a joy ride and as they were waltzing happily in and out of the clouds, Dick suddenly began slapping his pockets and then said:

'Damn! I've forgotten my glasses. You'll have to map-read us back.'

'But Daddy! I don't know *how* to map-read.'

On the other hand, Dick was too modest to remind David that he had also been decorated for gallantry in the field during the First World War. Dick had been blooded. David had not – through no fault of his own. Nevertheless men of David's generation, particularly, minded strongly about not knowing how they would have passed the warrior-in-action test. And that uneasiness can last the greater part of a lifetime.

By May of 1938 the mercury in the barometer of David's optimism had risen again. 'Things are now better at the Gargoyle and I have several plans for it to tell you about,' he wrote to Virginia in Paris. The Club sailed under an ostensibly democratic flag called The Committee. This was a somewhat fluid body recruited by David from among the members – a form of jury service – to come up with ideas for drumming up fun and funds. One such idea was that the Club should cast its net in a wider arc so as to ensnare new members from outer London, even from the suburbs, who would wish to bring 'the wife' up to town for a civilized night out with an excellent dinner and afterwards a trot round the dance-floor. The result of this initiative was to give rise to the complaint made by Constant Lambert, and quoted by Anthony Powell in his memoirs, that the Gargoyle dance-floor on Saturday night was 'packed with the two hundred nastiest people in Chiswick'.

*

The 'passionate idyll' was soon to be transformed to the complete and legitimate possession that David had desired for so long. Back in London after the summer closing of the Académie, Virginia finally gave her assent to the raising of the long siege. They would be married in September. Viola was overjoyed, her more worldly-wise sister, Iris, no less delighted, but with a word of caution which she intended to impart to David forthwith.

At long last David could turn from 'the tablet of your mind' and lay down the rich soil of experience which would nourish the song of passion he was to write five years later for Virginia.

A jungle striped pride issued from your loins
To meet a cosmic woman in your breast:
Carrier of terrible joy.
While laughter or mantling cheeks witnessed –
Change, as if by strangers
Their alternate dominion over your heart –
Cloud shadows on a landscape giving power.

You were composed of all things that you knew not of.
Strange joke of Heaven, to rule this primal kingdom
With a girlish mind.
As if a king gave all his power to a cherub zany
And got new pleasure from the arbitrary law
His magic fool laid down.

Pitiless as a flower, tender as a god, gay
As a spring wind
April on your lips – As winter's frost your mockery,
A summer's dawn in your regard
But a June rose was growing in your heart.

Viola had planned a Blessing at St Luke's, Chelsea, and her friend Christabel Aberconway had offered to lend her London house for the reception. Invitations were sent, wedding presents began arriving. But cruelly Viola was suddenly taken very ill. Within three weeks she was dead from lung cancer, aged fifty-four. In the end there was no Blessing but a routinely quiet marriage at Caxton Hall in November that year attended by rather more of Virginia's family – Great-aunt Aggie Beerbohm, brother David Parsons, Aunt Felicity Cory-Wright, Aunt Iris, Curtis Moffat and Ivan – than of David's – his sister-in-law, and Virginia's friend from the Slade, Elizabeth Glenconner only. There was one other witness at this civil wedding and, as always, keeping himself very discreetly in the background. This was Courtney Merrill who had taken over the day-to-day responsibilities of running the Gargoyle, not least of which was trying with firmness and tact to persuade errant members to pay the heavy bills they had run up there. Merrill was to stay with the Club to the end, proving himself a constant and loyal support to David while getting well-deserved affection and respect from members and staff alike.

On 24 November, David and Virginia sailed on the French ship *Champlon* to New York; on down to Nassau, then Cuba and finally

Mexico. They were intending to go on into South America, but after they had been away five weeks a telegram arrived from Christopher Glenconner urging David's swift return. David had left his erstwhile best man, Tony Mackeson, in overall charge of the Club – colonel, as it were, to Merrill's regimental quartermaster-sergeant. According to Christopher's telegram, Mackeson was making the most terrible hash of things at the Club and only David could do something about it. Mackeson had an unsettled disposition not helped, some thought, by having been exposed early-on by David to Matt Pritchard's philosophic sessions, a diet Mackeson found difficult to digest. Pam Mayor remembers often seeing him around this time at parties just leaning his head against a wall. Not long after David's return with Virginia, Mackeson walked into the revolving propeller of a small aircraft, spewing his brains over the flying field where it was warming up for take-off.

*

Hermione felt that she had weathered her divorce and David's subsequent marriage pretty well. Happily the theatre kept her busy. It was while playing in Beverley Nichols' *Floodlight* at the old Saville Theatre that the formidable drama critic Herbert Farjeon, longtime her professional admirer, came round to see her. There was no one in the field of revue and comedy to touch her, he said, and it was his intention to write a revue in which his wit would show her unique style of mocking bravura to best advantage. Hermione said that she had been hoping to be offered another dramatic role. Ever a sucker for flattery, it did not take long for Hermione to be won round by Farjeon. *Nine Sharp* opened at the Little Theatre in January 1938 and ran for two and a half years. Hermione became what one critic described as 'the undisputed queen of revue on the London stage'. But it was not, as it is phrased, all plain sailing.

Just before *Nine Sharp* opened the leading man had to leave the show quite suddenly. Bertie Farjeon had heard that the Australian dancer Cyril Ritchard was available. But would he be sophisticated enough for London audiences? Hermione said that Australians pick things up very quickly. He was indeed a beautiful dancer but he had something more – he had glamour. Take him, she said. Their partnership turned out to be a great success and together they created a dance which, in its way, has become a classic – a send-up of *Swan Lake*. The classical dancer and choreographer Frederick Ashton started them off with the right positions for the dance, dead-pan, dead serious. Gradually things go, with muted pain at first, from bad to worse. The sketch ends with Madame Allover (Hermione) belting Cyril over the head with the bouquet of flowers she has just been handed. As Hermione said, 'It was a number made to be stolen.' She once saw a man in the front row getting it all down in a note-book, every gesture, every little touch. The last time she saw Madame Allover was on American television in the 1970s when Sid Caesar and an American comedienne tried it.

But it was Hermione's delivery of Farjeon's witty one-liners which brought the house down night after night in the aptly named Little Theatre. One favourite scene was with Hermione, as the not-so-young wife of a famous elderly painter (a character based upon the beautiful Mrs Cowan Dobson), receiving one of her husband's sycophantic young admirers. Sickening of his gushing flattery, she turns away and walks slowly to the studio window. She gazes out dreamily. 'On a clear day,' she says in measured tones, 'on a clear day you can see half way to Chiswick cemetery.' Later in the scene, when being admonished by the great artist for taking an unseemly interest in what he terms 'a mere boy', she turns to him with her own solemn reproach. 'There's nothing *mere* about boys,' she says.

But the really dirty weather did not hit Hermione until *Nine Sharp* had been running almost a year and she herself was riding high on a surf of social success. *Nine Sharp* was, as she said, 'the hottest show in town'. She was not only extremely successful in her art but she was also greatly liked and admired by fellow professionals. And then it happened. She was in her dressing-room making up for a matinee performance. The call-boy had tapped on her door giving her the half-hour call.

'I looked in the mirror and suddenly froze. What had I done? The face looking back at me wasn't mine. A clown, someone whose face was daubed with streaks of greasepaint leered back. I clutched the arms of my chair and shrank back. What had happened? Had *I* done that? A knock came at the door and Bertie Farjeon came in. I saw his face staring above mine in the lighted mirror. I saw his jaw drop, his look of bewilderment. "Bertie?" My voice started to tremble. "Something's ... wrong." It was so difficult to do or say anything, as if I was swimming in an enormous sea and making no headway.' Hermione passed out. When she came to, the good Freddy was tucking her into the back of his Bentley. 'I can't bear it. I can't bear it', she kept whispering. The despair she had hidden over her break-up with David had at last broken her.

The newspapers made much of it. 'Revue star's mysterious illness!' they announced. 'Can the show survive without her?' they wanted to know. Farjeon had been obliged to engage five understudies to take over Hermione's numbers in the revue. But the takings at the box-office plummeted and the management insisted that another star be found to replace Hermione – Ivy St Helier. For six dreary weeks Hermione could neither think, write nor read, nor take any decision for herself. Quite untypically, she did not even want to talk. But she had a robust constitution and resilient nature. Eventually she felt strong enough to go back to *Nine Sharp*. The reception she received greatly reassured her; she knew she would get better and be able to cope with life again. And so it proved.

Hermione's performance in *Nine Sharp* won for her what must be the most obscure drama award in the history of the theatre. Hannen Swaffer, that great and imposing drama critic, decided that he would like to institute his own award to be presented to the actor or actress who had given the finest performance during the course of the year. It was, for whatever arcane reason, to be called The Golden Biscuit Award. Hermione won it first time round. By the third year of its institution, Swaffer had died and nobody ever took that particular biscuit again.

14

As the decade drew nearer to its close, the fear and the fury of war cast long shadows over Europe. People in Britain talked about 'the flap', the 'war flap' and warned each other not to get 'into a flap'. Pessimism was deplored. In the view of the Home Secretary, Sir Samuel Hoare, Europe (comprising three dictators, one of them Communist) was 'on the edge of a golden age'. Pessimism was 'muck' that was spread by 'panic-mongers' to 'jitter-bugs'.

Notwithstanding these tensions, the success of the revue at the Little Theatre continued unabated. It had become something like a club and people would drop in to see it two or three times a week. There had already been two versions of the revue and now a third was planned. Each time new material was added, new people came in, new ideas surfaced. The latest version would introduce a young girl, engagingly shy, whom Hermione and Farjeon had seen in a friend's house doing an hilariously funny turn for charity. They learnt that she wrote all her own material but had never even dreamt of doing it on the professional stage. Herbert and Hermione persuaded her to join them at the Little. Fearful and trembling she stood alone upon the stage and did a little sketch about naughty children. The audience howled with laughter and the shy young girl was never thereafter to look back from this instant success. Her name was Joyce Grenfell.

Hermione's healthy salary was boosted by her percentage of the box-office returns. However much money she might make, Hermione was still pathologically incontinent when it came to the matter of its retention. So when the question arose, as it already had, of Pauline coming to live with her in London (at least for the holidays) she found that she had not put anything aside with which to enlarge upon the mews house in Bayswater. Gwen was obliged to move into 'digs' and surrender her small room to Pauline. It was tacitly agreed that, in spite of Hermione's legal custody, Little David – at least for the moment – should continue to stay on down at Teffont. Word now came from Teffont asking Hermione if she would mind not coming to the Gargoyle any longer as it upset Virginia to see her there. Hermione's natural ebullience had returned on the high tide of her great London success and her need to 'let off steam' after the show frequently took her and her host of friends to the Club. She also felt she had quite recovered from the hurt of divorce, so when David telephoned out of the blue with this request, she was stunned into immediate acceptance. 'Of course', she said and hung up. And for the next few months she avoided going there. Then a message came from the Gargoyle asking her kindly to ignore Mr Tennant's demands; she and her friends were sorely missed. The Gargoyle needed her. Hermione reminded herself that she had been there at the Club's inception, at its birth, and had done much over the years to nurture its growth. She decided to risk David's wrath and Virginia's embarrassment.

This was for Pauline a particularly bleak and depressing time, spending the holidays in very cramped circumstances and in marked contrast to the freedom and relative grandeur of Teffont – a place to her always of magic and mystery. Nobody had explained that the reason for her banishment from that Eden was because her parents had been divorced. She only found this out quite some time later through climbing up on a chair in order to examine some newspapers Hermione had tucked away on top of a cupboard. 'Wedding bells to ring again for Hermione', splashed the headlines. They had not on that occasion, so Pauline felt more in the dark than ever. 'I never knew who was going to meet me from school. Some stranger with a car and an explanation as to why Mummy couldn't be there would just appear and perhaps take me out to tea. And then when he took me home I thought that perhaps I might be rather in the *way*.' What she most enjoyed in the holidays was going to the dogs on Saturday; to the grey-hound racing at the White City, with Gwen and her boy-friend. A cast back in memory to going out riding with David and his two greyhounds at Teffont, or coursing them over the downs. And what she looked forward to now was the promise Hermione had made her – the prospect of being sent to drama school.

*

In 1938, London's Bohemia lost one of its most versatile and engaging characters to his native land, the United States. In the twenties Curtis Moffat had turned the ground floor of his house in Fitzroy Square into a treasure trove of exotica, an Aladdin's cave filled with oriental carpets, African sculpture, T'ang dynasty horses, Russian and Greek icons, Lalique glass, jewellery from Mexico, the Andes, India, from Africa again – Nancy Cunard furnished herself there with the massive ebony and ivory bracelets that became so recognizable on her thin white arms – Eskimo carvings, buffalo-skin paintings and Indian artefacts from North America. Virginia, who had grown up in her parents' house on the opposite side of the square, remembers how they all loved to explore within Curtis's all too secret world. 'We never saw anybody actually *buy* anything' [apart, presumably, from Nancy] 'which was what, of course, was supposed to happen.' This ground-floor endeavour of Curtis had been financed by an indulgent American lady who now saw from afar the war clouds gathering over Europe and felt it expedient to withdraw her funds from the threatened area. Hence the recall of Curtis, much regretted by many.

Curtis, with whom he had had his only enjoyable experience of eating hashish (in jam), was also much liked by Augustus John, although with certain reservations. He was 'it must be confessed a bit of a sybarite. His quarters at 4 Fitzroy Square bore witness less to his reverence for tradition than to his taste for the up-to-date. He would be found reclining at ease, with some rare and exquisitely-bound volume open at his side, placed there as much to satisfy his sense of aesthetic propriety as for perusal. His fine eyes, which always subjugated me by their warm glow, seemed to smoulder with unaccountable amusement. Could it be his consciousness of the unknown, the unimaginable source of all this luxury, which so tickled him in secret? Rather than see this expression of happy irony clouded for a moment by financial care, I would have turned out all my pockets, and sometimes did; and I would be rewarded by the return of that beaming regard, in which love seemed to be mixed with some hint of derision, like the smile of a woman.'

One happy result of the retreat of Curtis from London was that his son, Ivan, inherited the Fitzroy Square house, or rather the use of the spacious top floor where, in one of the three bedrooms, 'Chile' Guevara had painted his mother Iris. As John remarked, Curtis in the twenties had imposed throughout these living quarters an art déco style which was now rapidly falling into a state of disrepair. And that, as Michael Law, a close friend of Ivan's and a frequent visitor to the flat, observed is about the worst thing that can happen to art déco. But there were a quantity of good pictures, a fine library with a number of first editions and the last remains of a superb cellar. Michael Law also particularly remembers an extraordinary collection of matching travelling bottles and phials of medications and arrays of syringes all sitting comfortably in specially and beautifully made leather containers – an hypochondriac's vade-mecum – each one designed to meet any contingency of illness or accident in any part of the world: frost bite, snake bite, sun stroke, wounds, burns, the worms and all manner of internal sickness – it was all there, waiting for misfortune to strike.

The flat and the cellar were to become a frequent source of comfort to the friends-for-life Ivan was now making – such as Dylan Thomas and Michael Law – through his apprenticeship in the world of documentary film making. One who did not belong to this rather exclusive world (Auden had been recruited in 1936 to write the verse commentary for the classic GPO film, scored by Benjamin Britten, *Night Mail*) but who was to become one of Ivan's closest friends was Philip Toynbee. Toynbee had formidable intellectual provenance his father was the pre-eminent historian, Arnold Toynbee; his grandfather on his mother's side, the remarkable Hellenist, Professor Gilbert Murray became, while relatively young, something of a British institution on acount of his trusty brain. Philip was also connected to one of the great landed families of England, the Howards of Castle Howard, where he had spent much of his childhood.

In 1934 Philip had run away from Rugby at the age of seventeen with the express purpose of joining up with Esmond Romilly, known to him then only by name, and at fifteen himself a fugitive from Wellington. This farouche schoolboy rebel had established his HQ at the Parton Press in Bloomsbury where he published *Out of Bounds*, a magazine whose startling purpose was to promote and foment radical revolution in England's public schools. Romilly's exploits had provoked much newspaper indignation: 'Winston Churchill's Red Nephew Runs Away From School', 'Red Menace in Public Schools', and so on. Ivan had contributed to *Out of Bounds* while still a schoolboy at Dartington, which was how he and Philip, two years his senior, first became aware of each other.

Philip was duly run to ground in Parton Street, expelled from Rugby and consented, under family pressure, to spend six months in a monastery cramming for an Oxford scholarship. While at Christ Church, and still very much under the influence of Romilly, Philip joined the Communist Party. He made a considerable impact, becoming the first (and quite possibly the last) Communist to be elected President of the Oxford Union.

Jessica Mitford (then Romilly's wife) has justly observed, 'Ivan occupied a rather special place in the spectrum of Philip's friends, for he alone spanned the gap between left wing politics and the deb dance scene.' Both had been involved in student politics whose principal focus had been on Spain: Philip as President of the Oxford Union, Ivan as a leading member of the Student Union at the London School of Economics. Ivan rightly deduced that there could be no better testing ground for Philip and himself to discover 'whether we're up to any good or not' than the Gargoyle Club. So he introduced Philip to this established arena of which he became an instant devotee. Ivan also arranged to introduce Philip to David and Virginia Tennant by taking him to stay at Teffont. On their arrival, Philip did not make a very good first impression on David's butler. His wild and battered appearance (Robert Kee observed of him at this time that: 'He looked like an Old Testament prophet with cirrhosis of the liver') was not helped by his clothes which always looked as if they had been slept in, as was often the case. The second impression was somewhat worse. As Ivan tells it:

> Immediately Philip, who had never met David before, darted into the dining-room and looked for a drink; he had a very keen eye for hidden bottles and decanters. He found brandy, *crème de menthe* and things, and put several of these down, and by the time we actually sat down to dinner, he was awfully drunk. And suddenly I saw to my horror across this lovely polished table – silver candlesticks and so on – a great, huge sea of dark red wine-vomit spreading. So I said 'For God's sake, Philip. . . .' and started trying to mop it up with a napkin.
>
> But David saw it, from the head of the table. He said, rather reasonably in the circumstances, 'Now look here, Philip, I don't think you can really quite do that,' and Philip winked at him and said, 'Let's be frank – I *have* done it.'

By contrast, Ivan's next catalytic act in the life of Philip was beautifully judged. Ever a seeker after goodness and self-improvement (and Communism was also a path), Philip had been casting about energetically in search of love that would assume the form of wife. 'How he loved – longed for love – suffered for love!' writes Jessica Mitford. He was recklessly promiscuous but, contrarily, longed for the stability of marriage. Virginia's brother David Parsons used to have a nickname for Philip: Plunger Abrahams. '"Abrahams"', explains Ivan, 'because of his fierce Biblical look and "Plunger" because he would plunge to the floor, plunge into this and that – parties, beds, causes. His passes at girls were in the nature of plunges.' The attentive Ivan, sensible of Philip's need to put an end to all that emotional skirmishing, was confident that his close friend Anne Powell, younger sister to Elizabeth Glenconner, was the very person to fit this bill. She herself was somewhat in rebellion: in her case against her conservative father, a one-time Colonel in the Brigade of Guards and a former Tory MP. Philip's *dégringolade*, his general appearance of anarchy would, Ivan felt, enchant her. Accordingly, he asked them both to tea with the warning that each was about to meet the person they would marry. They met, they got on famously, and within a few weeks they were engaged. In a letter to Esmond and Jesecca, then part-owners of a bar in Miami, Philip reported the Colonel's reaction when asked for his daughter's hand. 'It's wather embawassing, ye know,' he said. 'I've only met you four times and you were dwunk thwee of them.' Nevertheless, the wedding of Philip and Anne was celebrated at the Paddington register office shortly after the outbreak of war.

Ivan had done much to relieve the fading interior of the flat in Fitzroy Square by installing Natalie Newhouse in his bedchamber. Natalie was very much a child of the thirties – and late thirties at that. A street-wise gamine, small, pert, pretty with rich mouse hair, extremely seductive and meant to be, she strayed into the Cavendish when very young and felt instantly at home. Rosa liked her independent spirit and quick provocative mind. She might also have seen in her a likely recruit for the comfiture of officers in the event of a second world war. Ivan assumed territorial rights over this youthful gadfly. He introduced her into the Gargoyle where, as he said, she was to become 'the china-blue-eyed nemesis of many a member's inflated ego. Sharp-tongued and smiling, she would tuck the smile beneath her peekaboo hair style and the mouth would emerge angry, a sling-shot for acid words flung defiantly at the face of the offender of her curiously strong code – a code, in its special way both moral and rebellious. If the words thus flung did not suffice their object, then a splash of drink in the face might follow. Or, just as likely, laughter – mocking or forgiving. Generous and unrelenting with her favours, gregarious or seated alone with a scowl, Natalie – small in white shirt and green skirt – knew, it seemed by instinct, all that a far longer experience of life might have untaught her.'

Ivan and Natalie were introduced one evening in the Gargoyle by Cyril Connolly to the half-sister of Angela Culme-Seymour, Angela being now married to his Oxford friend, Patrick Balfour (Lord Kinross) and previously to the painter John Spencer Churchill, yet another of Winston's cousins. The half-sister was Janetta Woolley, a pale lovely Pre-Raphaelite seventeen-year-old. In spite of her manifest charms, Janetta had lived some of her young life in the shadow (one cast frequently across the Gargoyle ballroom) of Angela and her full brother Mark. The 'Cocteauesque' preoccupation of Mark and Angela with each other made them appear tantalizingly aloof to the curious onlooker. Indeed, it pleased some of their joint and several admirers to imagine that their principal romantic absorption was with one another, and this in spite of subsequent multiple marriages on both sides which in no way appeared to affect other amorous entanglements.

With Janetta in the Gargoyle that evening was Humphrey Slater. Slater had been an heroic and commanding figure on the Republican side in the Civil War, rising to be Chief of Operations in the International Brigades. As with the majority of those serving in these Brigades, Slater was a Communist. One reason for this was that for those with sufficiently strong idealistic motivation to want to fight on the Republican side – and Slater had – the most effective way to get into Spain through the closed frontiers was by joining the Party. They knew the secret routes. Even so, Slater had been imprisoned for some time by the French in Perpignan. Janetta and Humphrey had met very recently in Cassis, the little French fishing village between Marseille and Toulon where she was living with her mother in a small house, disdainful of convention, barefoot, wearing little else but shorts and singlet, a fierce expression and sometimes wielding a tall staff. Humphrey was there recuperating from typhoid contracted in Spain. They fell in love, and when the need to make some money brought Humphrey back to England, Janetta came too. Slater was now thirty-seven. He had been married to a rich wife. Before that he had graduated from the Slade and was an unsuccessful abstract artist. So he then turned to journalism for which he was well suited.

He was rescued from the sheen of journalistic virtuosity by his passionate commitment in Spain. But the Spanish experience had exhausted him, and Slater had yet to publish a novel and express some of the same bitter disenchantment that had already turned fellow Spanish war veterans George Orwell and Arthur Koestler into implacable enemies of Communism. Certainly, Slater did not relish the prospect of another war. 'I can't do it again. I've had my war,' he said that evening. One positive result of this meeting was the spontaneous friendship that developed between Janetta and Natalie. Instant recognition between gamine and rebel.

*

Life at Teffont, since Hermione's departure and in the enforced absence of Pauline, had become a great deal more ordered. There was no longer a weekly 'Comus rout' to contend with, instigator of black depressions. But 'the fume of empty bottles', as Philip joyfully experienced, was not entirely absent, and the disdainfully described 'carrion guests' were now restricted to the chosen and well-tried: the Mounts, Dick, as always, Georges Duthuit, the Mayors, David Parsons, also the painter

‘Spotty John’ Strachey (so called because of his pitted visage and also to distinguish from his namesake and cousin, John ‘Struggle for Power’ Strachey) with whom David liked to engage in rustic endeavours. Derek Jackson was also a frequent visitor. Virginia remembers one weekend when the congregation of the little church in the grounds of Teffont (on this occasion rather better attended than usual on account of the impending national crisis) was startled to see Jackson’s demon face suddenly appear at a window near the altar. ‘Disgusting God!’ he barked through it very loudly. (Jackson did give God a bit of a whirl sometime later when he thought he might become a Catholic in order to please yet another putative wife, and took instruction to that end. But it was no go. ‘I couldn’t swallow the story’, he explained.)

That July of 1939, David and Virginia, in spite of a general sense of foreboding, drove down to spend the summer in Cassis, so beloved of the discerning British. The sense of foreboding was made particularly acute by the German ‘lebensraum’ attitude to the Free City of Danzig (now Gdansk). This gave Poland its sole access to the Baltic Sea via the Polish Corridor established at the Treaty of Versailles.

In August, David, at thirty-seven outside the immediate conscription age bracket, felt it imperative that he return to England at once, leaving Virginia to follow. The Territorials, which David had joined when living at Teffont, were in any case being mustered so this was rather more than just a moral obligation.

A European war was made virtually inevitable by the signing, on 23 August, of a Non-Aggression Pact between Germany and the Soviet Union. The Pact also laid the seed of the facile view, which seems to persist even now in some quarters, that Communism and Fascism are two sides of the same coin. A view Philip was always very insistent about refuting. He refers to it in an *Observer* review written in 1976: ‘… Fascism and Communism were two very different phenomena: and that to equate them … is to take a crude and seriously misleading view of pre-war politics. Stalinism may well have been almost as horrible as National Socialism; the motives which led young men and women in England to become Fascists and Communists respectively were very different indeed.’ Philip, in marked contrast to some of his contemporaries – particularly those coming down the Apostle steps from Cambridge – was typically very open about his communist allegiance, both at the time and later.

*

By the time Virginia had returned to England at the end of August, David was already enrolled as a gunner in a light anti-aircraft battery stationed near Chesil Beach in Dorset. This straight and long-reaching stretch of the coast was one of the most inviting areas of the kingdom to the sea-borne invader. On it David now wielded a spade with the best of them, filling bags with its pebbly sand. Just before dawn on 1 September, six armoured divisions supported by eight motorized divisions of the Wehrmacht swept into Poland in the wake of relentless aerial bombardments. They were met heroically and futilely by the Polish cavalry. A new word had entered the English language: *blitzkrieg* (lightning war) and trench warfare thenceforth became a thing of the past. The next day, a Saturday, Virginia squeezed into a train crowded with evacuees to go down and stay the week-end with David in a lodging house near his camp. At noon on Sunday, 3 September, Chamberlain made this announcement to the House of Commons: 'This country is now at war with Germany. We are ready.' David and Virginia heard this broadcast on the one o'clock news. It was a solemn moment. But also one of immense relief for the country as a whole. The shilly-shallying was over.

The BBC was very restrained. Apart from regular news broadcasts throughout the day, there would be a sober diet of gramophone records relieved by a sensible talk by a doctor on first aid, and then the King's broadcast to the Commonwealth later in the evening. At five p.m. came the announcement from Paris of the French declaration of war. There followed a joint Anglo-French statement to the effect that the two governments would avoid the bombing of civilians and did not intend to use poison gas or germ warfare. It asked the Germans please to say that, too. They did not.

The following day one exceedingly combative figure was re-harnessed: 'Winnie's back' flashed the excited signal to the Fleet. Churchill was back in the Cabinet – now the 'war cabinet' – as First Lord of the Admiralty, a post he had held twenty-five years before at the outbreak of the First World War.

15

Despite the initial euphoria, fear was very present in the first few weeks of the war, particularly among the civilian population. By far the greatest fear, however, was not of the sea-borne invader, but of the nightmare descent of the storm-trooper from the skies. The issue of aged rifles to reinforce the pitch-forks, cutlasses and armbands of the Local Defence Volunteers (to be re-named, at Churchill's suggestion, the Home Guard) was not entirely reassuring. The design of the German military uniform, on the other hand, particularly in the shape of steel helmet and the automaton jack-boot, was psychologically very intimidating. It had an aura of invincibility. Something that Tommy's First World War tin-hat, normally worn at a jaunty angle shading the fag at mouth's edge, and the even older puttees wound round the leg from ankle to knee, definitely lacked. There was also the fear of the devastation that might be expected to fall on the big cities from aerial bombing, with the additional possibility of deadly gas attacks. Harrowing photographs such as crocodiles of five-year-old children parading in their gas-masks began to appear in the press.

These fears persuaded David that Virginia should not be allowed to return to London. Teffont, only rented in any case, had now been requisitioned by the army, the staff laid off, the cars put in moth-balls, furniture and belongings locked away. The solution was for her to go and stay with Gwyneth Johnstone's mother in Norfolk and a car (petrol rationing had not yet been introduced) was hired to take her there.

David had adapted remarkably well to being a ranker in the citizen's army. He had the advantage of being bigger, stronger, fitter and better-fed than the average conscript or volunteer. He was also older than most and time spent with the Territorials had given a military edge to his natural fine bearing. But more than anything it was his range of bawdy songs accompanied on his guitar that was to ensure his popularity. He became 'Dave' again to his mates, as with his fellow workers at the Leyland factory. In November he wrote to Virginia that he had been put up for a commission by his Colonel and was being sent to an Officers' Training Centre. There his abilities found due recognition and, on being commissioned, he was sent to Shrivenham in Berkshire as an anti-aircraft gunnery instructor. Dick Wyndham, meantime, had joined a Searchlight Unit. Greatly relieved, Virginia was now able to join David in Shrivenham where they took a room in the town. This was, she remembers, a particularly happy time in their lives. Then, at the beginning of April, David was granted ten days leave. The 'phoney war', as it was then called, showed no signs of becoming vital. Indeed, Chamberlain confidently informed Parliament that Hitler 'had missed the bus'.

It was a mark of the relaxed attitude to the war that David proposed that they should go over to Paris by train and then on down to Avignon in the south. There they would buy bicycles and tour through Provence down to the coast at Cassis and thence to Toulon. Philip and Anne Toynbee were also intending to spend two months in the South of France before he would be called up in June. There still remained a fair number of British residents in that part with no immediate intention of budging, notably P. G. Wodehouse. David and Virginia arrived in Avignon on her birthday, 9 April. They bought two spanking brand new *vélos* and set off in high spirits without bothering to read the papers. Had they done so they would have seen that the phoney war had taken a dramatic U-turn. The previous night Hitler had landed in Norway taking the Allies totally by surprise. Their hastily assembled expeditionary force turned into a fiasco. The crack French Chasseurs Alpins landed at Namsos without their skis; at Narvik, the British 203rd Field Battery landed without their guns; the Brigade despatched from England had one truck and three motorcycles, but were mapless; many of the officers, however, brought their fishing rods. All this has served to provoke the historian Alistair Horne's comment that 'of all the events of 1939–45, no single episode prompts the question "How did we win the second world war?" more forcefully than the largely forgotten Norway campaign of Spring 1940.'

Meanwhile, David and Virginia, in happy innocence of all this, were pedalling through the beauty of a Provençal springtime, the pink of the almond blossoms heightened by the white sulphur wash on their tree trunks, the wild narcissi thick on the ground. 'An idyllic tour,' as Virginia said. 'An amazing stolen moment before the onslaught of war.' On *vélos* they made better progress than the walking tours that David used to take with Dick and AJ – thirty miles a day rather than their twenty-two, but no wine until the day's ration of miles had been achieved. When they reached the great naval base of Toulon, they found the pride of the French fleet riding confidently at anchor, bunting on the rigging, the town's bistros and bordellos bursting with matelots. Within two months France would be defeated and much of this fleet would have been sunk by the British in the Algerian port of Mers-el-Kebir to prevent it falling (or sailing under its own steam) into enemy hands. What remained would later be scuttled when German tanks rolled into Toulon itself. Not long after David's return to military duties Hitler put his best panzer foot forward and, going at much the same speed as David and Virginia on bikes, occupied the Low Countries. Events across the Channel were moving at the speed of *blitzkrieg*. The BEF were caught in a desperate rearguard action on the French coast around Dunkirk. Ten days later the Germans were marching up the Champs Elysées in triumph – as they had done in 1871.

*

The Little Revue had finally closed early in 1940 and Hermione was now appearing in a production of Wycherley's *The Country Wife*. Her nightly trip to the West End was made from a charming eighteenth-century house in Kew rented to her by Mark Ogilvie Grant while absent soldiering. Mark had been re-introduced to Hermione by Johnny Bowes-Lyon, a wild and hard drinking young man considered by his cousin Queen Elizabeth, who was very fond of him, to be something of a problem. And so did he become to Hermione when he rented her mews house on her move to Kew. There had been an immediate attraction between Hermione and Johnny and, at the beginning of their love affair, she had seen his heavy drinking as no more than a wartime phenomenon, a natural thirst among the young for the pleasures of life before the threat of early death. But the reckless way Johnny indulged in drink 'like a madman without care or thought of what it could do to him', and his bombardment by telephone throughout the night pleading for her presence, to which, when she responded, it was only to find him slumped insensible on the floor, seemed to her a very premature but emphatic death-wish. In the event, events themselves anticipated his self-destruction. The young subaltern was killed in an ambush while serving with his regiment in France. Hermione mourned him sincerely – she had hesitantly agreed to Johnny's incessant demands that they should be married on his first leave from France and David had approved the idea from a distance. Nonetheless, she could not help experiencing a certain sense of release.

*

With the German conquest in the West, Goering was able to position the Luftwaffe on airfields well spread out but within easy striking distance of Britain. Moreover, the bombers could be given fighter protection over critical areas. London and the civil population found themselves now placed in the front line. Starting in the early evening of 7 September, wave after wave of German bombers with fighter escort flew up the Thames at two hourly intervals unloading their bombs on the docks, on the East End and on the City. Luftwaffe pilots returning to their bases in the Low Countries and Northern France, spoke of London being 'an ocean of flames'. The overture to the Blitz had started with a great bang.

David had earlier insisted that Pauline be removed from her boarding school which he rightly anticipated might lie in the path of the German bombers. Apart from Virginia, now pregnant with their first child, and his military duties, which pleased him since they involved instruction in a field of his competence, David's main concern was with the Gargoyle. National exigencies had more than decimated the attendance of the Club's regular members. (These exigencies included the forced detention in prison of Oswald Mosley under Regulation 18B, that is, without recourse to trial.) The main problem about the Gargoyle for David was that he could only be there very infrequently although his presence was all the more required since many of the trained staff were being called up. As Mark Culme-Seymour has pointed out: 'The centre of the focus at the Gargoyle would always be David. I remember very well the place was not the same if he wasn't around. I suppose he had a very strong personality, certainly a very changeable one: charming, generous, hospitable one evening; mean and rude another. It didn't really matter which mood he was in towards oneself, the place lacked some sort of sparkle if he wasn't there.' True enough. But for all that, there were two of Mark's friends, and close friends of each other since Oxford days, who did not find David's enforced absence from the Club too onerous a burden to bear. Peter Quennell and Cyril Connolly both knew David rather well, but neither altogether liked him. Pauline now attributes this to envy. 'David was what they would both have liked to have been – keeping their own brains, of course. They were envious of the looks, of the patrician style, and they were envious of the money. They all – the younger intellectuals – put David down if they could. Cyril and David always quarrelled. Cyril was so very bitchy to David and this hurt him although he would never show it. That was why they couldn't get on.'

David had by and large a kind, generous and an instinctive nature. But there was in him a shyness, in spite of or perhaps because of an intense inner reserve; and with it the appearance (and it could be very ill-concealed) of arrogance and disdain. This aroused in some an hostility he did not fully deserve. He certainly managed to get up Peter Quennell's nose – as did his brother Stephen in a rather different manner. In the early days of the war Quennell was working in one of the ministries as a censor. 'Stephen used to write me letters. Our private mail at the Ministry was stuck up on a green board, a criss-cross thing, and my fellow censors – a relatively unsophisticated lot – were surprised and curious because the letters I received from Stephen were heavily scented. They were so heavily scented the smell came right aross the room.' David's technique was more subtle, and more unnerving. 'He had a very odd habit, I found,' Peter said, 'of beginning to pay one compliments or trying to do something rather agreeable and then gradually changing his tune. I mean, you would meet him in the club and he would say "Come and sit at my table", or, "I've been longing to see you, Peter. After all you are an intelligent – *quite* an intelligent man. True, you have strains of stupidity like that article you recently published. It was pretty, but really it was one of the silliest articles I've ever read in my life. I mean, you mean well. What you lack in talent you make up in good nature and a sort of certain degree of subservience, perhaps. But, er..." And in the end, you know, the bouquet... he would present one with this great bouquet and then gradually take a flower back and then another. And then, similarly, the sort of wine he ordered.... "Peter, I'm going to order you some claret, I know you like claret... waiter, bring us a bottle of that Chateau-Lafite... but, on second thoughts, Dick tells me you've got absolutely no taste... waiter, I think we'll make that a bottle of *vin ordinaire* for Mr Quenel", carelessly mispronouncing my name. Well, David wanted to be a patron and he saw himself in one role as a gentleman entertaining people who were *not* always exactly... er, you know... and who could do with a bit of patronage, who were also rather hard-up and very glad to drink his wine. It was that, I think, really.'

Connolly had practical as well as social reasons for making war-time use of the Gargoyle. Since the beginning, he had not liked to do what fellow scribblers did, go to the Gargoyle for an agreeable cheap lunch. He liked to go with the brilliant butterflies at night. And all of a sudden he had become a brilliant butterfly himself who could cast disdainful glances at some of the ex-butterflies turning into old moths. Cyril had gone a long way to fulfil his early promise through explaining so eloquently and persuasively, in *Enemies of Promise*, published in 1938, why he had not done so. This book followed his first and only completed novel, *The Rock Pool* (1935), something of a damp squib. Much-despised literary reviewing ('Reviewing is a whole time job with a half time salary... where all triumphs are ephemeral and only the drudgery is permanent and where no future is secure except the certainty of turning into a hack') and the much respected money of his now absent wife had kept Cyril afloat between post-Oxford, and the war's outbreak. Then, a few weeks after the latter event, Cyril found an opportunity, at a party given by the writer Elizabeth Bowen, of raising once more an idea he had been nurturing for some time. This was the launching of a literary review, his literary review. The Maecenas he had been hunting for this project was the epicene Peter Watson. Elegant, gentle and shy, Watson had been living the life of an *haut pédéraste* in an eighteenth-century house on the Left Bank in Paris as discreetly as six servants and a remarkable collection of modern paintings would allow. This situation was made possible by his being one of the beneficiaries of a fortune made by his father in the First World War through the manufacture of margarine. Watson had resisted Cyril's literary overtures in Paris, but with conditions now so changed impelling a prudent retreat from his beloved Paris, Cyril moved confidently in for the kill at the Bowen soirée. In spite of certain reservations, Peter agreed to Cyril's proposal. But he made it a condition that Stephen Spender be asked to join them in a shadowy editorial capacity. Cyril felt no objection. Or if he did he was wise enough to be like dad and keep mum. He and Stephen knew each other and were friendly. Stephen, closely-linked with fellow poets Auden and Isherwood, had acquired a certain fame as a leading figure in the world of left-wing writers and intellectuals (in Orwell parlance, 'Parlour Bolsheviks'). He would be an asset, Cyril considered.

The magazine was to be a monthly review of literature and art. Art was to be Watson's primary concern, although on all major editorial matters he had decided to defer to Cyril as supremo. Considering the times – little magazines in 1939 were falling like autumn leaves, *Cornhill*, T. S. Eliot's *Criterion*, Julian Symons' *20th Century Verse*, *The London Mercury*, Geoffrey Grigson's *New Verse*, all lay lifeless on the ground – and considering the fact that neither Connolly, Watson nor Spender had any editorial – far less publishing – experience whatsoever, it was an amazingly bold and visionary enterprise. The magazine was to be called *Horizon* and the first issue – 2,500 copies – was offered to the public in December 1939. All copies were sold within a week, as was the second printing of 1,000. For the second issue a printing of 7,000 was ordered and that, too, was quickly absorbed by a grateful public. Had their paper allocation been greater, there is little doubt that this circulation could easily have been doubled at the outset. As it was, had it not been for Cyril's ability to knead the ear of Harold Nicolson, then Parliamentary Secretary to the Ministry of Information, the magazine might not have been granted any paper allocation at all. The successful German invasion of Norway, following immediately upon Chamberlain's 'missed the bus' speech, had cut off 80 per cent of Britain's supply of wood pulp and thereafter access to paper was a very tendentious issue throughout the war.

With the editorship of this brilliantly received magazine – one that was to be given sonorous recognition as a major contribution to the cultural life of the nation – Cyril was free once more to exercise the social skills which he had developed so successfully at Eton. Early numbers of *Horizon* were even laid out like the printed 'Lists' of Eton sports teams, the third issue featuring eleven 'players' headed by Auden, last man Graham Sutherland and with Cyril as twelfth man and non-playing captain. But Cyril did 'play' in so far as each number was introduced by his 'Comment'. The Comment – witty, provocative, idiosyncratic, arrogantly disdainful of accepted attitudes, intelligent in the extreme – gave to each eclectic issue Cyril's very personal, and sometimes petulant, bite. 'A magazine has to be eclectic to survive,' Connolly later wrote in his *Evening Colonnade*. 'It was the right moment to gather all the writers who could be preserved into the Ark.'

Recruiting contributions for the very early numbers at first proved a little difficult. An obvious person for Spender to approach, which he did, was his publisher at Faber and Faber, T. S. Eliot. He got a polite letter back but no contribution. He drew a blank also with Virginia Woolf whom he knew well. This may have been because she did not look kindly upon 'Smartyboots' Connolly. But Bertrand Russell, feeling that the young men – at thirty-seven, Cyril was the eldest of the three – deserved every encouragement, sent them an unsolicited offering. It arrived one morning when Cyril got to the mail first at Stephen's flat out of which they were operating. He read it. He did not like it. He found it too politically earnest and rejected it apologetically. The grounds he gave for the rejection were that 'Spender didn't like it'. A blatantly untrue comment which he forbore from divulging to the one supposed to have made it; who, indeed, did not even know of the manuscript's existence. Spender, understandably, was puzzled and dismayed to find himself the innocent target of hard looks from Russell whenever they met thenceforth. It was quite some time before the truth came out. In the telling of the tale Spender somehow managed to make it sound slanted against him while approving of Cyril's oneupmanship.

Cyril most adeptly turned the editorship of *Horizon* into a social act in which he called the numbers. He was an intensely stimulating companion, dangerous but easily wounded, generating in his circle an excitement in which the quality of mischief was not absent. He could be wildly funny, he was a parodist *sans pareil*, a master, also, of seduction and flattery. As Anthony Powell says in his memoirs, it was 'flattery of the best sort that can seem on the surface almost a form of detraction'. Ambience was very important to Cyril. Loving Europe and the Mediterranean, and France above all, he sought in beleaguered London environments where he could hold court in a cosmopolitan atmosphere. For Cyril this meant the Eiffel Tower (now re-named the White Tower), the gallery at the Café Royal and the Gargoyle. Philip Toynbee was one of the young Gargoyle members to be published in an early number of *Horizon*. 'I am quite well in with this new monthly called *Horizon* run by Stephen and Cyril Connolly', he had written to Esmond and Jessica Romilly in April 1940. 'They're rather too fond of fancying themselves an island of culture in the middle of anarchy, but I find their hopelessness rather sympathetic.' Another, less young, was Brian Howard, whose account of his retreat from France after Dunkirk it had published. Brian had very little achievement to show for the fifteen years since his dazzling days at Oxford. But, as Harold Acton tersely observed about his erstwhile great friend '... sitting in the Gargoyle or the Café Royal he could still impose himself by his superior command of language. While others hemmed and hawed he spoke with precision.'

*

By the beginning of December 1940, the Blitz had pursued its course of devastation on London without let for almost three months. But, with Virginia nearing the end of her pregnancy, and with the endless logistical problems in running the Gargoyle – all the Italian waiters in Soho (as elsewhere) had been interned as enemy aliens – David decided to close the Club. He enlisted the support of Ivan Moffat to assist at this bleak ritual.

> Starting late on a yellowish afternoon in December, David and I performed the simple ceremony of drinking the remaining opened bottles of the bar. The decision to close after three months of the blitz had not been lightly made. But the club had gradually become as deserted at night as the streets surrounding it. Some of the

regulars had taken to leaving London before nightfall. Others – though I doubt it – may even have taken to the shelters. Taxis were few and far between during the nightly alerts, and many of the patrons lived in seemingly far-off Chelsea and Hampstead. Even Kensington – on a night of prolonged bombing – seemed a longish walk away.

By the time the day had darkened and the mournful siren wailed, we had finished the Grand Marnier, the Cointreau, the Hine's brandy and the Crème de Menthe. Fiercer cordials now faced us. David having finished off the Poîre, and I the Slivovitz, he drained what was left of the Fernet Branca, declaring there was a bottle to be found somewhere of what he called 'strongwater' – a drink, he alleged, much favoured in the eighteenth century to induce vomiting. He produced instead a pale bottle labelled 'Alcool de Montpelier'. One sip of it was enough to tell me that if it wasn't strongwater it was the next best thing. David talked of longstanding Gargoyle members, seldom seen now, but whose memory recalled pre-war summer days on the garden roof: Dick Wyndham with his short leather jacket and his warm-to-predatory smile; stout St John Hutchinson (Hutchy), flushed with port and laughter despite foot bandaged with gout; my father Curtis; we talked of Freddy Mayor, of Augustus John who, in answer to an unwelcome query in the Club as to his health, had answered gruffly, 'I *was* all right.' David told again of his mother Pamela's dream about the vast Chinese horde decamped at the Gates of Glen in Scotland, and she all alone in the castle, which ended happily with the leader of the host bowing low and saying, in David's slight lisp: 'Fear not, for all things shall be arranged wisefully', and then the Mandarin chief turning and leading the far-flung host with its horses and yellow and scarlet banners over the hills and far away forever.

By the time David had started trying to define what the Gargoyle had stood for, bombers could be heard droning dully above the clouds. 'The thing is,' said David, 'the Gargoyle hasn't really stood for anything I wanted it to stand for for a very, *very* long time – except, of course –' and the lisp crept in – 'except of course for one's own *terribly* begrudging hospitality.' He did not smile, and I could tell that the night had entered a darker phase for him. David could stop being amused at any given point of an evening. He would then often go downstairs to his flat for what he described as his 'seraphic sleep'. Sometimes he would return after an hour smiling and fresh.

At other times – dark of cheek and avoiding of eye – he would go alone up to the bar and take a frowning and lonely nightcap. On the occasions when Virginia would be in the Club, he would seek her out in these moods, but more often than not he would sit them out alone. On this particular night, and as there was a lull in the bombing, he decided upon a brisk walk up Oxford Street. It was on my way home, and I accompanied him. As we walked a little unsteadily up Dean Street, David said: 'To think that we shall never be laughing inside the Gargoyle again!' He seemed to take a momentary and grim satisfaction from the thought, because he went on: 'And it might well be the best thing for all of us. In short a blessing in so thin a disguise that even Dr Watson could see through it.' By the time we reached Oxford Street, the clouds had parted beneath a small bright moon. Oxford Street was totally deserted and still. Far away over the suburbs a single plane could be heard droning, and the tiny red specks of anti-aircraft shells could be seen in the sky. It sounded as if just one plane and one gun were involved. I remarked on this. David nodded. 'Well, good night.' He had a way of terminating an evening in that brisk manner.

But there was to be 'laughing inside the Gargoyle again!' A great deal of it and more raucous than ever before to refute David's gloomy prognostication.

16

Over at the Cavendish, Rosa was opening 'Cherrybums' of Bollinger to welcome those, previously known or not, who had returned from Dunkirk. Once more she had taken on a chirpy new lease of life now that the doors of her hotel were open again to warriors and heroes. Hermione, when the bombing was too severe or she had other reasons for not wishing to return to Kew, would often bed down for the night in one of Rosa's empty rooms. So it was that she was present at one of those thanksgiving celebrations where she was introduced by Rosa to a tall, good-looking officer in the 12th Lancers wearing the bright new ribbon of the Military Cross. '"'Ere, darling. This is Dozey. Dozey's a good boy, aren't you, Dozey. Very kind. You look after 'Mione now, Dozey." She floated away.'

'Dozey' was Captain J. H. Willis, but always known as Dozey for a reason Hermione never discovered. Nor, she claimed, even when they were married, did she ever learn what the two initials stood for. Meanwhile Dozey and Hermione ducked under each other's respective wings: she missing the dead Johnny, he suffering from the wound in the head he had been dealt at Dunkirk. Dozey was, as Rosa had said, extremely kind. He did Hermione a major service by introducing her and Little David, prep-schooled and adrift, to his aunt Mamie Eccles, owner of a large estate in Dorset. Mamie took one look at the small boy and said, 'Poor little rat. What you need is a home.' She took Little David back to her country house which became his home, and he, the son she never had.

Dozey kept proposing to Hermione – marriage understandably being more frequently and recklessly undertaken in war time – and she kept refusing. David then noticed a newspaper gossip item about the two of them. He wrote to her at once. 'Don't for heaven's sake get married unless I say so', he warned, ending up with the obscure threat: 'I'm looking through a glass darkly.' It pleased Hermione to think that David did not really want her to get married at all. But Hermione did marry Dozey without really knowing why. Perhaps she thought it might be regarded as her war effort. 'I didn't love him, I thought he was a darling, I was very fond of him, but I shouldn't have married him. In wartime one does crazy things....'

It might equally have been thought crazy to leave leafy Kew and rent a flat above the tobacconists, Salmon and Gluckstein, a well known landmark in Piccadilly, itself a target for German bombs. But Hermione did that too; her neighbours being a jolly tart and a morose cabaret artiste. Dozey, however, in spite of suffering severe headaches from his wound, was still serving with his regiment, now stationed in Suffolk. Hermione enjoyed the lively social life, the parties, all the comings and goings, a characteristic of the general reshuffling of social roles. She enjoyed it for a time. But the creaking boards could never be out of earshot for long. Rehearsals for *Rise Above It*, a new revue in which she was to star, were about to start. Back to Piccadilly. That revue – destined to be another hit with a long run – was to launch the famous partnership of the two Hermiones – the lubricous Baddeley and the astringent Gingold.

Since Shrivenham, David had twice been subjected to the vagaries of army postings and consequent separations from Virginia. He had made provision for the birth of their daughter, Georgiana, by buying a small but practical house in the village of East Knoyle not far from Teffont and Clouds. Apart from delighting in their first child, Virginia felt very frustrated and 'out of things', stuck by herself in a small Wiltshire village when many young people of her age and sex had all the excitement of enlisting in the Services. She would have liked to have done something dashing like Dick's daughter Joan, who had just joined the Waafs. The crisply uniformed Waafs (Wrens had the bonus of being issued with black silk stockings to add to their allure) were jovially referred to by the aircraftsmen as 'officer's groundsheets' or 'pilot's cockpits'. 'You can have a different boyfriend every night if you want to – it's whizzo!' was the enthusiastic greeting one new recruit received. Young Joan, even before joining the Waafs, had been enjoying her war in Chelsea. 'The bombs are lovely, I think it's all thrilling,' the seventeen-year-old Catholic virgin wrote in her diary during the Blitz. 'What a life never knowing if you're going to be bombed or seduced from one moment to the next!'

With his new family settled and the Battle of Britain apparently won in the air (after June 1941 and until the advent of the ballistic missile onslaughts, German attacks were largely in retaliation for mass bombings of German cities), David decided to bow to the entreaties of many members and re-open the Gargoyle. The month he chose, June's end, coincided with Hitler's fateful decision to break the pact with Stalin and invade Russia. Within a week German panzer divisions had captured

Minsk, over halfway to Moscow, and reached Kiev in the Ukraine. A new phase of the war had begun and a new phase in the life of the Gargoyle also.

With the war, the cross-currents of social life multiplied exceedingly and a more hybrid membership, shaken to the surface in the time of emergency, was now thrust upon the Club's owner. The London based Free French were drawn to the Gargoyle; writers, poets, intellectuals and artists in flight from Europe found a form of refuge there. People from societies where the culture of the café was all-important – Vienna, Poland, the Balkans – found in the Gargoyle a place where information and ideas could be exchanged in a way that they would be familiar with but one that was almost unknown elsewhere in this country. Feliks Topolski, Romain Gary, Arthur Koestler, Nanos Valaoritis, Karel Stepanek, George Weidenfeld were among those who were to feel, if not entirely at ease, at least on familiar territory in the Club. David was most fortunate in being able to re-engage two key figures in the well ordered running of the Gargoyle: Courtney Merrill, the manager, and Charles, the *maître d'hotel.* A new club secretary was also brought in, the comely and most efficient Miss Ransley. Charles, from the Haut-Savoie, had been with the Gargoyle five years or so and was an invaluable asset. He had great address, a powerful smoothness, a charming round red face and neat well-cut hair. His knowledge of good food and wine was comprehensive, his pursuit of perfection zealous, and when occasion warranted he could be tyrannical with his staff. It was largely due to Charles that the Club kept to its standard of producing good French-style country food so reasonably and served so well.

There was one significant change in the outward appearance of the Gargoyle on its re-opening. This was the absence of the great Matisse canvas, *The Red Studio*, from the wall of the downstairs ballroom. In one of those moments when he felt himself to be on the verge of ruin, David had allowed his other Matisse, *The Studio, Quai St Michel*, to be acquired by the predatory Douglas Cooper for a derisory sum. These sudden panicky needs to shore himself up were brought about by uneasy awareness of past reckless extravagances, exacerbated in this case by prophecies of war, and almost always resulting in some unrealistic if not wholly impractical act. Cooper turned a quick profit by selling the painting to Kenneth Clark whence it went in due course to the Phillips Museum in Washington, DC. The Gargoyle, however, was not entirely divested of Matisse. Disposed about the bar and vestibule were twelve superb lithographs, studies of a dancer. *The Red Studio* had in fact been off the ballroom wall since the start of the blitz when David had prudently had it brought down and stored in the basement of the Redfern Gallery. Perhaps as a reflection of creeping disenchantment, the disenchantment he had expressed to Ivan when they closed down the Club, perhaps because he had just got bored with the picture itself, he now told the Redfern Gallery to put it up for sale.

With the re-opening of the Gargoyle, Ivan played a seminal influence in peopling the place with 'young turks', who, for whatever reason, were ineligible to join the forces. He brought Dylan Thomas, wooed back from Wales where he had taken refuge when the bombing in London began. The wooing was done by Donald Taylor who ran Strand Films where Dylan and Ivan also worked. Strand was one of many companies, with the Ministry of Information's Crown Film Unit, that produced Government-sponsored documentaries. British Documentary, a radical movement established ten years before, had set out to awaken the British social consciousness. Now with the urgent task of converting the country to a war footing, documentary was given a unique opportunity to promote the war effort: informing and instructing and raising morale throughout the land. The dedicated film makers of documentaries, drinking at the Highlander or the York Minster, always just known as 'The French', would often find their way up or down Dean Street after closing time, drawn to the nightly follies to be witnessed at the Gargoyle: Paul Rotha, Arthur Elton, Edgar Anstey, Basil Wright and the most original and exceptional of them all, Humphrey Jennings (*Fires Were Started*, *The Silent Village* and *Diary for Timothy*) amongst them. But in the fraternity of war there were still separate tables as Utopia viewed Bohemia across the dance floor. To Ivan and Dylan the Gargoyle became an imperative; as it did to Dylan's friend Ruthven (then working on *Horizon)* and to Ruthven's friend Johnny Craxton and to Johnny's friend Lucian Freud. One day at *Horizon*, Stephen Spender, who knew Ruthven was going around a lot with Johnny and Lucian – 'a crazy experience' – according to Ruthven – said (in Ruthven's words), 'with no thought of wit, giving me a carefully considered, balanced opinion, "You know, Ruthven, that so far as Lucian's concerned, I'm afraid his grandfather lived in vain."' Spender has a slyer wit than Ruthven allows him here.

The young turks were very moderate spenders but they did bring a stimulating ingredient into the Club. An exception to the moderation nearly occurred when, on one occasion after work at Crown, Ivan and Dylan went into their favourite pub in Dean Street, The French. Ivan confided to Dylan that he had a hundred pounds in his pocket – an unheard of sum for either of them to be carrying, or even owning in those days. Dylan, said Ivan, took the news with delight and laughter. To the Gargoyle, then. In the cabin-trunk lift Ivan asked him what, in the best of all possible worlds, his favourite drink would be.

'Oh, champagne', said Dylan unhesitatingly and in his most serious voice.

'Well, then', said Ivan. Charles, standing in as barman, looked at them with no great relish.

'Two large champagne cocktails, Charles, if you please', said Dylan resonantly.

Charles cocked an eye at him.

'They'll be three pounds ten each, Mr Thomas.'

Dylan didn't even glance at Ivan, but his voice was an octave lower as he said:

'Two milds-and-bitters, Charles, if you please.'

Attendance at the Gargoyle would be augmented when the frontiers of Fitzrovia were crossed, usually after dark and after the pubs had closed. These raids were sometimes conducted by the exquisite Tambimuttu, the Sri Lankan who had edited *Poetry London*, a Forces-pocket-sized magazine, since 1939. The magnetic young Tambi took to the pub life of London bohemia, in Andrew Sinclair's phrase, 'as to the bitter born'. He preferred to conduct his business in The Wheatsheaf, The Fitzroy Tavern or The Hog in the Pound, which, if inconclusive, had then to be continued deeper into the night. Tambi had been shrewd and persuasive enough to get backing for *PL* from the well-established publishers Nicholson and Watson. They also had access to large stocks of paper. *PL*, under Tambi, was very much more than a gatherer of unconsidered trifles from the high tables of *Horizon* and *Penguin New Writing*. It published, among much else of value and interest, Henry Moore's 'Shelter Sketchbook'. Contributions to *PL* from poets and others were subject to exceptional hazards, however. Garnered from people Tambi had arranged to meet, or met haphazardly in the pubs, and stuffed by day in the pockets of clothing that covered his slim form, at night they would be placed for safety in a large Victorian chamber pot with floral design residing under his bed. Waking up one night overcome by the intake of bitter that had not yet been expressed, he sleepily used the pot for its intended purpose. Manuscripts of untold worth had then to be speedily rescued and dried. Offerings that managed to avoid some similar treatment might be aired by Tambi in the Gargoyle, reading from them in his deep, melodious voice, his long, black, prehensile fingers turning back on their double joints like flower petals as they peeled over the pages.

A rather older turk now began to make frequent and noticeable appearances at the Club. This was the volatile Guy Burgess. He would often fetch up there with Brian Howard with whom he was very thick at this time and who was now a fully fledged member of MI5. (Guy did not become a fully fledged member of the Gargoyle until 1943 when Brian, his entry key, having been sacked from MI5, was doing conscripted penance as a humble aircraftsman in Buckinghamshire.) Guy had recently rejoined the BBC, but for some time before the war he had operated as a freelance agent for the Secret Intelligence Services – expenses only, but cash. In fact, he was now operating for three masters and one mistress. The mistress, in fiscal terms only, was Mrs Charles Rothschild, the mother of his Cambridge friend Victor, the late Lord Rothschild. Guy had made such an impression on her (he had asked himself down to stay at Victor's house in the country) with his political insight and grasp of world affairs that she decided to engage him on a retainer of £100 a month to advise her on her personal investments (vast and widely spread) instead of the family banking house in the City. After the BBC and the SIS, the third and most revered master was, of course, the KGB, then known as NKVD. At the outbreak of war Guy had been briefly with the D Section (sabotage and propaganda) of MI6. Guy had been personally recruited to the KGB by Harold 'Kim' Philby while in his second year at Cambridge; Philby in turn having been induced by Anthony Blunt. All three Trinity men were also invited to join that most discriminating of secret societies, the Society of the Apostles. The fourth member of the (known) Cambridge Comintern, Donald Maclean, was never selected for that honour. He had to be content with seduction by Burgess. An adventure not to be repeated by Guy in later life: 'All that soft white flesh! It would be like going to bed with Dame Nellie Melba.' Apart from the three masters and a mistress, Guy also had three ruling passions: good talk (normally his own brilliant exposition of provocative, even outrageous, propositions), sex (young, male, 'rough trade') and drink (wine, whisky and port. To this day a particularly large beaker of port is known at his old club, the Reform, as a 'double Burgess').

Philby was the oddball of the Cambridge comintern in that he was exclusively and energetically heterosexual. There have to be temperamental as well as ideological or purely venal reasons for choosing to become a spy. A love of danger has to be one of them. This was a tremendous inducement to one of Philby's reckless, buccaneering temperament. Although preoccupation with good serious communism was an intelligible position and an honourable position to take in the thirties (at least until the Hitler–Stalin pact), being a homosexual adult of the establishment was not so generally acceptable. So if that was what you were, a covert homosexual, you had to hide it. And if the hiding of it gave you the extra charge of excitement – as in some cases it undoubtedly did – then the temptation was there to feed that excitement with something even more daring.

Not that Burgess, off duty, bothered overmuch to hide his inclinations. But for Maclean and for Blunt public exposure of sexual deviation would have been deplorable. That is why the Gargoyle, with its tolerance of any form of sexual aberration, was so attractive to Guy and Brian and their shadows. But it wasn't just sexual aberration for which there was tolerance in the Gargoyle. It extended also to a certain form – often a boisterous, public-school form – of bad behaviour. So where better a safe house for Maclean, so addicted in later years to rough and tumble bad behaviour, than the Gargoyle.

After Cambridge and until the war Kim Philby was working in journalism. He covered the Spanish civil war for *The Times* from the fascist trenches and was later decorated by Franco. Up until then he was often to be seen at the Gargoyle; his 'proper' club being the Athenaeum, as was his father's. Even before he was to become the archetypal traitor of modern times, and in spite of the distressing speech impediment, he had an extraordinary charisma and a charm to which both sexes were susceptible.

Philby was much admired at MI6 and was soon put in charge of the Iberian department. Among his sixty subordinates were Malcolm Muggeridge and Graham Greene. A firm friendship grew up between Greene and Philby – in 1942 they would lunch together in London almost every day – which even his eventual defection could not despoil.

While having some sympathy for Philby, Muggeridge was appalled by Burgess the only time he met him. This was when Muggeridge was taken to Victor Rothschild's London flat in Bentinck Street, where Guy sometimes stayed, and found there a gathering of displaced intellectuals – 'John Strachey, J. D. Bernal, Anthony Blunt, Guy Burgess, a whole revolutionary "Who's Who" ... (Burgess) gave me a feeling such as I have never had for anyone else, of being morally afflicted in some way ... A true hero of our time ... hip before hipsters, Rolling before the Stones, acid head before LSD. Etonian mudlark and sick toast of a sick society....'

It was perhaps for the reason that Guy and Brian were so often in the Gargoyle after its re-opening, and so often misbehaving drunkenly, that Philby, no slouch himself where drink was concerned, but who was carrying out his double life so effectively, deemed it politic to avoid the place. Brian, especially, could be a grave embarrassment. There was the time, before his fall from grace at MI5, when having started their evening at the Gargoyle, Guy, Brian and Gerald Hamilton (the original wicked Mr Norris of Isherwood's *Mr Norris Changes Trains*) departed in search of seamy adventure in a louche Soho basement club. While they were there the place was raided. When the police came up to their table, Brian, by this time very drunk indeed, replied to their polite request for his name and address by saying 'My name is Brian Howard, *I* live in Mayfair. No doubt *you* live in some dreary suburb.' Hamilton later remarked to Guy, who had behaved with typical assured nonchalance, that in his view this was a *most* tactless way of receiving the attentions of the civil arm.

*

David was himself suffering the bite of suburbia on his new posting to the quasi-patrician setting of Blaise Castle near Bristol, a largish early nineteenth-century seat built by the Harfords, a local banking family, and now requisitioned by the military. The suburban bite provoked him into a display of his own, and not untypical, form of bad behaviour. The unit to which he was attached was concerned with radio-location of aircraft (radar), its development having proved to be a major contributor to the stemming of the Luftwaffe tide. David's personal style was not something his fellow officers had come across before, and he increased their suspicion by the practice of ways they thought to be odd. Why, they wanted to know, did he have to take two, sometimes *three* baths a day? Was he a closet Lady Macbeth? Perhaps he was compulsively engaged in some guilty ritual? And why, when he locked himself in the bathroom, did he always leave his boots (shoes for the evening bath) outside the door? These and other matters puzzled them. Not for David the small talk with a glass of sherry before the evening meal. For this bleak ritual he tended to arrive late, tight of jaw and taciturn. He had, they noted, formed a rather close liaison with the senior mess waiter. He was happy to give the good corporal his time to instruct him in the art of decanting the wine for his personal and copious consumption from the cases he had sent up from his cellar in the Gargoyle. They did not know what to make of such lordly behaviour in a temporary army captain who had no time for his service peers.

For his part David did not even bother to try and find areas of social contact with his fellow mess mates. They were to a man what Stella Benson was pleased to call 'Upper Tooting' (Brian's 'dreary suburbia'). 'Upper Tooting' denoted for Stella a typical breeding ground for middle-class social vices: philistine attitudes, a tendency to be over-mindful of 'Ps' and 'Qs', self-satisfaction and complacency in an immoderate degree. David concurred. He was at all times happy and at ease with the 'other ranks' where he felt more natural and where spontaneous responses obtained. But now he found himself cast as one of those whom he had always tended to despise even when obliged to patronize. Worse – *they* appeared to be patronizing *him*. And doing it with barely disguised contempt, too. David seethed inwardly. The inner seethe manifested itself in a curious – even possibly unique – form. It involved the salute. As is well-known, the salute is aimed at the uniform and not at the person inside it. That at least is the theory and established practice. David reversed this by interpreting the salute as a personal issue. It was not just that he objected to being saluted *at*; what he disliked even more was having to salute *back*. He felt that acceptance of the salute involved both parties in humiliation. One dare not try to imagine what he might have suffered had he been called upon, for example, to take the salute of a whole regiment.

This matter of the salute began to weigh upon David heavily. He became so obsessed by it that it assumed the gravity of a complex, a term not much used in those days. Something had to give. On a certain evening David came down to the mess for dinner, late as usual and well charged, but no more than normally, with ardent spirits taken in the privacy of his chamber. He sat down, not tight of jaw, but wearing a distant self-protective smile which he never realized could be read by the keen observer as an insult. The wine he took to help the process of desensitization was duly placed before him and swiftly polished off. The well-trained mess waiter produced the second decanter. Meantime the padre was regaling his brother officers with a few off-colour stories. Unhappily this night the wine failed to produce the required anaesthesia. Instead, David felt the lava of indignation swelling up within him. It erupted suddenly on the conclusion of one of the padre's stories. As the appreciative chuckles died down, David clenched his fists and raised them to shoulder-level. Slowly he turned to the man of God, declaiming loudly: '*I* don't want to hear you telling dirty stories – I want to see you raise the banner of Christ.' A long moment of silence. The padre looked at David softly. 'David, God doesn't mind us drinking.

God doesn't mind us smoking. He's just like you and me.' David let out a strangled shout: 'I hope to God He's not like *you*!'

The CO and the other officers rose silently to take coffee in the adjoining room. The padre came round to the back of David's chair and laid a gently forgiving hand on his shoulder. 'David', he said, 'would you like to come and see me in my little office tomorrow. Shall we say at ten?'

David might have done well to remember his grandfather, 'The Bart's', urbane counter to foolish behaviour: 'Don't be angry with him. Perhaps he's not quite a gentleman, poor fellow.' As it was he failed to make an appearance in the little office the next morning. He failed, indeed, to manifest himself anywhere within the confines of Blaise Castle. Nowhere could he be found and his batman confirmed that his sheets had not been disturbed. A solemn conclusion was reached in the Orderly Room that having 'got pissed and blown his top' with old padre the night before, the snotty bugger must have gone AWOL. The CO, an old 'dug out' from the First World War took a 'dim view'. He briefed his adjutant to telephone Mrs Tennant at East Knoyle if her spouse did not 'show' for dinner. Virginia was greatly astonished and alarmed when the call came through. She had no explanation to proffer. Being unable to drive and, in any case, being shackled by little Georgie, only a few months old, she felt not only fearful but very helpless. She did not know what to think: she hardly dared to think. But she started to telephone: first the Gargoyle, then any close friend that could be reached. No one had anything to offer except comforting words. These only brought on greater fears: Virginia began to think that David might be dead.

The one place she did not think to telephone was the Cavendish Hotel. Had she done so on the following morning, one of the eager amateurs manning the Edwardian switchboard there might just have put her through to the previous Mrs Tennant where, sitting in uniform on the end of Hermione's bed, David was to be reached. No Virginia, Hermione had noted sleepily when he came in and plonked himself down; no Dozey, David had observed. Enter Rosa with a wicked grin. 'Wot you two doin' 'ere. I thought all this was over and done with?' David glanced at her darkly. Rosa realized this was no moment to be waggish. 'When you sorted yourselves out, better come down for a glass of wine in the Elinor', she said, and shuffled off, fur coat over nightie, Kippie III at her heels. Hermione, now fully awake, sensed that all was far from well with David. He had arrived late the previous night, it transpired, and taken refuge in the Cavendish. Rosa had told him Hermione's room number, but oblivion was what he sought – oblivion through a glass darkly.

It was now the week-end. His absence would have been noticed. David was uncertain of his next move. 'They'll think I've just gone off on a bender. But I can't go back. I just can't bring myself to go back there. Can you understand, 'Mione? I'm expected to ask the men whether they've cleaned their ears! These are people I might have been in the ranks with. It's a *grave indignity* towards them. You do see – *I can't go back.*' Such feelings of sensibility had never been Dozey's problem. But, understand or not, Hermione did help David reach the only two sensible decisions left to him. The first was to telephone his CO, the second to telephone a distraught Virginia. His CO told him to report to the RAMC hospital, Millbank, in Westminster and Virginia was just so relieved to hear from him she could hardly speak.

Matters now moved quite fast. At Millbank he was seen by an RAMC psychiatrist who recommended that he should be kept for a few weeks at an officers' rehabilitation centre and then come before a medical board which would determine his future military usefulness. This was in Hertfordshire and at least a thankful Virginia was able to visit him there; and later, when David came up before a medical tribunal, he was dealt with kindly. Perhaps it was thought he was not a suitable case for disciplinary punishment, or, if kept, he might prove to be more trouble than he was worth. So he was invalided out of the service as being 'temperamentally unfit'. A just conclusion. That was in December 1941. David and Virginia then went for a sojourn at the Ritz Hotel in Piccadilly to get over the shock.

17

In the same month of that year, the Japanese delivered their massive, Sunday morning shock attack on the US Pacific Fleet in its home base at Pearl Harbor in Hawaii. In two hours they sank or destroyed five battle ships, fourteen smaller vessels, two hundred aircraft and killed over two thousand four hundred people. The war in Europe, fought so bitterly along a thousand-mile front in Russia, and by the British on the northern shores of Africa in infinitely warmer and more fluid conditions, had escalated overnight into global conflict. The first US troops to set foot in Europe since the great war landed in Northern Ireland on 26 January, 1941.

One small consequence of these momentous events was that Ivan Moffat forsook his mistress, Natalie Newhouse; his home, the decaying sybarite's flat in Fitzroy Square; his work with Strand Films and his cronies in the Gargoyle for the GI's uniform and the American training camp at Lichfield. On Ivan's first appearance in the Club so dressed, Alex Alexander made his little band strike up *Over There*. Philip Toynbee, who took mischievous relish in other people's discomfiture, even if he had not engineered it himself, was highly amused by Ivan's embarrassment. Philip was now frequently to be found in the Club where David was once more conducting the night under his civilian baton. Having been rejected by the Guards (too independent-minded according to the present Duke of Devonshire, himself a successful candidate) Philip had been given a more appropriate commission in the Intelligence Corps, whence he had been seconded to the Ministry of Economic Warfare in London. As such Philip naturally found himself on the building's fire-watching roster. On Philip's arrival at the Club one evening – this is now 1942 – David gave him a rather quizzical reception. Ivan, reunited with Natalie and sitting at David and Virginia's table, witnessed the scene.

'How David should have known on any given night that Philip was supposed to be standing vigil on the roof of the Ministry, I do not know. Although David had his seemingly vague side, he had surprisingly sharp awareness of his friends' talents and shortcomings. On this occasion, sensing disapproval, Philip sought to ingratiate himself by remarking cheerfully: "By the way, David, I saw your brother Christopher at the Ministry yesterday." David's jaw tightened and darkened and his tongue flicked out and back again. "Philip I've come to the conclusion that you're not only something of a snob but what's more that you are a damn bad fire-watcher." Philip, his face creased with mock repentance, betook himself alone to the bar.'

David and Virginia were now able to come up to London more often during the week and stay in the flat beneath the Gargoyle ballroom through having the good fortune to engage an East Knoyle resident, Mrs Janet Brickell, as their cook-housekeeper. Mrs Brickell had a small boy about Georgiana's age and so it came about naturally that she took over the role of nanny as well. This steadfast young woman was not only an indefatigable worker (becoming, under David's guidance, an excellent cook), but she was also to prove a loyal and trusted friend to them both when the going got rough.

Another neighbour employed by David, Mr Street, an ex-miner whose little home was built next to the Tennants at Holloway House, became an invaluable adjunct to their lives there. On David's somewhat shamefaced return from his not really dishonourable discharge from the army, Street had greeted him with 'So, you've bin finished wi'all that rubbish, then.' A remark of such tact that it endeared him forever to David. Although partially crippled from working long years down the pits, Street was a very capable handyman-gardener and well able to engage in the tellurian play which David found so necessary to his well-being. This consisted of such things as building pig-sties, foxproof quarters for chickens and ducks and clearing and planting up a wood David had bought which marched with the garden.

'It was so difficult to get the things, what with shortages and ration-cards, that Mr Tennant wanted for all the people he would bring down to Holloway House,' Mrs Brickell remembers. 'He liked to feed and wine his friends well, he did. Yet in a way, even with bombs falling all over the place, it was such a happy time. People were all so friendly and helpful. It was a different world then.' Among those Mrs Brickell would cater for were John and Rosemary Strachey, Robin Mount, Ivan Moffat and Natalie, Robert Newton (whom Natalie was to marry), John Sutro now a film producer, Dylan (and sometimes Caitlin) Thomas, and Pauline.

When Dylan came down Virginia would take the precaution of removing all china objects from the chimney-place in the living-room – Staffordshire shepherds and shepherdesses and so forth. This was not just because a lot of wine was being drunk, which it was, but because David and Dylan liked reading aloud to each other, switching for preference between Milton and Shakespeare. The threat to her precious objects, Virginia felt, lay as much in the mounting resonance of pitch in their voices as in the expansive gestures accompanying their declamations. During an interval for refreshment in one of these readings, Pauline told Dylan how much she had liked his first book of poems. Dylan said, 'These are the real achieved poets. You see I'm just a poet of promise. At least, Edith Sitwell thinks so.' Virginia remembers that once David and Dylan stayed up talking, singing, reading to each other and sometimes fighting 'for the whole night and into the whole of the next day and through the following night – food and sleep totally ignored'.

Pauline had recently been on the cover of *Picture Post*, the hugely successful national weekly magazine. *Picture Post* was founded by Edward Hulton and edited by Tom Hopkinson. It used pictures rather than words (photojournalism) to put its message across. This was a nice blend of reality (the war), middlebrow didacticism ('Has Britain a Mission?') and attractive light relief (Pauline and Other Animals). It promoted the Age of the Common Man and became during the war, and for some time after, little short of a national institution. In the 1942 issue with Pauline on the cover was a two page centre-spread under the title 'Mr Cochran's very youngest Lady is a schoolgirl'. 'At fifteen', *Picture Post* claimed for her, 'Pauline has the looks of a young film star, the assurance of a society hostess, and all the coltish charm and restless enthusiasm of a schoolgirl, which make an irresistible combination.' Pauline's first professional engagement had been with the Italia Conti annual production of *Where The Rainbow Ends* in which Noël Coward had also made his début. Pauline appeared in the programme under 'Bears, Pigs and Wolves etc.'. Rather lowly. But she was soon promoted to Fairy with a little speech. She then went to the Webber-Douglas School of Dramatic Art, evacuated near Petersfield. While in her second year there Hermione, an infrequent communicator, suddenly rang up to say there was this wonderful, wonderful offer from Cochran. He had seen her in a school production of *A Midsummer Night's Dream* and immediately saw her potential as a Cochran Young Lady. He wanted her at once for his new show to be called *Big Top* and starring Beatrice Lillie. Pauline was dismayed. She didn't want to be a 'show girl', she protested, she wanted to be a straight actress. 'It's a tough life the theatre, and the sooner you get used to it the better', growled Hermione. And so Pauline was dragged away from her lamenting teacher. 'She would have been our finest Sheridan actress', she wailed.

David, whose permission had to be obtained, insisted rather prudishly that she would have to have a chaperone while in the theatre. Hermione scoffed. How Louise would have laughed. But David was adamant. Pauline was his creature and would so remain. 'I was so ashamed,' Pauline said. 'I was the only chorus girl *ever* to have a duenna. It made me quite different. Not part of the chorus anymore. Luckily I was taken up by Bea Lillie who looked after me the whole time.' And the duenna, a kind Quaker with bad rheumatism, was free to catch up with her knitting. Bea Lillie (Lady Peel) was a tremendous draw in the theatre. As a revue star she was in the same league as Hermione, but very different. 'The key to her success is that she ignores her audience. This is an act of daring that amounts to revolution,' was how Kenneth Tynan would assess it. With Bea in the lead and Cochran behind her, Pauline's first big show was assured of success.

The Gargoyle was now running extremely successfully, more than paying its way, and generating its own excitement, laughter and challenge. It did not need orchestrating nor did it need the conductor's baton, which in any case was occasionally seen to fall from the hand. The tiny lift was like an overburdened donkey, obliged to operate almost ceaselessly by day and by night, hoisting up its cargo that was for the most part uniformed and multi-national, to be disgorged into the elegant vestibule. Such a high proportion of smart and varied uniforms appearing in his Club which had always prided itself upon its informality of dress, made David feel the ambivalence of his own position. Although turned forty he looked much younger, and he looked fit and strong, which indeed he was. It did not seem entirely honourable in these dramatic times to have only a frivolous occupation, and one which could hardly qualify, as did Cyril's at *Horizon*, for a 'reserved' status.

Therefore, a little over a year after his medical discharge from the army, David applied to rejoin the BBC. As one of the star voices of 2LO in the old days of broadcasting at Savoy Hill, David's return was warmly welcomed. He was to be a Home News Reader. 'But', warned the *Evening News*, 'after an interval of thirteen years he will find that there have been many changes in the technique of announcing.' Perhaps the BBC might have been warned that there had been a few changes in David as well. One of the innovations that he now brought to Broadcasting House was sartorial. The BBC had thoughtfully provided beds at BH to accommodate announcers on early morning duty, who would otherwise be exposed to travel in the blackout, so they could take their rest and come fresh to the microphone. David would often avail himself of this provision when required to read the Home News at 7 a.m. But since this would normally follow a rather late night at the Gargoyle, or even later elsewhere, he would surprise the engineers by appearing in front of the early morning microphone in immaculate dinner-jacket or tails, thus reversing the edict laid down by Reith who had only insisted on his announcers being so dressed for the evening news. But it certainly provided comfort and a source of pride for Virginia, glued, like most of Britain, to her wireless set when down at East Knoyle, to hear '... and this is David Tennant reading it' in his own mellifluous tones.

With Pauline safely launched in Cochran's circus, Hermione had been tempted to return to the legitimate theatre by the offer of a part in a play adapted from his novel by Graham Greene. This was *Brighton Rock* in which Richard Attenborough, a comparatively untried young actor, was to have his first leading role. During rehearsals Greene left them completely alone, but when they were in Oxford on tour before the West End opening, Greene gave a small party for the cast to meet him for the first time. 'I found Graham unusual,' Hermione reported, 'Instead of being confident, as such a successful writer had every right to be, he was shy. Perhaps we extrovert theatre people overwhelmed him.' Perhaps. More probably, the quality of aloofness and detachment that Graham Greene bore dampened even Hermione's gregarious nature. The opening night of *Brighton Rock* (to be filmed after the war) at the Garrick Theatre was all they had hoped for. After their curtain calls, Hermione (the good cockney Ida) led Dickie Attenborough (the vicious young Pinkie) and his 'moll' Dulcie Grey to the front of the footlights to introduce two new stars in the audience. At that moment there was the sound of the most fearful explosion. Everyone in the theatre thought they must have been hit. But no. It was the nearby '50 Shilling Tailors', wiped off the map of London.

David was likewise erased from the news-reading room of the BBC. The white nights had begun to take their toll. The evening dress, frequently slept in, had become increasingly less immaculate; the speech had begun to slur. More than once, BBC staff were unable to revive him at the appointed time. David could no longer hold the job down. He was asked to leave. David returned to East Knoyle for some rehabilitating activity with Street in his wood, to contemplate events and to ponder his future.

The tide of war, in 1943, had turned quite dramatically in favour of the Allies and with this improvement in the Allied fortunes, David's cousin Dick was now also declared redundant to the British war effort on medical grounds. He had been suffering unendurable stress due to a passion only partially requited for one of the London-based Paget twins. These were young birds of rare feather – beautiful, artistically gifted, serious minded and modest. The twin in question was Mamaine, later to marry Arthur Koestler. But Dick wanted to marry Mamaine now, and it was his frustration in this ambition that led him to nervous breakdown. After a routine examination, Dick's active involvement with the military was severed. He went, not into the Ritz, but directly into the London Clinic. In those days the Clinic, amongst its other healing activities, was willing to play a not dissimilar role to the one which his old home, Clouds, now offers to those in the grip of unfortunate compulsions and addictions. But it was the heart that Dick needed to have dried out, and here the Clinic could not oblige. And so he was released to assuage by the waters of Tickeridge Mill a restive impatient spirit fed, as his friend Peter Quennell observed, by some secret disquiet.

David's present predicament was rather different. He, too, needed to be dried out, but preferably by alcohol indoctrinated leeches. The problem might have been much worse were it not for David's strong constitution and the epicurean principle he applied to himself over what he consumed. With Churchill he could have said, 'My tastes are simple. I only like the best.' Nonetheless, the burden of the drinking was beginning to tell on Virginia, the more so since she was once again pregnant. David then took the, for him, unusual step of seeking advice as to what might lie behind his belief that where drink was concerned the only place worth going was too far. This quest led him to the chambers of the Freudian analyst Karen Stephen, a cousin by marriage of Virginia Woolf. The course of analysis that followed failed to achieve its objective. For one thing, Dr Stephen's unpalatable advice to David was that he should leave Virginia. But as David explained with innocent candour, 'the *transference*, you see, went the wrong way. *I* was supposed to fall in love with her, but she's gone and fallen in love with *me*.'

When the run of *Brighton Rock* drew near its end, the musical comedy star Leslie Henson came round to see Hermione in her dressing room. He was forming a new revue company for Basil Dean, Hermione's first employer on the London stage and the founder of the wartime Entertainments National Services Association (ENSA). Henson wanted Hermione to join his company which would be going overseas to entertain the troops. It would be a tough assignment, he said, and only paid fifteen pounds a week. Hermione protested that she had just signed a contract at a very large salary to star in a new revue, *Sweet and Low*. Henson looked downcast, said nothing. Hermione reflected. It had been quite some time since she could claim Dunkirk hero, Dozey Willis, as her war effort. 'Don't worry, darling,' she told Henson, 'of course I'll come. I'll just have to break my contract and learn to grow poor gracefully.' Which for the next eighteen months or so is what Hermione did. She followed the drum with Henson's company and beat it, too, with good effect not far behind the lines; first in North Africa, in Sicily just after the invasion, and then in Naples when it had fallen to the Allies, but the main thrust north was still held up by the German resistance at Monte Casino. Her old partner from *Ballyhoo* and *Rise Above It*, Wally Crisham, was with her in Henson's company to which was later added Bea Lillie and Joyce Grenfell. Hermione was obliged to show Bea how to adapt her sophisticated manner of appearing to ignore her audience and to bang the drum in the way the troops appreciated. She remembered a number called 'Rhythm' in which Bea shook her bosoms all over the stage. 'Try that,' advised Hermione. Bea did. 'She shook her very low bosoms and everything else she possessed and the boys loved it. Sweet and low, that's what they wanted,' Hermione said.

Hermione went overseas secure in the knowledge that she *had* put her daughter on the stage – in spite of Noël Coward's warning chant to 'Mrs Worthington'. Before leaving England she had introduced her to Bill Linnit of that powerful management team, O'Brien, Linnet and Dunfee, while Pauline was still in *Big Top*. Linnet took one look at her and said, 'That's the girl I want for *She Follows Me About*', a Ben Travers farce they were about to put on. So into *She Follows Me About* went Pauline, the keys to Hermione's Piccadilly flat in her handbag.

*

With their second child, Sabrina, about to be born, David encouraged Pauline to take the place once held by her mother in the Gargoyle and from which Virginia was now necessarily absent. Pauline, otherwise rather lonely, was only too happy to comply and she would go there after the show almost nightly when she would frequently join up with Ivan. Ivan in Pauline's life was pleased to assume an ostensibly avuncular role. This must have been frustratingly hard once her nubile attractions had become so pronounced. There was also her bookish side which erudite Ivan much appreciated. Aside from her thespian gifts, Pauline had acquired from David, whom she loved and admired inordinately, an appreciation of literature and of painting. Among the contemporary poets whose works she greatly admired and many of which she knew by heart was Louis MacNeice. MacNeice, then working at the BBC as, in his own words, a 'radio practioner', was, and has strangely so remained, one of the least sung among his richly gifted generation of poets. But he was much admired by his peers, not least by Auden. Ivan used to make her recite 'The Earth Compels' and other of his works late at night in the Gargoyle. Then, with a look of mock apprehension, 'We're not going to let her meet Louis, are we? He'll just fall in love with her if he knows she knows all his poems by heart.'

Ivan was able to play this, and other, roles through a fortunate if well deserved situation which arose once America had become deeply committed to the war in the West. General Eisenhower, shortly to be appointed Supreme Commander of the Allied Expeditionary Forces, had expressed himself dissatisfied with the film record of the war. Accordingly, SPECOU, the Special Coverage Unit of the US Army Signal Corps, was formed. This was headed by the Hollywood film director George Stevens, whom Eisenhower had encountered serving as a major with the American forces in North Africa. Stevens was a splendid choice. On his return after the war he was to make such Hollywood classics as *Shane, Giant*, and *A Place in the Sun*. In the meantime, he was charged with assembling small mobile units of professional film-makers capable of providing expert coverage of the forthcoming campaign to liberate Europe. Assigned to each of these units was a writer who, in caption and description, was to write it like it was. The novelists Irwin Shaw and Harry Brown were two such; another was the playwright William Saroyan; and then there was Stevens' future screenwriter, Ivan Moffat.

SPECOU, otherwise known as the 'Hollywood Irregulars', was attached to SHAEF (where Philip Toynbee now rested his elbows), the Supreme Headquarters Allied Expeditionary Force. Ivan was thus strategically placed to render signal social service to his fellow GIs (some of them commissioned, with rank counting for little), the writers and crack cameramen, the sound men and assistant directors, by guiding their eager footsteps towards the Gargoyle. They, and fellow explorers from the neo-Georgian fastness of Grosvenor Square, began to congregate almost nightly in the Club. After the claustrophobia of an enforced and provincial insularity they had found elsewhere, they were captivated by the spirit of abandon and open discussion they found in the Gargoyle. There was Cyril Connolly surrounded by his court listening to what Sonia Brownell had to say about the latest work from European Resistance writers; here were the 'Burnt Men' of Communism and the singed radicals still arguing over the defection of Auden and Isherwood to America. And who in the heck were those two guys in kilts sitting over there holding hands? Neo-Romantic painters? Well, well. And isn't that guy – the one who looks like he's going to take a leak under the stairs – Bob Newton? The one who Willie Wyler wanted so bad to play opposite Merle in *Wuthering Heights*? But Sam insisted on Olivier? For these Americans new to Britain, it was the unpredictable happenings and encounters in the Gargoyle which appealed.

It was exciting, too, for the young Wolf Rilla who had come to England from Germany as a boy before the war and who was to follow his father, the actor Walter Rilla, into films. Wolf would become not only a film director (*Village of the Damned*) but also a novelist and writer on film. In the meantime he was working for the Foreign Service Department of the BBC in Bush House in the Strand whose top floor also then housed the Political Intelligence Department of the Foreign Office. Wolf was brought to the Gargoyle by the ubiquitous Ruthven Todd. 'I was enormously impressed by its sophistication, intellectual glamour and mirrored walls,' he recollects. 'I used to feel very brave and devil-may-care spending air raid evenings on the top floor, in the company of glamorous *illuminati* insouciant of bombs. I remember the noise and the table-hopping – everyone seemed to know everyone. Closing hours seemed to have no significance. After hours, or when he went to bed, Tennant used to give the keys to the downstairs bar to Ruthven who used to help himself and everyone liberally from it. I never remember who, if anyone, paid. The appeal to the very young man I then was, was its literary and showbizzy *New Yorker*-ish air. There was a definite feeling of being privileged to be a member of this cosmopolitan *Sturm und Drang*. Among those in the American forces I remember particularly Harry Brown because of my falling deeply under the sexual spell of his glamorous Swedish model wife, Ursula, who all but seduced me in public at the piano in the Tudor Room which I used to play after hours. She was sophisticated in a Gertie Lawrence kind of way, but also intellectual, gold-digging, hard as nails. And I remember William Saroyan who told me how and what to write and actually was a bit of a bore but very sweet and ungrand. Then there would be Dylan Thomas reciting bawdy verses and warning everybody off a well-known actress because she had the clap – horse's mouth, he said. And Bobby Newton who took a completely irrational dislike to me and offered to 'knock my block off'; Tambimuttu, and Brian Howard bizarrely linked up with Douglas Byng in the perambulating search for young men. And through it all, floating serenely and somewhat absentmindedly, Tennant.'

This serenity, even when floating on a sea of alcohol, would be apt to be challenged when, for instance, coming down the stairs into the ballroom enthusiastically humming arias from *Traviata* David would be faced with 'Ain't Giving Nothing Away' from his own four-piece band – like some absurd confrontation of taste in the saloon of a transatlantic liner. Alexander's famous 'dirty number', to which Waaf officer Joan Wyndham liked to sing along, went as follows:

If you want it – you've got to buy it.
We ain't giving nothing away.
If you need it – and really crave it
Then by God you'll have to pay.
  You can have it in a saucer
  You can have it in a cup
  You can have it lying down
  Or you can have it standing up
But ... [da capo]

Nor, in Virginia's experience, was the intellectual insouciance to the bombing in the Gargoyle quite as general as Wolf Rilla has suggested. 'I remember the bombs falling terrifically one night when Irwin Shaw and William Saroyan were there. We all stayed down in the ballroom after the club closed, Ruthven, Augustus, John Young, Humphrey Slater and everybody, and suddenly the bombing started. Nobody paid any attention. We were all engrossed watching Ivan doing wonderful imitations from Shakespeare. Irwin Shaw looked at us amazed. "What are you all doing? Shouldn't we be doing something – like getting under the table or something?" He was told to shut up by Humphrey and the rest of us.'

Slater, the Spanish Civil War veteran, had been called up in unusual circumstances (for one thing he was the same age as David) and was now a captain in the army. He had been living in dire circumstances with Janetta Woolley in one room in Bristol, both then working in ammunition factories, when he was approached by his friend from the International Brigade, Tom Wintringham, to become an instructor at a school for Home Guards that he was starting at Osterley Park just outside London. Humphrey was to run tactical training courses, Roland Penrose, another friend, would lecture on camouflage, and so on. Humphrey ran his courses brilliantly, the whole enterprise was greatly successful, with people coming from all over Britain to attend. *Picture Post* devoted a number to it. Amazingly, it was all done on an unofficial and voluntary basis. This, and its success, made the War Office anxious. It all had to be made official they ruled. Consequently Humphrey was called up as a private. John 'Struggle for Power' Strachey raised a question about the absurdity of this in the House of Commons. So Humphrey was made a captain. Once he had been promoted captain he was made to feel morally obliged to regularize his union with Janetta. They then got married and she became a somewhat rebellious captain's lady. The Communist Party now got wind of all this carry on. They wrote to Humphrey upbraiding him for following a line diametrically opposed to the Party line in becoming involved in an imperialist war. Not only that, he was also being subjected to the bad bourgeois influence of Janetta. The combination of the two was too much. Humphrey's card was torn up.

But Wolf Rilla was right to complain about the combustible Bobby Newton. He was always likely to pose an unpredictable threat. Quite apart from David, the Gargoyle with Bobby, Brian Howard, Philip Toynbee, Guy Burgess, Dylan Thomas, Nina Hamnett and Augustus John alone, had rather more than its share of heroic drinkers. Augustus used to say 'I drink in order to become more myself.' Bobby tended to do exactly the opposite. Whatever the professional role he happened to be playing at the time (and with film as well as theatre there was often more than one) it would be brought with him into the Club. Thus Pistol from Olivier's film of *Henry V* might have to contend for possession of Bobby with a character from Noël Coward's *This Happy Breed*, or, worse', with Slim Grisson, the vicious psychopathic gangster in *No Orchids for Miss Blandish*, a long-running theatrical canter through sex and sadism, brutality and perversion at the Prince of Wales theatre. Bobby electrified London theatregoers with his performance which was known on occasion to be so highly charged that he and it both came over the footlights and into the audience.

In order to escape the temptation of extravagant excess that London offered, Bobby signed on from time to time as a cook in an undemanding branch of the Merchant Navy cobbled together for the emergency. This was the Small Vessels Pool based at Plymouth, whose business it was to find temporary four-man crews to pick up auxiliary vessels from the builder's yard and deliver them, hugging the coast as a prophylactic against submarine attack, to the post where they were required to do the donkey work of fetching and carrying for the fleet. 'There's no better place to dry out than on the briny,' Bobby was persuading David one evening in the Club. 'They're always looking for cooks in Small Vessels.

The galleys are tiny, but you don't mind. You love to cook. Why not come down with me and try it out – sign on for a few weeks?' It was a fortuitous suggestion. Things had turned rather quiet in the Gargoyle recently. Britain, since the beginning of 1944, had become a vast armed camp in preparation for the biggest land, sea and air operation of all time. Large-scale military exercises were taking place in many parts of the land, and these involved George Stevens' SPECOU and a great many other units which had contributed personnel to the Gargoyle white nights. David welcomed Bobby's idea enthusiastically. Action. And he would be in uniform again – of a sort. But better still he would be living and working among the 'other ranks' where he knew he would feel at home.

18

'Dave' proved a signal success with his coastwise shipmates from the Small Vessels Pool. In his tiny galley he produced a flow of rather high-class nursery food. Not just the seaman's familiar diet of fries and over-cooked stews but proper baked pies, pastries and plum duffs. They quickly came to accept his 'Oxford' accent and perfect 'reader's' enunciation. But in any case the trusty guitar and repertoire of bawdy songs prevented any social ice from forming. A particular favourite was the sea-shanty 'Nautical William', which Nina had taught him:

> 'Where am I going to sleep tonight?' said Bollicky Bill the Sailor.
> 'You may sleep within my bed, Sir', said the fair young lady.
> 'There's no room for two in a bed', said Bollicky Bill the Sailor.
> 'You may sleep within my thighs, Sir', said the fair young lady.
> 'What shall I find between your thighs?' said Bollicky Bill the Sailor.
> 'You shall find a nice pincushion', said the fair young lady.
> 'I have a pin that'll just fit in', said Bollicky Bill the Sailor.

With David away at sea for quite long periods and no longer jolly week-ends at East Knoyle, whatever the state of the war, Virginia forced herself to conquer her natural shyness by coming up to London by herself and giving small parties for trusted friends in the flat below the ballroom. When David was there to ease the strain of exposure in the Club – the loss of 'ordinary' life with very little 'going out' but always out on display herself – Virginia found her shyness less paralysing. It was also true that David, despite a peacock bent, sometimes found the display a great strain. 'But then', as Virginia explained, 'we sort of hid in each other, which somehow made it all right. And of course he was so rude at times. That could be a bit of a help, too. One felt safe with him under his rude protective cloak – his vitriolic umbrella.'

Harry Weatherall was a trusted friend and a Gargoyle member. He was also a frequenter of the Cavendish and an ardent and longtime admirer of Daphne Fielding, chronicler of the life and good times of Rosa Lewis, whose then husband, Henry Weymouth, kept a permanent set of rooms at Rosa's. Harry brought Rosa round one evening with one or two others for drinks with Virginia. Everything about Virginia had a delicacy which stopped just short of feyness, and which often found expression in treasured possessions. Not the least treasured was a collection of minuscule and exquisite sea-shells garnered from sacred places, such as the honeymoon beaches of Nassau and Cuba, which had played a significant part in her life. These were laid out in a mosaic of loving care on a large dish. Rosa, on entering the flat, was tempted by what she took to be inviting cocktail delicacies. She grabbed a handful and thrust them into her mouth. Her sturdy teeth, expecting something soft and delicious were caught unawares. They baulked. Out spewed the shells, followed by an 18 carat gold tooth. This was hastily retrieved by an embarrassed Virginia from the chaos of tiny crunched shells on the carpet.

Up in the ballroom some of the mirrored tiles of eighteenth-century French glass had been dislodged from the walls in the bombing raids leaving gaps not unlike missing teeth. But the large majority remained to reflect a frenetic activity inside the Club itself, sponsored by the drama being played out across the Channel.

D-Day, 6th June, 1944: that great historic day for which the whole nation and all those to whom it played host had worked and waited for so long fell at the appointed hour upon the beaches of Normandy. After ferocious combat, the invasion was secured and the Germans forced back. Hitler's 'secret weapon', the much-vaunted flying bomb, was then launched from the Pas de Calais. As many as 150 a day were being loosed over the South of England and London. This prompted the second mass exodus of children from the city. Flying fast and low, the 'doodle-bugs' or 'buzz-bombs' often came over in broad daylight watched by those on the ground guiltily praying the buzzing would not stop and thus wishing it on to someone else. As long as you could hear it you knew you were safe. It stopped, as programmed, when the jet fuel had run out, and you had about fifteen seconds before the great explosion hit the ground – and you, perhaps. The sudden silence of the sinister weapons after the homely buzz induced an excitement of pure terror.

Hitler had something to be excited about when, in the same month as the Normandy landings and while listening to a report from his military staff about the rapidly deteriorating situation on the Russian front, a violent explosion shattered the conference room where they were gathered. Hitler was unhurt. Once more Hitler had been saved by the accident of circumstance. He, of course, took it as a 'thumbs up' sign from Providence. But Providence was letting the dictator down. The Allied armies, driven by rival charioteers, Montgomery and Patton, advanced rapidly after the Normandy breakthrough. In August Paris was taken without battle. By February 1945, with Eisenhower's armies advancing from the west on Berlin, already a wasteland of utter desolation, and the Russians under Marshal Zhukov from the east, it was apparent that Nazi Germany was about to be eliminated.

David, on a coaster steaming north from Fife in Scotland, felt part of this optimism. This was helped by his finding the briny not quite as dry as Bobby Newton had claimed. At his whim, David saw fit to dispense from his tiny galley a most efficacious nostrum against the bitter cold that blew off the shores of Ultima Thule. His recipe: take one pound of best (or worst) butter, add to this another pound of demerara sugar over which should then be poured a pint of boiling water; stir and add to mixture a bottle of Navy rum. Imbibe while hot. This prophylactic eased the passage round the northernmost points on the Scottish mainland, Dunnet Head and Cape Wrath, and thence down to the protective harbourage at Oban across from the Isle of Mull. From there he wrote yearningly to Virginia of the Mediterranean, and of planning an explorative thrust into Portugal when the war was over.

*

Pauline, meanwhile having played the juvenile lead in Esther McCracken's *No Medals* in the West End with Fay Compton, was placed under film contract by the all powerful Rank Organization as a 'Rank Starlet' at £500 per annum. She was still living in the Piccadilly flat, from which Hermione was often absent, and felt suddenly very flush. Another play was offered, written by two very young Gargoyle members, Simon Wardell and Kieren Tunney. This was *Day After Tomorrow* directed at the little 'Q' Theatre near Kew Bridge by that fine Shavian actor, Esmé Percy. After the performance Esmé would often give Pauline a lift back to the West End. Driving home one evening, a form of which she had vaguely been aware curled up in the back of the car – it could have been a large black-haired dog under a rug – stirred itself and started to engage them both in very animated conversation. 'Oh, Pauline, this is Lucian, Lucian Freud', said Esmé helpfully.

To people who knew him at the time Lucian was a comet of astonishing brilliance. In the freshness, originality and immediacy of his responses he evoked Baudelaire's dictum '*Le génie, c'est l'enfance retrouvée.*' 'He was an original', said Johnny Craxton. 'He had no great theories about art but marvellous ideas about life and people. He also gave the impression of being incredibly good-looking in his curious way. No wonder everybody fell for him.' Lucian's infectiously engaging and dynamic personality had an appeal that transcended any conventional sexual barriers.

Lucian, Pauline admits, was a very persuasive and persistent wooer, and in time he won her. As Lucian's first wife, Kitty, later said to Pauline, 'You must realize you were for him the first step up the ladder.' There may have been other steps, of course, and other ladders; but perhaps never quite such a young and promising one. What first really impressed her about him, Pauline said, was when on going with him one evening to Shepherd Market, he approached each of the tarts stationed there, addressing them familiarly by their first names. To one and all of the sorority there was just 'Luce', a term, evidently, of endearment. Lucian became, and, when he was in England, for many years remained, an almost nightly communicant at the Gargoyle. Or, as Harry Weatherall liked to have it, at 'The Agony in the Gargoyle'; adding that above where the lift stopped should have been written: 'Abandon hope, all ye who enter here'. When David cast off his seaman's sweater, he was not best pleased to find this young man, virtually unknown to him, who had himself served at cabin-boy age with the Small Vessels Pool, to be so very much at home in his court. Still less pleased that Pauline, in her role of part-time hostess, had extended the hospitality of the house rather liberally to the then impecunious Lucian.

The seaman's sweater, of heavy-duty cable stitch, when cast off went to the indigent Dylan Thomas. It was never recovered, somewhat to David's chagrin. Whenever he caught Dylan wearing it and demanded its return, Dylan just lifted it up exposing a fair, blameless skin and pleading 'Look. Nothing underneath.' Dylan hated solitude and was always loath to go to bed. He was so often the spark which could ignite an otherwise unrewarding occasion. In the lugubrious night-club Dylan would clown about, innocent of the surrounding disenchantment and not drunk in any conventional way, mocking sexual endeavour and himself with playfully exaggerated claims of his own achievement. Augustus remembered a rather different Dylan when sitting one night with him and David in the Gargoyle. 'The latter, trying to draw him out, asked, "Do you believe in multi-matrimony?" Dylan replied, "No, I don't, I believe in one wife only." And he was very serious. But at the time he wasn't married, nor had he visited the USA.' Nor, you can bet, was it the answer David was hoping to hear. John's last word on Dylan: '... at the core [he was] a typical Welsh puritan and nonconformist gone wrong. He was also a genius.'

David was pretty indulgent to Dylan – particularly in the matter of loans, or when the matter of his unpaid bills at the Club was brought to his attention by Mr Smellie at his firm of solicitors. Poor Dylan was so often in debt. In 1945, he wrote to Cyril Connolly: 'Do you remember our conversation if that's the word in the Gargoyle some nights ago about fifty pounds that I think you said you thought I should have for my poem but for your fear that I should spend it? Spend it of course I would, but certainly not all on what I don't know why I shouldn't spend it on anyway. I'm so much in worry and debt that the money would be wonderful *now* ....' Dylan did get it – but not quite 'now'.

David had indeed been generous to Dylan but there was also that element of 'one's own terribly begrudging hospitality', he had mentioned to Ivan. 'Well,' as Pauline has said, 'my father was a Scot. He felt the blood leaking out of his veins. Richard III said "I'm not in a giving *vein* today." Sometimes very generous, sometimes he suddenly seized up and said it's too much.' But then after all, Dylan was the prime example of a worthy recipient of the form of patronage David had in mind when he originally conceived the function of the Club. Not that he had expected to fill the role of patron himself; at the same time he felt he had to set an example.

Peter Quennell took a less tolerant view of Dylan than either Edith Sitwell or Augustus. 'I drink to correct the imbalance between the disorder outside and the order within', was the neat explanation Dylan offered Ivan Moffat. But it was not good enough for Peter Quennell.

The night Peter witnessed Dylan drinking someone else's wine out of his own shoe made an indelible impression upon him. 'There was a period at the Gargoyle when people were divided between those who had come up to town with the wife. They were called the "dentists" or the "Wimbledon set" and were assiduously courted – in principle if not in practice – by David and Virginia, who felt the shaky fortunes of the Club might have to depend on them, I mean, they paid their bills while the likes of Dylan, and quite often myself, did not. And then there were people like Dylan and Brian Howard and every kind of rascal. Such a "dentist" couple were sitting quietly with a bottle of red wine in front of them when Dylan seized it from their table and with some mad idea of Grand Dukes drinking out of other people's shoes, he whipped off his own shoe which happened to have a great hole in the sole and poured the wine into it. Some of it went into Dylan's great maw, the rest spouted out of the hole in the shoe. An indescribably grotesque scene.'

Sometime after lunch on 26th July 1945, David was to be seen leaning out of a window in the ballroom of the Gargoyle and shouting down to surprised passers-by in Dean Street, 'We've won! We've won!' This was not a reference to the unconditional surrender of Germany which had taken place in May so much as to the sensational landslide victory of the Labour party at the polls giving them an absolute and overwhelming majority for the first time in history. So when the Big Three sat down at Potsdam to chart the course of post-war Europe, only Stalin remained from the previous occasion at Yalta. Churchill was now replaced by Attlee, and Roosevelt, who had died on the eve of victory, by Truman. At this conference no agreement was reached over where Germany's frontiers should be drawn. So down slammed the Iron Curtain. And David was out of his political closet.

*

Lucian, under Pauline's eyes, once had his own consciousness raised in the Gargoyle in somewhat similar circumstances to those described by Peter Quennell. 'Sometimes', as Pauline said, 'the "dentists" formed up against the artists. One evening a man came up to Lucian sitting there with an arrogant, saturnine expression on his face, dragged him to his feet and gave him a right to the jaw saying "There's one for you", then lifting the bedraggled fellow up again gave him a second cuff – "And another one for your beastly old grandfather."' Part of Pauline's relationship with Lucian was shared with Johnny Craxton and a very beautiful young girl called Sonia Leon, known as 'Spider' because of her immensely long thin limbs, who was to become the fourth (but not the last) Mrs Peter Quennell. They spent much time in the Gargoyle but 'we also went to the cinema a lot and to sleazy places in the Harrow Road that Lucian had discovered and loved and sometimes up to Hampstead where Johnny's parents – a heavily artistically committed family – had a house. I remember one lugubrious evening with David Gascoyne reading his poems. Very good, but the audience full of long ladies with gloomy faces and enormous amber beads hanging down and clanking and deathly serious. Very off-putting.'

But with the war ended and the long VJ night celebrated on the Gargoyle roof, there was once more a change in emphasis among the frequenters of the Club. There were those returned from 'The blaze and havoc of war with its loves and deaths', often unexpectedly young and outwardly unmarked by the experience and with accounts of heroic deeds that had to be modestly told. There was George Millar sitting in his Rifle Brigade uniform in the dining-room of the Cavendish writing

Horned Pigeon, his book of his escape from a POW camp in Germany; there was W. Stanley Moss writing about the amazing exploit of two young men's capture of a German general from the fortress of occupied Crete, in which Billy Moss played Horatio to Paddy Leigh Fermor's Hamlet. There was the recently demobbed RAF pilot Robert Kee whose book *A Crowd Is Not Company* was to establish itself as the precursor of a new genre in the writing of war experience. There was the Free French flyer, Romain Gary, whose masterpiece, *The Roots of Heaven*, had still to be written. There was the Hungarian writer Peter de Polnay, whose *Death and Tomorrow* told at first hand of life in Paris under German occupation. There was the dashing, polyglot Xan Fielding whose meeting in the Club with Daphne Bath would lead to marriage. There was Paddy Leigh Fermor himself, and others such as the much decorated bomber pilots Kensington (Ken) Davison, who had often piloted his friend Derek Jackson on tricky missions, and Alan Cairns whose admiration for Virginia could scarce be contained. And the Navy always had a presence in the Club when Michael Law closed his desk at the Admiralty hard by. Then there were the war correspondents: the beautiful American, Lee Miller, once a favourite of the surrealist photographer Man Ray and later to marry Sir Roland Penrose; Sam White, the Australian who was to become the doyen of the foreign press corps with his weekly column from Paris for Beaverbrook's *Evening Standard* which ran for years and years; and the world-famous antipodean Alan Moorehead, among them.

But nothing could dislodge Brian Howard of forked tongue and cloven hoof swivelling on the bar-stool waiting to release his unexpended venom on suitable prey. For at this time in his life, sexual hubris still out-boxed what Maurice Richardson referred to as 'Brian's daemonic drive to self-destruction'. Hating pretension in others, Brian's own pretension was to eviscerate the nascent pretensions of the young. And if you had the impudence to be not only young but a reasonably good-looking and not evidently homosexual male, watch out! John Richardson, who broadly answered to such a description, was accosted one evening by Brian peering into the vestibule to see what the lift had just brought up. It was John, quite young and wearing a dinner jacket with a carnation. 'Who do you think we *are*, my dear. Noël *Coward*?' 'I was horrified by this evil, predatory queen, who I hardly knew, insulting me for no reason at all', said John. 'He seems to be a recurring decimal in the Gargoyle. Everybody's memories always include Brian Howard.' 'At least, my dear,' Brian once said to a fellow believer, '*I* am a has-been.

That's something *you* can never be.' Virginia did once dislodge Brian from his stool. He was just about to mouth some fearful obscenity when she turned on him and said: 'For once I'm not going to listen to this.' And with her finger to his chest she pushed him back very slowly until both Brian and bar-stool crashed to the ground. 'He looked quite amazed and rather pleased', said Virginia. As he did on another occasion in the Club when Paul Potts the People's Poet turned his hooked nose and bald noble head and said to Brian with a directness picked up from service with the commandos, 'The trouble with you Brian, you know, is that you wear your crown of thorns on your arse-hole rather than on your head.' A smile of gratified acknowledgement, like a slow burn, worked over Brian's mouth.

Brian was by no means the only constant occupant of the Gargoyle bar-stools – just the most challenging one. 'Here', the painter Michael Wishart remembers, 'lined up like swallows eager to migrate to gentler climes often sat Roy Campbell, Louis MacNeice, John Davenport, Dylan Thomas, Humphrey Slater, Constant Lambert, Patrick Kinross, Philip Toynbee and other clever bards who drank more than they danced.' And past them were paraded, under escort, the *belles de nuit* on their descent to David's intended Paradise, the basement in the skies answering to Alex Alexander's metronomic beat. Spotted among them might be Wishart's future wife, the painter Anne Dunn one of Cyril's loves; Lucian's future wife, Wishart's cousin, Kitty Epstein; and Caroline Blackwood (another of Lucian's future wives), Doon Plunkett, Antonia Fraser (then Pakenham), Venetia Murray (Basil's daughter), Henrietta (Law, to be), Anne Valaoritis, Charlotte Star Busmann, Margaret Lygon, Sally Ann Howes, Jennifer Renwick, Isobel Lambert, Elizabeth Smart, Barbara Skelton (who married three of the Club's habitués – Connolly, Weidenfeld, Jackson), Joan Eyres Monsell, Jocelyn Rickards, Olivia Manning, Glur Dyson Taylor (wife no. 3 to Peter Quennell), Elizabeth Jane Howard, Joy Craig (Bobby Newton's sister), Jennifer Heber-Percy (once Fry, then Ross), June Churchill (Randolph's wife), Hermione, of course, with her attendant court of *mignons*, 'gaudy enough', said Wishart, 'to make Henri III, last of the Valois Kings, spin in his tomb with envy', Janetta Slater (soon to be Kee), and Ivan's Natalie now Bobby Newton's. 'Could any other lift,' asks Michael Wishart, 'have hauled up such a fateful, intermarried catch?' Once when the elevator jammed, Michael was caught in the toytown lift with Natalie, who said to him: 'What's the point of the lift sticking if you're not going to fuck me?' To which inquisition Michael loftily replied that as far as he was concerned pot-holing was an aphrodisiac.

The immediate post-war years brought together again or for the first time many kindred spirits in the Club. 'It was in the Gargoyle I first met Philip Toynbee,' said Paddy Leigh Fermor.

I was once taken to luncheon there with David and Hermione while still at school. It seemed then – sometime in the early thirties – the acme of smartness and sophistication, quite extraordinary, with sun streaming in, quite unlike its nocturnal character, full of rather fascinating and famous people, with a savoury dash of Bohemia. [Paddy's post-war eyes saw it in rather a different light.] Though it still had an aura of twenties and Bright Young People smartness, it was now definitely Bohemian in character, rather shabby and tremendous fun – a last haven after the changes of the Café Royal. It was very difficult to stay away, and seemed like a never-ending party night after night and with constant changes of partners, and, as years passed, a certain permutation of partners.

In that world, and of those times, Philip Toynbee was a much loved and life-enhancing figure. I'd often heard of him in a vague way before we met – which was just after the war – and it's odd that our paths didn't cross sooner. Whenever he was in London Philip gravitated to the Gargoyle at night like an iron filing. So did Joan (Eyres Monsell, now Leigh Fermor), who had known Philip long before, and I, often with Xan Fielding. It was a marvellously exhilarating time. Hangovers were drowned like kittens next morning in a drink called a Dog's Nose or a Monkey's Tail: a pint of beer, that is, with either a large gin or vodka slipped into it. It worked wonders.

Snatches of conversation, lifted, I think, from Gargoyle occasions at which Philip participated: Henry Bath overheard saying to Julia Strachey, sitting next to him at dinner – they'd never met before – "Now – take the sexiest thing of all: SEX! I say – you are married, I hope?" Julia: "Yes." Henry, triumphantly: "Well, then, you see what I mean!" And again, over lunch this time, with Philip, Cyril Connolly, Stephen Spender and some others. Towards the end, when the talk had taken a rather gloomy turn, Cyril quoted Yeats's line: "Too long a sacrifice makes of the heart a stone," and heaved a sigh. So did the others. They were all about to subside into a mood of gentle melancholy, when Stephen said "Yes, Cyril, but that's not why *our* hearts are stones"; and the talk revived.

Other post-war occasions I remember vividly were the time when

Johnny Minton got tremendously tight and improvised a sort of solitary apache dance, by himself on the dance floor, flinging off his outer garments as it advanced, but falling far short of Seven Veils. And then Philip and Raymond Carr – the latter already head of a college – sitting side by side, both dressed in dog-collars, watching Freddie Ayer demonstrate that he was an accomplished soft-shoe dancer. It was a delight to see the famous Logical-Positivist flickering and twirling about the room as nimbly as Fred Astaire.

It was true, as Paddy says, how well Freddie's 'stainless steel mind' (e. e. cummings' phrase) could persuade his nimble feet to cut a nifty rug. In which pursuit his frequent and favourite accompanist at the Gargoyle (the exercise of dancing was still conducted in pairs in those early post-war days) was the delectable Australian painter and (subsequently) *femme fatale*, Jocelyn Rickards, who focused upon the Grote Professor of the Philosophy of Mind and Logic at University College, London, a, then, 'single-minded devotion'. In the enjoyment of this activity – the dance – Freddie was unconsciously emulating an earlier Gargoyle member of comparable intellectual stature, Pamela's friend, Sir Oliver Lodge, physicist, spiritualist and ballroom dancer. The Gargoyle was important to Freddie not only as a dancing gymnasium but, surprising in the liveliest of men and one who shared Bertrand Russell's sexual as well as his philosophical enthusiasm, as a social catalyst. 'The Gargoyle made me a social figure,' he explained to the author.

> I wasn't a social figure before the war, I was an academic figure. I'd written this book which was very successful, in fact is the original source of whatever fame I have: *Language, Truth and Logic*. But it wasn't known much outside academic circles [but within them, at least, it was recognized to be the most exciting and influential English philosophical book of the decade – the thirties]. My first wife, Renée, didn't care much for social life. We lived before the war a very quiet life really – partly in London, partly in Oxford – seeing friends, indeed, but almost entirely academic friends. I'd almost no friends up until the war who weren't in themselves dons. And then in the army I did make friends, but in the way one makes friends in the army, one goes out drinking with them and in so far as one had any social life at all it was at places frequented by fellow Guardees, rather disreputable night-clubs like The Nest, where I was invited to get off with tarts which on the whole is not my style. I was surprisingly good at getting on with people I wouldn't have been

expected to get on with ordinarily, Guards officers and so on. And I managed to adapt myself to them but I wasn't really a great success with them, and then suddenly after the war I developed and began to know all sorts of people I hadn't known before – writers, painters and so on. The Gargoyle was very largely responsible for that. I mean both cause and effect ... cause in that it was through my beginning to know them and be known *by* them that I went to the Gargoyle, and the effect in the sense that once I was there I then got to know them much better, and to like them and be liked by them. So I think I really date the beginning of my life as a kind of social figure: someone who might appear – indeed, I just have appeared [1985] – in *Talk of the Town* in the *New Yorker*, from my Gargoyle life. And I think this might be true, also, for certain intellectuals from different fields – V. S. Pritchett, for instance, and J. Z. Young. I think that was the Gargoyle's point, really. Most dons, you see, don't see many other people than other dons.

Like Guy Burgess, with whom he was at school and who in the early days was one of his very few extra-mural friends, Freddie loved talk. He believed supremely in the value of conversation and brought to it an elegance and intensity that Guy could not match. And in the Gargoyle it was possible to talk. Once Johnny Craxton was sitting with Peter Watson at a table with Graham Greene and Freddie Ayer, and Greene was challenging Freddie to furnish arguments from the depths of his agnosticism to demolish the religion he had embraced. 'Talk me out of it', he said. 'De-Catholocize me with your logical positivism.' 'And all this perfectly serious exchange was going on', said Johnny, 'in a Club where there was dancing and all this terrible kitsch music which Lucian and I, who were very keen on good jazz, black American music, greatly despised. But this unbelievably old-fashioned music didn't interfere with the conversation. That was the good thing about it. People could sit on the banquettes and those little gold chairs and have proper and improper conversations and Brian Howard could go from table to table telling people terrible, cruel home-truths – and the band played on, without drowning it all.' Michael Wishart was another who applauded the opportunities for conversation that the Gargoyle offered. 'It was possible in this vertiginous Pleasure Dome,' he mused, 'not only to see the person addressing one, but also to hear and understand what they were saying. As with the post-conciliar Mass, this was occasionally an advantage.'

Freddie's effort at de-conversion evidently met with honourable failure. A failure of a different sort greeted the tender Guy put out to seduce Johnny. 'Would you like to come back to my flat?' he offered. 'Would you like to be whipped – a wild thrashing? Wine thrown in?' Johnny said no, he didn't want to be whipped at all. 'I was terrified. I tell you who saved me. He was sitting opposite. Philip Toynbee. Toynbee the once acknowledged Commie, Burgess the covert one. A nice irony.' That scene ended with a tussle between Guy and Philip rolling about on the floor amongst the dancers, threatening Alexander's drum.

Johnny Minton, a teacher at the Royal College of Art, was a charismatic and widely loved figure in post-war Soho. 'When I remember the Gargoyle, I think very much of Johnny', the poet Elizabeth Smart said. 'And then there was this dancing – proper dancing. Johnny was the most uninhibited dancer. Often just by himself. It was when I was just dancing around – I don't know who with, not George [Barker] anyway – and a man stood up at a table where he was sitting with a ravishing woman and said, "As one novelist to another, I like the way you dance." It was Henry Green. I've always thought – what did he mean by that? Did he mean he didn't like the book that I had just published and I didn't think anyone had read, but that he liked my dancing better?' How sad that Elizabeth could have doubted that of all people Henry, a writer of such rare sensitivity, would not have instantly recognized *By Grand Central Station I Sat Down and Wept* to be a masterpiece. In Brigid Brophy's view her majestic prose-poem of tragic lament to love and loss, which to their shame created little stir among the critics when it first came out in 1945, must rank amongst the first half dozen in its genre, in the world.

The Gargoyle had a tremendous appeal for Elizabeth Smart. 'There were all those passions: people falling in love with each other and somebody's wife was there with somebody else and things of that kind getting out of hand which made it lovely. There was nobody sitting there just munching. There were real passions flying around and there were people tearing each other's eyes out, but it was mostly for love or jealousy or something reasonable like that. The people were rather beautiful, too; and there was the fact that David, and especially Virginia, were so glamorous. They didn't fuss about things too much.'

While all this was going on, and without much fuss, David did take Virginia to the Promised Land of Portugal. Nonetheless, significant strings must have been tweaked for this to happen given the very stringent travel and currency restrictions about to be imposed by the new Labour Government. David hired a six-seater plane from Croydon and they took off for Lisbon. But the plane ran out of petrol and so they landed instead at Oporto. '*Heaven* after the war years', said Virginia. From there they went by bus and train to Seville, Cordoba, Granada and ending up in the charming and quite unspoilt fishing village of Torremolinos. This trip confirmed the identification mystique David felt for Spain, first seeded when he went there with Pamela in the twenties. A still-existent feudalism in the country appealed to the hidalgo in him, more deeply rooted than his recent political emancipation. Here, or hereabouts, was where he wished to settle.

19

Pauline was now in Baghdad. This had come about through her marriage in August of the previous year (1946) to a most suitable suitor, the determined and inscrutable Julian Lane Fox Pitt-Rivers. Julian had been engaged as tutor to Feisal, the eleven-year-old boy-king of Iraq, who would be assassinated in 1958 at the instigation of Colonel Nasser of Egypt in order to make way for a socialist republic. When he had asked Pauline to marry him, Julian made it clear that he was not prepared to share her with the 'twelve and six pennies' – the price then of a seat in the stalls. So it was to be goodbye to the boards for Pauline. The marriage had been solemnized at St George's, Hanover Square, a splendid affair with David giving her away and Hermione beaming her delight on the large congregation. 'Luckily the Church wasn't overcrowded as so many people were up in Scotland shooting', explained Pauline. Grouse would have been a very welcome addition to the table, which in the great majority of cases was where the birds would never reach. The nation's table was extremely bare: rationing had been brought back on a near wartime basis. Bread was rationed; butter, margarine and cooking fats were cut from eight to seven ounces weekly; the meat ration remained at 1s. 2d. per head per week.

Hermione, though regretting Pauline's defection to Arabia felix, kept her own feet firmly on the boards in all weathers. She was in a huge West End success, *Grand National Night*, written by Major-General Campbell Christie and his wife, whom she had met in Malta while touring with ENSA. Leslie Banks was the male lead and there were two female starring roles, the good sister and the bad sister. Hermione played them both. She had also found a romantic replacement for her previous attachment, Sir John 'Buffles' Milbank, who had died on active service with his regiment in the last days of the war. This was Francis de Moleyns, the younger and impoverished brother of an Irish peer, Lord Ventry, and a 'charmer'. Francis was in the Gargoyle celebrating some wartime event with fellow ex-flyers on the same evening as 'a kind friend had arranged a very jolly party for me [Hermione] ... with, of course, David'. Francis spotted Hermione and came over uninvited and sat down at their table. Hermione, as she said, was 'hypnotized from the word go ... the best looking man after David I had ever seen'. Whoever gave the word 'go' it was emphatically not David.

Hermione's new demon lover taught her a number of things she did not want to know, such as how to cast a fly and how to use a 12 bore shotgun. He also tried to teach her something she knew only too well – how to spend money recklessly. Hermione was getting a very large salary from the play and it was not hard for de Moleyns to persuade her to become a principal investor in a number of schemes aimed at making the desired quick and easy money. One was the opening of a sea-food bar in Victoria, near the Chester Square house Hermione had taken. All might have gone well had de Moleyns not regarded the 'takings' as something there to be taken.

David and Virginia's relationship also left something to be desired. It was not just his drinking which imposed strains, so much as the Lothario factor which still refused to lie down. Anne Valery, the author and dramatist, recalls her first meeting with David as a young girl in the Intelligence Corps on leave from the army. It was among the 'Cherry-bums' and old polo sticks and uniforms from the Boer war in Rosa's cellar during an air raid.

> David started to talk to me and tell me about his club and invited me to go there the following night. I longed to go even though Rosa took me aside to give me a quiet warning. But I didn't get another chance to go until just after the war. And when I did it really changed my life as, I think, it did for many young people in those days. In my case it was through meeting the Greek poet Nanos Valaoritis there, who had escaped somehow from German-occupied Greece and arrived, via Cairo, in London. Through meeting Nanos and eventually marrying him I became a literary groupie. Sonia Brownell (later married to George Orwell) was the head groupie, of course. God, what a prickly number she was. But to give her her due, she was the one who edited *Horizon*. Cyril would come and go, but Sonia would do the day-to-day slog.
>
> The Gargoyle was a wonderful place and it was the only place then, possibly now, perhaps ever, where a woman could go alone without her character being impugned. If you were alone, Merrill would send over to your table some smoked salmon, which I didn't happen to like, and some brown bread and butter and you never received a bill so long as you were alone. When I first went I was

taken by Anthony Carson and when we got to the top I recognized it instantly as a place I had been taken to by my nanny for a children's party. Then David spotted me and came up and said 'Ah, my dear, so you've come at last.' I felt very grand because I was already known. But with David living on the floor below there was always this slight hazard because sometimes he would stand at the lift gate outside his flat and if he saw someone he rather fancied going up – the lift went up oh so slowly – he would open the lift gates on his side and there you would be stuck and there would he be, having thwarted you from reaching the Gargoyle, saying 'Come and have a little drink with me first.' You were not let in without let, as they say.

There was also the time when David decided to take the beautiful ex-wife of one of the Club's members for a week-end in Paris. Everything was to be the high perfection of civilized living – a very comfortable but discreet hotel; they would eat wisely but not too well at the most selective restaurants and drink only the best wine in moderation; they would go to the theatre, visit art galleries, gaze at splendid buildings. David even arranged – in the days when you could get into your *wagon-lit* at Victoria station and remain undisturbed until the train's arrival in Paris – for Moyses Stevens to have flowers delivered to their reserved table in the restaurant car. And as they sat down in the train to nourish themselves in preparation for the consummation of their great passion, David ordered whatever it was he had before lunch – five dry martinis, say – from which point on that week-end became the whitest occasion ever spent by two beautiful people on pleasure bent.

Virginia, of course, had a great many of her own admirers, the writer Anthony Carson being among the most impassioned. But, as is well known, sauce acceptable to the gander is not necessarily meet for the goose. David was not a *mari complaisant*. He did not view attentions paid to Virginia kindly, any more than he had easily tolerated Hermione's worshippers. This led to a certain domestic tension. Nevertheless, apart from the not infrequent withering aside from David, this tension was never allowed in the Gargoyle to degenerate into the marital histrionics indulged in by some of the Club's members.

*

Johnny Minton was a very particular example of a new energy drawn from the world of young painters – Francis Bacon, Rodrigo Moynihan, Robert Buhler, Eduardo Paolozzi, Lucian Freud, ex-painter now critic David Sylvester, and the dread inseparable Colquhoun and MacBryde with their haggis accents and swinging kilts worn so far south of the Tweed. They bubbled up in the lift night after night before going down into the ballroom to puncture or burst. Johnny Minton's bubble would never burst suddenly as sometimes happened to Philip Toynbee or Dylan who would go cleanly as if they had been picked off by a sniper's bullet. With Johnny there would be very often a slow and somewhat melancholy deflation. It was Minton who first brought Francis Bacon up to the Club. Francis remembers that evening well. 'Dan Farson came across the room to where I was sitting with Johnny and some of his friends and he said "Are you Francis Bacon?" and I said "Yes" and he threw his glass of beer in my face. That was my introduction to the Gargoyle.' Since Farson has often publicly acclaimed his great affection for Francis, it can safely be assumed that this opening gesture was issued in the spirit of flirtation rather than of gratuitous aggression.

> But the thing is [Francis says] the place, because people probably were so drunk, was really made for rows. I've seen greater scenes than I've ever seen in my life in the Gargoyle – except for one's personal rows. They were nightly. They went on not only for hours, they went on for days. It was like one of those instalments where it says tomorrow you'll get such and such – well, you certainly did in the Gargoyle. It was great fun, really, in spite of the rows. And there were marvellous evenings without rows. I remember once meeting Sartre who was there with his governess, Simone de Beauvoir, sitting with Sonia Orwell. Lucian and I were both invited over to their table. Sartre got up and sat on it waggling his short legs and said, 'Who is that good looking one?' jabbing his Gauloise at Lucian. I do remember Sartre was very, very charming. He said "when you come to Paris ring me". But I never did.
>
> I used to go up there after the Colony Room closed with Muriel Belcher and Carmel, with so many people who used the Gargoyle. People like George Barker, Rodrigo Moynihan and Gerald Hamilton, and of course Natalie Newton and Henrietta Law [Francis used Muriel and Henrietta as his models on several occasions]. Natalie and Joy Newton – Craig she then was, I think – always had rows. They both rowed with everybody and of course Robert Newton himself was well made for rows, too. I think the most interesting thing *were* those rows – like instalment stories.
>
> Cyril Connolly went there a lot. I never really knew Cyril. I used to see him not long before Sonia died, quite often at her place. I

always got on terribly badly with Cyril. I think he probably hated me as much as I disliked him. I found him profoundly unsympathetic. In *Horizon* I think he did one of the best magazines that has been done for many years in this country – but that's another story. He approached you always as though he wanted to be wounded, which is a horrible way of approaching people. You only had to see his whole furtive look. And Brian Howard. The amazing thing, I was always told he was supposed to be so witty. I never understood him as being witty at all. In any case, wit is such a very rare thing: wit is generally a very acerbic commentary on behaviour. I never heard it from Brian. But I miss the Gargoyle very much. It was a sympathetic place to go – why I don't know. It is an impossible thing to analyse.

On Francis' issue of rows, Robert Buhler recalled one (happily, with only a single instalment) in which Buhler was the antagonist and Francis an heroic defender.

I fell foul of James Pope-Hennessy [the author and, then, Literary Editor of *The Spectator*]. Sitting one night at a table in the Gargoyle were Lucian Freud, Francis, Prudence Branch who I was living with, Johnny Minton, Pope-Hennessy and a couple of his paratrooper 'rough-trade' boys, and myself. Pope-Hennessy and I didn't hit it off. With the drink I have an unfortunate tongue – like so many people. Evidently I had said something about his brother John [an authority on Italian painting and then a keeper at the Victoria and Albert Museum] which offended. Anyway Prudence, Lucian, Francis and I left. When we got to the bottom in that rickety little lift we found James and his two paratroopers waiting for us. They had gone down the fire-escape stairs – much quicker. As we got out, I was immediately set upon by the two paratroopers. Now Lucian – we were all out by this time – Lucian was very brave. He jumped on the back of one of the bully boys while Francis kicked at his shins. Every time one of the paratroopers came near him, Francis just kicked – in a very lady-like way, I must say. In spite of their determined efforts, I got quite badly bashed up.

They were horrid, those two brothers, in their different ways. When I recovered I sent James Pope-Hennessy a solicitor's letter in which the solicitor, who was a bit of an ass, referred to it as 'that Florentine behaviour'. Then Eddie Marsh – obviously James had got on to him for assistance – rang me up and said, oh, do drop it. I was 'disturbing the waves of social equilibrium' – his euphemism for threat of homosexual exposure.

In spite of the threat of 'Florentine behaviour', the Gargoyle was, as Bobby Buhler said,

> the only place which wasn't a 'set', like the literary set, the social set and so on. It was a meeting place for all sorts of unexpected people. And yet it had already been sieved through, so you wouldn't get very unlikely strangers there, you would get people you had either heard about, vaguely knew, or their friends.
>
> Then there was that time David Tennant – it was one of David's promotional gimmicks – got hold of a whole lot of Burmese dancers, ballet dancers, and they were strutting their stuff with old Alexander doing his best to keep up in the background. Meanwhile Philip Toynbee and Lucian had been quarrelling noisily over a girl at a table and this finally led to a sort of wild and messy punch-up. Unfortunately this was a running battle which then settled down to take place amongst the dancers in mid-number. The dancers – you couldn't tell what sex they were – were very beautiful but the magic, I'm afraid, was rather broken by these two Westerners taking drunken lunges at each other amongst the exquisitely graceful formal gestures of the little Asians. So that ended in disaster with the dancers wrapping their skimpy clothes round their loins and mincing off in a collective huff.

David's well-intentioned efforts to salvage the Club's ailing finances were all too often undone, as with the Burmese dancers, by 'insiders'. Joan Wyndham went one evening with Bobby Newton and Natalie for a 'special evening' laid on for rather grand people. 'But Bobby peed on the floor', she said, 'and the evening was a fiasco. Regulars took no notice, but the "grand" people all walked out.' Another own goal. Some of the regulars then let loose. Natalie threw a bottle at Joan's head and had to be forcibly hauled off her by Arthur Koestler, recently married to Dick's ex-mistress, Mamaine Paget. A somewhat different gladiatorial contest arose between the physically ill-matched artist Feliks Topolski, with the build and address of a smallish but fit Turkish pasha, and the tall, lanky man of letters, Peter Quennell, a natural exponent of the straight left. The *casus belli* was Barbara Skelton, *femme fatale* extraordinary. Barbara had been bombed out of her little room in Mayfair above a dress designer for whom she modelled and had, since the war, settled, according to Feliks, 'for living in a basket, as it were. She was this beauty, an odd beauty because it was not real beauty, but tremendously desired by all men all round. And being utterly silent and not offering really anything and not going along with any situation but at the same time, in consequence, being the most desirable object in existence. In the early days she was mysterious with this lovely cat-attitude of not settling anywhere but just carrying the basket of essentials and moving from one person to another. At that time she was mostly using as bases, Peter Quennell and me. And so, if she stayed with me and after a few days became unbearable – because she was unbearable basically – she would simply without much explanation take her basket, slink off along the wall and go to Peter; and then reappear in a week or two to stay in my bed with no things said. And that's how it went on for a while, for quite a while – for years, actually.

'On this evening I sat downstairs with Barbara and John Davenport and Peter sat by himself at another table. And Quennell was fuming obviously, because he was full of jealousy, full of possessiveness ... which I wasn't, that was not my line. And then we moved to go and Peter, who had followed us out, went for me. Peter looked a very forceful character, he was always falling into these fights. I was not a fighter but had this strange quality which I carried since my school days of being very strong. So he went for me and pulled his fist at a sort of distance aiming at my face and let it go. Then I don't know how it happened but in a second somehow that fist didn't land on my face and I had him by the front of his jacket and pushed him away. He just flew into the corner and fell down completely squashed on the floor. But then I had these ridiculous thoughts based on cinema, or whatever, that now one has to complete this act to do something final. I went to him for a few steps and didn't know quite what to do so I ended by just fluffing his hair.'

This *coup de grâce* was the ultimate indignity for Peter. The hair since Oxford days had contributed much to his animus and as such attracted the malice of Brian Howard, who, according to Harold Acton, took exception to its Shelley-like fall across Peter's brow. 'My dear, you can't think how *démodé* you look, with that tumbling jonquil. So greenery-yallery. It just isn't done these days. Where is your *comb*?' demanded Brian. But whatever line it assumed – straight, fringed or pulled back – Peter's hair was always immaculately brushed; but ruffled – never! Save, gently, by the loved one – by Barbara's feline paw.

The lift had now arrived and leaving the disconsolate Peter rearranging his coif on the floor, the three descended; Davenport, a Cambridge boxing blue, profuse with congratulations to Feliks. Peter, it was later learnt, sustained not only damage to the ego, but two broken ribs. As Feliks said, 'A simple ridiculous story but very typical of the Gargoyle. It was really a very high-brow place, a place of the upper strata; intellectually as well as artistically and socially. So somehow the scuffles among people who were not professionally able to fight – like Philip Toynbee and Guy Burgess and Peter and myself – were rather ridiculous things.'

An even more ridiculous event occurred on the night the Club was raided, and not by the police. 'There were quite a lot of us there that night,' Anne Valery remembers,

> I had gone up to that barn-like ladies loo with all that space and proper lavatories with floor to ceiling mahogany doors – out of which I once surprised Lucian emerging with Henrietta Law – and there was Caryl Chance spitting on her mascara and saying, 'Jesus Christ! I married one millionaire by the time I was nineteen. I'm certainly going to marry another before I'm twenty-two.' The 'another' Caryl had in mind was Tony Strickland Hubbard of Woolworth fame sitting downstairs with Wendy Abbot, re-christened Henrietta when she married Michael Law. Hubbard once got hold of Henrietta by the legs and spun her across the dance floor and she went into Alex's drum – head first. Spun her right between the kilts of the otherwise inseparable Colquhoun and MacBryde.
>
> On this evening we were all sitting together at a table – it was quite late – and suddenly two men appeared at the top of the stairs in raincoats and felt hats and said 'This is a raid'. Apparently they had come up in the lift and jammed it at the top so nobody else could come up. They held up the bar on the top floor and got the takings and then walked slowly down the steps on to the dance floor, hands holding something threatening in their pockets, and said 'This is a raid'. We were all fairly sloshed by this time and I remember Caryl saying in that nasal drawl of hers: 'Oh, don't be so silly, darlings, you look absolutely lovely and I'm going to dance with one of you,' and threw her arms around the one nearest her which embarrassed him acutely. What happened then was absolutely ridiculous because you can only hold up a place if people believe that you really are a gangster. Nobody in the Club, apart from Caryl, took any notice of them at all. By this time the barman upstairs had managed to untie himself and telephone the police. The next moment the police came pounding through the fire-escape exit door and grabbed the crooks, whom they obviously knew. With the arrival of the police everyone

started milling around and shoving drinks up their jumpers because it was 'after hours'. Caryl, in spite of the police presence, was still trying to dance with one of the hoods and Hubbard was saying 'Christ, I don't believe this!' I then heard one of the crooks say, 'I've never seen such disgraceful behaviour in my life!' And the police said, 'Oh, yes, it's not a place to come to.' So the police and the crooks went off commiserating, followed by indignant shouts from the members, some of whom were now coming alive to what was happening. 'Don't you want my evidence, officer?' they wanted to know. Kitty Epstein, who I had come with that evening, just sat there smiling sweetly. That was before she was married to Lucian.

Tony Hubbard had put up the money for *Circus*, the literary magazine started by John Davenport which went bust almost at once. 'The reason why Hubbard got involved in *Circus*', explained Anne, 'was that Davenport was teaching at Stowe when Hubbard was there. Tony says that while he was learning the violin, Davenport seduced him. That's as may be. Anyway, that's how Hubbard got into Davenport's life – during the violin lesson. So when Hubbard got the use of some of his Woolworth money, Davenport got on to him smartly and persuaded him – in between the lower depths of the Mandrake and the heady heights of the Gargoyle – to put up ten thousand pounds or so – a lot of money then – to launch the speedily doomed lit. mag.'

The Mandrake was a very sympathetic little club dug out of the cellars in Meard Street beside and below the Gargoyle run by a large and imposing Russian called Boris who supposedly had decapitated a rival in his native land. Its *raison d'être* was chess. It was a Chess Club where you could concentrate on the board over your next moves in a quiet and serious atmosphere. It was also a place where you could drink in the afternoons. On that account it quickly assumed an additional function as a launching pad for the Gargoyle – a place where loins could be girded, friends gathered, the spirits stiffened for that challenging arena up above.

The kilted Roberts (Colquhoun and MacBryde) were not the only arresting sartorial aspect of the post-war Gargoyle. Mark Culme-Seymour might arrive in a paisley dressing gown. Lucian Freud sometimes sported tartan trews which, it was said, caused Princess Margaret to raise an interrogative eyebrow. 'An old Portuguese tartan, ma'am,' was the explanation. Lucian would also partly disguise himself under a very odd-looking cap which he said he had taken off the head of a drowned Dutch sailor found on a lonely beach in his maritime years. Dennis

Craig, Joy Newton's second husband, always wore hairy tweeds and was never, even in the ballroom, without his walking stick – like an African tribal symbol of authority. Bobby Newton, too, favoured a stick with which to bang on tables to give emphasis to his needs and punctuate his dramatic turns. And Sylvester Gates, married to Pauline, Bobby's other sister, in a drunken fury at the bar hit the unfortunate Quentin Crewe over the head with *his* stick – Quentin even then in a wheel-chair. Extravagant behaviour for a deputy chairman of the Westminster Bank. But it was David Sylvester's US Army combat jacket that excited most notable attention. 'That was my passport to immortality that thing', says David cheerfully. 'I had picked it up in Paris in '47 when I was researching an article I was doing for Benedict Nicolson (then editor of the *Burlington Magazine*). The first time I met Barbara Skelton, at the Gargoyle, I was wearing it. Then we went out for dinner a couple of nights later and I disappointed her very much by wearing a suit. She didn't like that at all. Then Evelyn Waugh saw me in this thing – I wore it all the time in those days – and started having nightmares about me. He wrote bizarre letters to Anne Fleming and Christopher Sykes about the horror of the impact it had made upon him. ("I saw the most extraordinary man named SYLVESTER and cannot get him out of my dreams night and day. He was an art critic and looked like an American soldier of the most alarming kind." And "Never an hour passes but I think of Sylvester."'

*

In May 1948, Dick Wyndham was killed by a sniper's bullet in Palestine. It happened just four days after the conclusion of the British mandate there and the proclamation of the new state of Israel. That this was given instant recognition from the White House by President Truman, stunned delegates to the UN. Dick had been appointed the *Sunday Times* war correspondent in the Middle East, and he was in Palestine to cover the hostilities which were the predictable result of no boundaries having been declared for the new State. The cause of his death was characteristic of a certain recklessness in his Irish blood from his mother's side. His daughter, Joan, simply attributes his demise to the fact that he could not resist dressing up. For the purpose of his newspaper coverage Dick had been accredited to the Arab Legion in Jordan, to which a number of British officers were attached as instructors. Naturally he had adopted their particular and very stylish head-dress worn with khaki uniform. 'Daddy was always dressing up in Arab robes,' said Joan. 'I remember as a child he would have my mother carried around on a palaquin, she dressed as a *houri* and he would be the young Arab princeling. Given the chance of wearing the authentic Arab Legion uniform, of course he couldn't resist it. So when, dressed like this, he climbed up onto a ridge outside Jerusalem to photograph the Arab lines in full view of the Hadassah hospital, a Jewish sniper just potted him.'

Dick had worked as a foreign correspondent in the Near East for some time, a role he relished. It eased his restless spirit and fed his sense of adventure and amorous curiosity. Whenever he was back in England he would train a sun-lamp over the bald tonsure on the crown of his grizzled pate to enhance his rascally allure. At one time he was writing for the *News of the World*, owned by his friends Derek Jackson and Philip Dunn, a paper whose interest in the vagaries of human nature has not changed over the years. Nor had Dick's practice of them. To the wags of Fleet Street, Dick became known as the paper's 'whipping boy'. Dick had huge expense accounts, Joan remembers. 'He kept this suite in the Hyde Park Hotel where he would give amazing dinner parties (rationing not withstanding) for people like Cyril, David, Christopher Sykes, Freddy Mayor, Ralph (Bunny) Keene, Tom Driberg and Peter Quennell – with attendant *houris*, of course. I found him one morning at breakfast in the hotel with a huge piece of paper. "What are you doing, Daddy?" I asked him. "I'm making out my swindle sheet," he said.'

Dick often managed to scoop his fellow journalists by using his own aeroplane to get there first. This may not have made him too popular with them. On the other hand he was often crashing it. 'He was very vulnerable, I always thought', says Joan. 'He crashed it in the heights of Afghanistan and spent a week walking back through the mountains of Iran and got frost-bite in both his feet. I was in hospital and he staggered in to see me on crutches wearing a sheepskin coat to the floor. He looked wonderful – Bessarabian. Of course he was a "spook". I am convinced of that. He was a field man using his newspaper assignments as a cover. He was a great friend of Geoffrey Keating out there who was a spook also. [Keating was a shadowy, nevertheless ubiquitous figure, who worked in the Middle East for BP. He appeared to know "everybody" and go "everywhere". Even the Queen was overheard to remark irritably of his damson face: "Who *is* that man I seem to see everywhere?" "Everywhere" often being where Keating had no official business.] Of course, unlike Kim Philby, Daddy and Geoffrey only spied for us.'

Joan Wyndham had predicted in her diary that when she was demobbed from the Waafs at the end of the war, she would take her £60 and go to the dogs. Very much to the contrary. But she did step briefly into her cousin Pauline's discarded shoes when she became involved with Lucian Freud. 'When I first knew him he had this bloody hawk which he would take with him on the underground. The hawk *hated* Lucian. He would take it on the Circle Line wearing his grandfather's overcoat with a fur collar from Vienna and much too big for him with the hawk attacking him and trying to peck his beady little eyes out. It caused quite a hoo-ha. People weren't used to eccentrics in those days. Lucian told me he had worked in a circus. I didn't believe him for a second. He psyched this wretched animal – it was terrified of him. It used to get the odd dead mouse thrown at it in his studio, but finally it died of starvation before Lucian had finished drawing it. An endless performance.'

Pauline had returned with Julian from Baghdad when his tutorship of the young Feisal came to an end. He then went up to Oxford to do a post-graduate course in anthropology and the young couple were obliged to live quite frugally. By chance Pauline met the film producer Anatole de Grunwald. He had a project that he very much wanted to film: Pushkin's *The Queen of Spades*. Thorold Dickinson would direct and Edith Evans was to play the old Countess. The actress whom he had wanted to play the Countess as a young woman had fallen out. Please step in, Tolly begged Pauline. A serious film project with an excellent cast and a fine director with an offer of £50 a day – Julian had to agree that Pauline must accept. She did and the film was a success. It first appeared in the year of Dick's death. Pauline's beauty was shown to good advantage in period costume and the controlled intensity of her performance impressed Wardour Street. It was a time when 'period' films were rather in vogue and this resulted in Pauline receiving a great many offers of further work. But she turned them all down, deciding to shut her theatrical make-up box for good and go and live with Julian in Spain. 'That was the reason, really, I wanted to go and live in Spain, because Daddy went every year. He was a passionate follower of the bulls and used to go all over Spain to see Belmonte fighting them. He had been an Hispanophile for a very long time.'

*

The last time David and Virginia went to Spain together was in 1952. They went together but came back separately. Janet Brickell herself had only just returned to Holloway House having taken a two-year sabbatical, the first time in her life that she had been away from the village where she was born. 'The old gardener [Street] told me that things were going wrong with Mr and Mrs Tennant and I couldn't believe him. They seemed so happy I had finally come back and David went so far as to say it was like home again with me back. Then they went out to Spain for what was to be their last time together. Virginia returned home after a few weeks alone so I could tell something had seriously gone wrong. Mr Tennant stayed on in Spain until Virginia had left East Knoyle. Then he came back for a bit until the house was sold. David's insistence on their going to Spain was a last forlorn attempt to salvage their marriage. But, as Virginia said, "It came too late. Ten years ago I would have adored it, loved nothing better. But the idea of going to Spain then and setting up house – I just *hated* the thought of it. David was so disappointed. I know it was a bitter disappointment to him, but by then I had got to know Henry [Bath] and the whole thing changed. I would have stayed with David forever if it had not been for Henry. That was the crux of the thing. We had fallen in love. It started four years before at the Chelsea Arts Ball. That changed everything. It was so sad, really, a time of emotional agony for me. Because I still *loved* David. But there you are."'

*

The year 1950, which was to prove such a sad one for David, opened quite promisingly. The Club celebrated its silver jubilee in January with Compton Mackenzie as guest of honour. This was attended by 'men of letters, artists, stage and film celebrities, people of title and social consequence'. The press reports read like those of the opening night; only the company had changed. To mark the moment, David had the innovative idea of mounting an exhibition of paintings by members of the staff (catalogue introduction by David Sylvester). The six exhibitors – Sunday painters, should they be so lucky – were all drawn from those who had long become accustomed to behave in the Club with the legendary stoicism of the sinking *Titanic*'s crew. That they remained so loyal and constant in the face of provocation, says much for the affection that David inspired in them. Provocation, the temptation of Alex Alexander's drum and the sudden overturning of lovingly laid tables apart, could vary from Dylan's insistence on dancing with a busy waiter to take his (Dylan's) 'mind off things', to Donald Maclean stubbornly refusing to leave the Club when very drunk unless accompanied in the lift by the homely presence of Mrs Calder, the Scottish custodian of the ladies cloakroom; to Miss Ransley, Club Secretary, coming downstairs to the flat with the announcement: 'I'm sorry to have to tell you, Mr Tennant, but Mr Toynbee's throwing salt cellars about'; to the more mundane activity of dodging the bread roll missile.

Hanging over the aftermath of these celebrations was the realization for David that a very serious shift in affections threatened, and all too close to home. This was partly due to the effect of Henry and Daphne Bath's marital schism. '... my marriage to Henry could not survive', Daphne has written in her autobiography. 'During and since the war we both developed along different lines, so that divorce became inevitable.' Added to which, Xan Fielding, once safely put down by Barbara Skelton, formed an attachment for Daphne that would not be denied, and that would, after the divorce, result in their marriage. It was, in fact, in the Club where Xan disported almost nightly for some years after the war, that he first got to know Daphne. Xan's presence there could sometimes be an unwelcome reminder to David of his own personal discomfiture. Although it was true that some cracks had now begun to show in the mask of a matinée idol faced with an endless run of late-night shows, David had emphatically not lost his stylish ego-puncturing capability. He once turned to Xan sitting at his table, and whose critical attentions he had begun to find rather aggravating, and said: 'You, Xan, are nothing but a *tiny wasp* attacking a *rather fine fruit*.'

When David returned from Spain the protracted procedure of divorce, obligatory at that time, was well under way. The social changes that had been taking place since the war seemed to him more marked. The certainties as well as the tensions that had excited and given strength under insular siege had receded across the waters. People had moved, associations loosened, responsibilities, and often loyalties, changed. Peace had brought its own anxieties and new insecurities. There had been a notable number of suicides among the Club's members. People were said to be falling off the edge. The survivors of the old Gargoyle establishment appeared less frequently. Clive Bell was an exception, there, as ever, to dance rather primly wearing a winged collar with his black tie, the only person in a dinner jacket. In the atmosphere was a distancing of place, a cooling of time, like a night-club taken over by the dawn.

One who had not yet fallen off the edge, but was swaying perilously close to it, was Donald Maclean. In May 1950 Maclean had returned from a disastrous spell as Head of Chancery at the Embassy in Cairo. He was in a very sorry state. Excessive drinking, lapses into homosexuality, manic rages and acutely embarrassing outbreaks of violence led to his being gratefully released by the Ambassador. The establishment in London accepted that he was in the throes of a nervous breakdown compounded by acute melancholia. He was treated for this by a woman psychiatrist who diagnosed his drinking problem as a result of a guilt complex over his treatment of his wife Melinda. But the guilt went rather deeper than that. It lay heavily on his chest and he badly needed somewhere to throw it off. His friend Mark Culme-Seymour had the solution: Gargoyle Club membership. In the absence of David in Spain, Virginia proposed him, Courtney Merrill seconded and on recognition of his cheque for four guineas (foreign membership) Donald Maclean was made a member in August.

Mark and Donald had been friends since before the war. It was Mark who had introduced Donald to Melinda in Paris and Donald in turn had been instrumental in helping Mark to escape on the day the Germans marched into the City. Now, reunited in London, they lunched together once a week and were frequently in each other's company in the Gargoyle at night. Mark describes him lurching one night from table to table barking out that he was the English Hiss (Alger Hiss, a US State Department senior 'establishment' official who had been shopped by Whittaker Chambers, a self-confessed former Russian agent, and had come up before the House Un-American Activities Committee at the beginning of the McCarthy hysteria). 'Not', said Mark, 'that anybody took the slightest interest.' This compulsively indiscreet and reckless behaviour was going on at a time when Maclean was holding an extremely important seat at the Foreign Office as Head of the American Department. He was also trying once more to 'make a go' of his marriage by living out of temptation in the country with his two children and Melinda, now once more pregnant. Another example of his precipitate conduct was when he attacked Goronway Rees in the Club. Rees was a close friend of Guy Burgess whom Maclean had known at Cambridge. He blundered drunkenly over to the table where Rees was sitting with a party of friends and bearing down belligerently said: 'I know all about you, you bastard .... You used to be one of us but you ratted.'

Robert Buhler was in the Gargoyle one night with Mark and Donald and Daphne Bath and one or two others. 'I remember Donald kept on saying he worked for Uncle Joe [Stalin], and Mark turned to me and said "Do you think he really means it? I think he does!" I said "Don't be so fucking stupid. It's just *pour épater*. I mean head of the American desk at the FO? He's pissed and wants to take the piss out of us." Donald then got too drunk and Mark said he'd put him up for the night and we took him back to Mark's flat in Sloane Avenue Mansions and he had a bit more to drink and became totally impossible. It almost seemed as if he had had an epileptic fit and by that time he was on the floor. So Mark said, "You sit on him and I'll try to bring him round". Mark squirted a soda syphon over his head and I sat there getting wet, but it was no good he was quite out. How wrong I was and how right Mark was. Obviously Donald felt in the Gargoyle he was free to say anything he wished and even if he had been believed, seemingly only by Mark, people might not have felt it was a particularly urgent issue.'

Maclean knew that he was under surveillance but he did not know that the MI5 investigations started in 1949 into the source of the security leakage from the Foreign Office had narrowed the suspects down to two. In May of that year there was only one name on the list. It was that of Donald Maclean. This was a situation of which the FO was largely unaware, or else he would never have been given the American desk. Only a handful of authorized people in the country were in the know, and one unauthorized person – Guy Burgess. Guy had returned from the embassy in Washington on 7 May, 1951 in disgrace, his Foreign Office employment in suspension, but with this highly secret and, for Maclean, vital piece of information which would lead to their joint defection. Burgess and Maclean left England on the night of 25 May. On the evening of the 23rd Burgess had dined at the Gargoyle with Barley Allison, not then the perspicacious publisher she was to become, but one of the first British women diplomats to be promoted above clerical level and an ex-MI6 operative. Barley told the author shortly before her death that she had remained convinced that it was never Burgess's intention to remain in Russia once he had achieved his act of derring-do by getting Maclean there. 'Guy intended to go on to the Middle East. To Egypt or one of the North African countries and start a new life there. I know it.' If she was right, then how naive he was.

Also in the Gargoyle that evening was Anne Valery. She was roundly abused by Burgess when she asked to borrow the salt on his table. 'He was unbelievably rude to me, so I just got up and grabbed it.' Some time later Anne was working on a television series for Granada while a documentary on Burgess and Maclean was being produced there. 'They did a mammoth research lasting over a year and were always looking for a third (Blunt) and fourth (Philby) and fifth (?) man and also looking for the "letter box". When I saw the documentary privately I said afterwards to the producer, the obvious place for Burgess and Maclean to exchange and collect messages, the perfect place in the whole of London, the one place where the Home Office, the Foreign Office, Bohemia, the sodden aristocracy, the odd Russian, the odd Hungarian could *all* go without it looking odd at all was the Gargoyle. The producer said that's very strange because he had no idea what the Gargoyle was and it kept on coming up again and again and again in our research.'

The 'human interest story of the century', the defection of the two diplomats to Russia which broke on 7 June, 1951, was also the last related dramatic event during David's tenancy of the Club he had founded and which had been for nearly thirty years, his life. The actor-manager playing out his part in the wings; the self-appointed ring-master with a taste for the whip, yet having a vicarious dependence on the circus of his own creation; David Tennant, the 'grise' of his own 'eminence', decided the time had now come to bring down the big top, to sell up and go.

With the guy ropes severed, the 'crystal man' felt as light as helium – but directionless. God would, surely, still fill the sails; but from which direction would the wind be blowing? It blew him across the Irish Sea and down into a place of magic above a white beach by a lake tucked into the Featherbed Mountains near Dublin. This had been a hunting-lodge once owned by the family of Rose La Touche and then bought before the First World War by Ernest Guinness, second son of the first Earl of Iveagh. Luggala, as the place is named, had in time been given by Ernest to his third, and some say preferred, daughter Oonagh. David had known the bewitching Oonagh since she was a deb in the thirties when she would often be brought to the Gargoyle, and he liked her very much. And he knew that she had recently and sadly been divorced from her second husband, Dominick, 4th Baron Oranmore and Browne. Some barely conscious instinct might have directed his course to Dublin in the expectation that not only would the sails of his barque be filled but its now rather empty hold as well.

His wild flight brought him to Luggala just as dinner for thirty was being served in the main hall. David's timing was unfortunate. This was August and the Dublin Horse Show was in full swing and for which a house-party at Oonagh's for largely non-horsey folk was standard procedure. Three Rollses and sundry lesser vehicles had been waiting to take the house-party to Dublin for dinner at the Shelbourne Hotel, but a last minute whim had dictated a change of plans. So a six-course dinner for thirty had to be provided by the kitchens at Luggala – and no Rosa Lewis to take the strain. David appeared suddenly in the doorway of the dining-hall like Mercury – black hair, black suit, black shoes, wild eyes in a pale disdainful visage. He must have been startled to find Oonagh sitting at the head of her T-shaped table flanked by her Praetorian Guard – Maurice Richardson, Claud Cockburn, Terence Kilmartin, Robert Kee *et al.* – most of them members of his own club, now up for sale.

Oonagh's Guinness-blue eyes, framed by thick black interlocking eyelashes, hardly ever showed surprise. Anger, yes; surprise hardly ever. She simply indicated to Cummings, her infallible factotum, that another place should be laid for Mr Tennant. David ignored the place hurriedly made available for him and went next door to drink alone. His message was for Oonagh and Oonagh's ear only. When at last opportunity arose for David to bend Oonagh's ear in private it was to say that the Gods felt, or anyway David Tennant felt, that marriage between them would be made in Heaven. But David's timing was again off. This was not the moment in Oonagh's life to lay such a proposition before her. Oonagh's heart was lodged elsewhere. She straightened out his black shoes and said she was sorry but she was afraid she could not, if he saw what she meant. But David had passed quite out. In the morning he had left again. In long retrospect, and in the light of subsequent events in her own life, Oonagh often regretted her refusal of his twice-taken hand.

Epilogue

The Gargoyle years and two marriages now irrevocably behind him, the future to David did not look altogether promising. However, he was still a relatively rich man and, to women, immensely attractive. But his existence in London seemed empty. England had lost its allure, so David now set his sails to catch a favouring breeze that would blow him once more to the sanctuary of Spain. He went back to Torremolinos on the Andalusian coast, first visited with Virginia and still pristine, and took a house there. He was not alone for long. In all his adult life David had never been without a woman at his side, but now, though locally comforted, he felt keenly the loss of Virginia. 'That was what broke him, I believe, in the end,' Pauline later said.

In due course, his youngest daughter Sabrina came out to live with him and a governess was engaged to instruct her. But in spite of climatic and economic advantages, self-banishment had brought with it the disagreeable sense of being *dépaysé.* To ease this discomfort, he sought to share it by inviting himself to stay with a fellow exile, Alec Waugh living a downy existence in Tangier. David and Alec would have briefly overlapped at Sherborne had not Alec been sacked before David's arrival for the 'usual reasons'. The 'usual reasons' left far behind him, Alec had as his good companion a very lively and twice married lady called Marion Wrottesley. David and Marion were not total strangers. Marion had often been taken to the Gargoyle and had even rendered signal service to one or two of the younger members still unweaned from sexual ambiguity. David stayed happily with them in Tangier until Waugh was called back to London for the publication of his new novel. David was dismayed at the prospect of returning alone to Torremolinos and asked if he might not borrow Marion for a bit. Leave was granted on the condition that Marion's two young children went too. And so they did. But David never gave Marion back. She was to assume in time a new and somewhat reluctant role – that of David's third, and last, mother-in-law.

David had sold the Gargoyle as a going concern with all contents save the paintings (some of which, like the twelve Matisse lithographs, were also sold) for the discreditable sum of £5,000 to a London caterer called

John Negus. 'The interesting thing about the Negus time', said David Sylvester, 'is that he was so lost. This man tried so hard to keep the place going as it was, but he seemed so out of his depth and all his customers patronized him. I don't think the Gargoyle ceased to be enjoyable in its decrepit days. It was odder. But it was still basically the same because it was the only place in London to go after midnight where you could sit comfortably and drink and find interesting people to talk to. There was nowhere else except very expensive places. And Annabel's is no replacement for the Gargoyle – in any way.'

For this reason, even if the older members now dropped off, many of the younger members, not a few of whom were descendants of the Souls, continued to use the Club. And also, as Raymond Carr has said, it was still so remarkably cheap. 'You would have to be pretty rich to live the life you and I lived then,' he told the author, 'and we were anything but rich. The Gargoyle was the centre of my social life for many years, but my children could no more afford the equivalent than fly.' Raymond, whose wife, Sara, was a granddaughter of Pamela's sister Mary Wemyss, continued to go to the Club habitually with such friends as Nicholas Mosley and his wife Rosemary, an ethereal, outwardly listless beauty, Simon Asquith and Hugo Charteris (Raymond being, in the company, the only exception to direct Soul descendancy). They went, that is, until a certain night – 'The Night of the Daily Mail'. On this particular night in 1956, the Club's management (it was now owned by the band leader, Harry Roy) had decided to introduce rock 'n' roll to the upper crust. 'The whole evening seemed odd from the beginning', said Raymond. 'I don't think we had taken in that there had been changes in ownership since Tennant. We kept on seeing these flashes. They could have been little fireworks, or anything. It never entered our heads that they came from photographers. And then the next day there were these enormous photographs of Nick and Sara (shoeless, tieless and dancing, it must be said, in quite an abandoned way) and Little David Tennant with Deirdre Grantley. It was a very, very unpleasant article, with two cartoons, about, you can imagine, the upper classes letting their hair down, decadent, that kind of thing – I really thought it might get me the sack at Oxford [Sir Raymond Carr has recently retired as Warden of St Antony's College]. They knew it was the first time rock 'n' roll had been played there and they had got two people with titles, Oxford don, that sort of thing ('It's decidedly U to rock around the clock, darling', gloated the *Daily Mail*). My wife's family were outraged. That was the end of the Gargoyle as far as I and my friends and quite a significant number of other people were concerned. We all simply banned it, we weren't going to have that sort of thing. It could never have happened in Tennant's day.'

The party was now definitely over for the Gargoyle Club as David had conceived and created it. The place changed hands shortly after this disgraceful affair and became a strip-tease joint. After 1979 it was best known as the weekend Comedy Store, the gong-them-off revue of stand-up comedians which brought fame to Alexei Sayle and others. A number of once-a-week ventures followed, ending in 1982 in a Sixties soul disco hosted by David Ogilvy, a former pageboy to the Queen. Since then the Matisse mirrored ballroom walls, the oak Tudor Room and all the interiors have been stripped for conversion to its present function as a sophisticated studio complex providing, in the heart of the commercial film-making industry, all technical facilities for the making of such products and popular videos.

The Gargoyle that David had created was a world of expectancy. There was much beauty to be found there and a sufficiency of beasts to charge the atmosphere with excitement. An immediate flow of adrenalin was released from the moment the grille of the lift door closed and the shaky ascent to uncertainty began. It was also a place that generated an inordinate amount of laughter. Irwin Shaw asked Ivan Moffat one night at the Gargoyle why there was so much laughter going on in London. Had there been as much during the Blitz? Ivan replied that although they had been grim days indeed, he could not, ironically enough, remember times when there had been more laughter either – and no more so than in the Gargoyle. David had a nice understanding of where the good source of laughter lay. 'Laughter is nothing to do with telling jokes in pubs,' he insisted to Virginia, who had always been amazed and delighted by David's zest for hyperbole and exaggeration. 'What matters is that it should well up from inside you.' 'Daddy's humour was evanescent', said Pauline. 'But there was no hint of maliciousness in it. It was like an artesian well, bubbling up and irrigating the land around.'

But the artesian well had somewhat dried up, Hermione found when she went out to visit David in Spain, and the emotional land around had become arid. He had by then bought several hectares of land in the hills above Fuengirole and just below the little untouched village of Mijas and there he built, among the olive groves, the first of his four villas. The 'Unsinkable Hermione Baddeley' (her phrase) had recently survived two torpedo attacks: the first from bankruptcy brought about in part by the improvident Francis de Molens; and secondly from a coruscating love affair with film-star-to-be Laurence Harvey, who had succeeded him in her favours. She was much dismayed, on her arrival, at what she found at the Villa Palomar. There was no sign of David. Finally, in an aromatic fug that would not have disgraced Los Angeles, she made out a figure in some disarray lying on a bed of cushions in the middle of the room. A frail-looking girl, an ordinary unhappy-looking young girl dressed in the uniform of the western world, blue jeans and a T-shirt, got up and introduced herself as Shelagh, daughter of Marion now, at David's bidding, in retreat in Majorca. Shelagh knew that Hermione had been asked over to get rid of her, she said, but she was besotted by David and refused to leave. She was convinced that in time he would fall in love with her.

David finally appeared and Hermione agreed to stay on a few days in that distressing atmosphere. But 'There was too much alcohol around, too much cheap Spanish wine and brandy and David was surrounded by people he would not have given the time of day to in England. David had changed: he had always loved good wine and interesting company, but now he could no longer carry his drink and his temper was erratic. And I wondered if there was something else …'

David and Shelagh Rainey were married at Caxton Hall in London in 1963. The auguries were not propitious: more than forty years separated man and wife; moreover, the young wife was the mother of a child supposedly by a close relation of King Juan Carlos. This had led to her arrest and deportation from Spain. But now, as David's wife, she could safely return. As her wedding present, David bought Shelagh 'Sheelagh's Bar' in Torremolinos, a very fancy set-up which soon began to attract the Costa glitterati. 'Every night I would dress up to the hilt wearing a Balenciaga or some other designer dress,' she recently told a lady from the press. 'We had twelve waiters all beautifully dressed, and they each played on different things in the bar … It was the very first loud music bar. We had the Rolling Stones there, film stars, a Prince, a "limpiabotas", a fisherman – everyone.'

In the same year Sabrina, David's youngest daughter, married the writer Jonathan Gathorne-Hardy, Eddie's nephew. 'At El Palomar night was turned into day,' says Johnny. '"Breakfast" was taken at about 6 p.m., "lunch" at 1 a.m., "dinner" just before dawn.' And all the time the young wife was having a high old time attracting custom to her bar. Such goings on could not go on indefinitely for David. His delayed reaction to the prolonged nightmare was nervous breakdown. He came back to England and went to a nursing home in Hampstead and slowly recovered. Hermione, then starring in *The Killing of Sister George* at the St Martin's Theatre, helped him to convalesce. David tried to avoid seeing old friends, but one day Peter Quennell bumped into him on the corner of Kings Road and Sloane Square. 'He was looking absolutely dreadful – very, very gaunt, terribly unshaven and, er, pathetically amiable. Seemed, for once, quite pleased to see one.'

One night over dinner in London, David told Hermione that his nephew Colin (now Lord Glenconner) had suggested that he come out to Mustique, an island in the West Indies where he had bought a considerable amount of land and intended to build. Pauline, now into her second marriage, had agreed to go with him alone. 'I shall be happy to leave a rotten part of the world,' he said. It was not on Mustique that David eventually decided to build but on the neighbouring island of St Lucia. The house was constructed on a typically grandiose and impractical scale and on a height where there was no water to be found. It was intended to underwrite all this extravagance by inaugurating an inter-island airline service. A suitable aeroplane was acquired, a pilot engaged and Pauline was to learn to fly and become a partner in the enterprise. And then there was the drink. In spite of his efforts at regeneration and Pauline's efforts to stiffen his resolve against it, the drink refused to let David go. 'Darling, it's all right on *champagne*', he told Pauline. But it was not all right because David had about five bottles before lunch every day. Then Pauline discovered to her dismay, and while in the air with him, that the pilot David so admired had a secret fear of flying. Unwisely he grounded himself and was instantly killed on his motorbike, so the whole project fell through. 'A turkey meet for the plucking', a citizen of St Lucia observed of David.

It was true that most of David's fine feathers had now gone. The splendid head had become engraved with accidie and the powerful frame had become so reduced he looked like a survivor from a Japanese prisoner of war camp. The next thing that Hermione heard – she was now working in Hollywood – was an urgent telephone call from Pauline to say that it was suspected that David might have cancer and she was flying him back to England for treatment. But when seen by the doctors there this proved to be a false alarm.

Instead of returning to the unfinished and waterless house in St Lucia, David now elected to go back to the 'rotten part of the world' in Mijas. It was not to be a happy homecoming. Shelagh was still there and the bar was still flourishing, but not long after he had settled back into the villa, Shelagh threw herself out of a bedroom window and broke her back. She had, it appeared, been the victim of somebody introducing a drug into her drink in Torremolinos.

David had been warned by the doctors to abjure from any form of alcohol lest dire consequences prevail. He did not and they did. He died, in 1968, from a heart attack. His brother Christopher had his body flown back to England and buried in the little churchyard at Wilsford beside Pamela. All three of David's wives were at the funeral, the last wearing black over the eighty pounds of white plaster in which she was still encased.

For David, at least, God had finally emptied the sails. 'You see I am,' he was wont to say by way of self-explanation, 'I am the crystal man.' What did he mean by that enigmatic phrase? A crystal can be cut in many ways, and certainly David had many facets to his character, but a crystal is above all bright and clear, and David's nature was far from transparent; it was often dark, obscure and clouded. 'The world to him', Pauline said, 'was like a house that needed decorating.' David had tried to set about the task with an innocent heart. But the endlessly peeling wallpaper had proved too much for him.

If it was Pirandello who said that a man has to invent a character for himself that he can believe in and take seriously, then perhaps it can be said that David never found such an author within him. There was a flaw in the crystal and he could not see himself clear.

Index

NOTE: Ranks and titles are generally the latest mentioned in the text